EVIL INFLUENCES

EVIL INFLUENCES

Crusades against the Mass Media

Steven Starker

Transaction Publishers
New Brunswick (U.S.A.) and London (U.K.)

Library of Congress Catalog Number: 88-29174
ISBN: 0-88738-275-4
Printed in the United States of America

Library of Congress Cataloging-in-Publication Data

Starker, Steven, 1942–
    Evil influences: crusades against the mass media / Steven
Starker.
        p.   cm.
    Includes index.
    ISBN 0-88738-275-4
    1. Mass media—United States.   2. Mass media—Moral and
ethical aspects.   3. United States—Popular culture. I. Title.
P92.U5S645 1989
302.2'34'0973—dc19   88-29174
                                                                            CIP

Contents

Part I

Introduction and Background

1

Threats to Mind, Morality, and Society

Each new technology creates an environment
that is regarded as corrupt and degrading.
Yet the new one turns its predecessor into an
art form.

—Marshall McLuhan
Understanding Media

Millions of Americans daily awaken to their favorite radio stations; they breakfast to the accompaniment of radio/TV news and weather reports or else read their morning newspapers. Those who drive to work are likely to turn on the automobile radio, while bus and train riders devour their newspapers and magazines. Some workers manage to listen to the radio throughout the day, others spend their time reading and responding to messages on video terminals. The unemployed may remain at home to watch the "soaps" and the daytime game shows on television. Their children, at school, are provided movies, slides, videotapes, and computerized educational materials as part of their day's activities. At the end of the workday, the exodus from the office is marked by the purchase of the evening newspapers, magazines, and/or further radio listening. Arriving home, the television is already on for the kids, or it is turned on almost immediately. For many, it remains on all evening. Magazines and novels are also consumed in the evening, while the television or radio provides comfortable and familiar background patter. Weekends find millions flocking to the movies, renting videotapes, and playing video games. Saturday morning the kids are glued to the television for the cartoon shows. On Sunday morning the churches compete with televised sermons and fat weekend newspapers, including color comics and multiple advertising inserts. If the various mass media are somehow malevolent, as so many suspect, they certainly have ample opportunity to exert their evil influences.

There are well over 150 million TV sets in use in the United States; many families have several. They are found in living rooms, family

3

rooms, bedrooms, kitchens, and playrooms. In newly miniaturized forms, they are finding their way into our pockets as well. A recent national survey reported that viewers ages 2 to 17 watch an average of twenty-five hours of television per week, far more than the "experts" would like. Moreover, many viewing hours are spent with the shows that concerned parents and educators find distressing: *He-Man, Transformers, Thundercats,* and other fantasy-adventure cartoons. Children are also exposed to hundreds of associated toy, candy, and cereal commercials. Equally distressing to many, rock video is available seven days a week, twenty-four hours a day, in over twenty million homes. Comic books, which enjoyed their "golden age" in the 1940s and early 1950s, are back. Not only have they regained readership, but they have invaded the bookstores. Waldenbooks, in 1985, reported among comic best sellers such titles as *Secret Wars II, GI Joe, Transformers, X-Men,* and *West Coast Avengers.* The purported evil influences of mass media, then, often are targeted toward the nation's children. An important part of their daily lives, the media inevitably influence the shape of America's popular youth culture. This is one reason, certainly, for the intensity of the attack upon media. Like other animals, humans fight fiercely against perceived threats to their young.

Although much debate regarding mass media has focused upon their effects on children, their presumed evil influence is by no means limited to the young. Adult Americans, after all, have at their disposal some 1,500 daily newspapers and another 7,600 weekly or semi-weekly newspapers; sales approach some sixty million copies daily. They spend about half their leisure time watching television, listening to many of the nation's 400 million radios, and choosing among the 60,000 different magazines and journals available. Each year they are offered another 40,000 or so new book titles. Opinions regarding the threat to adults from this mass media bombardment range from concern about an overdose of "kitsch" (artistic trash) to predictions of the destruction of society and culture as we know it.

Visions of exactly how the omnipresent media will destroy us have been varied. There are those who, like Orwell, fear the mass media to be the foundation of a *1984*-like totalitarianism, in which citizens will be manipulated through propaganda and lies and completely lose their privacy, initiative, and individuality. Others fear the creation of a society of passive, withdrawn, and illiterate "videots." Still others, like author/educator Neil Postman, see America drowning in electronically produced trivia, irrelevance, and an all pervasive entertainment mentality:

Our politics, religion, news, athletics, education and commerce have been transformed into congenial adjuncts of show business, largely without protest or even much popular notice. The result is that we are a people on the verge of amusing ourselves to death.[1]

Over the past three decades, serious research efforts have been under way to determine the impact of the media upon human development and behavior; these are beginning to bear fruit. The crusades against mass media, however, preceded these efforts by many years. In fact, virtually all of the arguments rallied against the media were firmly in place well before the relevant research had been undertaken.

A Hostile Reception

The story of the mass media in America reads much like the case history of a public health menace. Each technological innovation, or new media application, promptly has been declared a serious threat to the character and mental abilities of children, the behavior of teenagers, the morality and intelligence of adults, and the sanctity of the American way of life. Newspapers, comics, paperback books, magazines, romance and detective novels, movies, radio, television, video games, and recently computers, have all engendered critical books and articles by alarmed experts. Parents and educators have been exhorted to monitor, police, and control all such "evil influences," lest they contaminate the health and character of the nation's children.

Organized into community groups, Americans often have taken militant action against the offending media. Comic books have been burned in public ceremonies, novels have been banned and blacklisted, publishers have been harassed and jailed, video games have been regulated or restricted, investigative committees and commissions have been formed, and so on. Our adult population repeatedly has been chastised for succumbing to the temptations of the "boob tube," reading "junk" magazines and novels, attending and liking the "wrong" movies, and otherwise permitting their brains and their morals to deteriorate in a morass of media mediocrity. A great many of us have taken these warnings to heart, attempting to modify our habits, or those of our children, or simply learning to be appropriately secretive and to feel guilty.

The charges regularly leveled against the media include these:

- stimulation of violence, sadism, and criminality
- undermining of sexual morality and legitimate authority

- promotion of passivity through narcotization, hypnosis, and desensitization
- substitution of fantasy for reality; promotion of escapism
- promotion of stereotypy, distortion, oversimplification, and irrelevance
- deliberate emotional manipulation and exploitation of consumers
- destruction of literacy
- weakening of family ties
- destruction of artistic integrity and creativity in society
- homogenization of culture at the lowest common level
- promotion of materialism and conformity

Surveying the voluminous body of literature attacking the media, it may seem surprising that America and its inhabitants have survived at all. The critics, after all, have always had some good points to make. They have been sufficiently convincing to alarm millions of parents and teachers, again and again, regarding the latest threats of page and screen. One might almost expect the combined effects of comic books, paperbacks, horror movies, daytime television, tabloid newspapers, video games, and similar evil influences to have overwhelmed us by now, creating a nation of illiterate cretins.

While critics have enjoyed only the most short-lived success in their efforts to curtail and control the various media menaces of the past two hundred years, the nation has nevertheless survived. (A few intellectuals may claim that the great majority of Americans have, indeed, been morally and intellectually demolished.) The most likely explanation for our continued intellectual and cultural existence is that the evils purveyed by the various media have repeatedly been exaggerated. That is, granting the validity of many individual criticisms that have been offered over the past two centuries, the overall picture remains considerably less grim than anticipated by the critics. This becomes increasingly clear as one reviews the many dire warnings of the past. The latter are too readily forgotten in the heat of contemporary media controversies.

The business of choosing a particular form or application of the media upon which to blame a host of psychological or social problems has become a recurrent theme in America and generally contains elements of oversimplification and scapegoating. The idea that a single source of evil influence is the key to understanding much of human behavior perhaps derives from America's Puritan religious heritage. Satan, father of all evil, is transformed into a contemporary form with which we can do battle. Such a "single-factor" theory of evil has the virtue of making our lives seem far more comprehensible and controllable. All we need to do is to get rid of television (comics, rock-and-roll, movies, magazines) and things will be right with the world once again. This sort of thinking, although rejected by virtually all serious observers of society, manages to appear and reappear over time, finding new targets for its concerns and influencing millions.

As observed by media scholar Donald N. Wood:

> The 'dime' novels of the nineteenth century, the 'scandalous' Hollywood films of the 1920's, the comic books of the 1940's, and (of course) television today—all in turn have been condemned for glorifying violence, contributing to juvenile delinquency, promoting promiscuous sex, increasing the national crime rate, and generally undermining the moral fabric of our country.[2]

Enunciations of Evil: A Sampler

In the beginning there was the spoken word. Evil influence was simply a matter of listening to the "wrong" people, to bad advice. In ancient Greece, for example, Socrates was condemned to death for his innovative use of the medium of speech. His approach to philosophy and discourse, which encouraged doubt and questioning in all matters, including government and religion, was deemed a corrupting influence upon his youthful students. An "evil influence," Socrates was removed from Greek society by outraged citizens seeking to preserve and protect the values and morals of their culture and their children.

Ascendency of the written word over the spoken word was not achieved without some misgivings, as can be surmised from reading Plato:

> . . . this discovery of yours will create forgetfulness in the learners' souls, because they will not use their memories; they will trust to the external written characters and not remember of themselves. The specific which you have discovered is an aid not to memory, but to reminiscence, and you give your disciples not truth, but only the semblance of truth; they will be hearers of many things and will have learned nothing; they will appear to be omniscient and will generally know nothing; they will be tiresome company having the show of wisdom without the reality.[3]

The written word, nevertheless, came to dominate religion, education, communication, and the arts for many centuries. By the nineteenth century, many critics evaluating new applications of the written word agreed that they contained the germs of evil influence. One literary form, in particular, was found deserving of condemnation—the novel. Consider the remarks of Coleridge (1856):

I will run the risk of asserting, that where the reading of novels prevails as a habit, it occasions in time the entire destruction of the powers of the mind; it is such an utter loss to the reader, that it is not so much to be called pass-time as kill-time. It conveys no trustworthy information as to facts; it produces no improvement of the intellect, but fills the mind with a mawkish and morbid sensibility, which is directly hostile to the cultivation, invigoration and enlargement of the nobler faculties of the understanding.[4]

Particularly at risk were young women, for whom the novel constituted an unacceptably exciting stimulus, which could readily overload frail nervous systems. O. S. Fowler (1875) warned:

It is doubtful whether fiction writers are public benefactors, or their publishers philanthropists. The amount of nervous excitement and consequent prostration, exhaustion, and disorder they cause is fearful. Girls already have ten times too much excitability for their strength. Yet every page of every novel redoubles both their nervousness and their weakness . . . Those perfectly happy in their affections never read novels, because *real* love is so much more fascinating than that described.[5]

Journalism, in the form of the printed newspaper, was also judged by some experts to be responsible for a decline in the mental health of urban Americans. Neurologist George M. Beard (1881) wrote:

The sorrows of any part of the world, many times greater than the old world as known to the ancients, through the medium of the press and the telegraph are made the sorrows of individuals everywhere . . . With the extension and complexity of populations of the globe, with the rise and growth of nations and peoples, these local sorrows and local horrors become daily occasions of nervous disorders. Our morning newspaper, that we read with our breakfast, has the history of the sorrows of the whole world for a day; and a nature but moderately sympathetic is robbed thereby, consciously or unconsciously, of more or less nervous strength.[6]

With the arrival of motion pictures, however, the projection of moving images was soon deemed by the periodicals of the day to be far more threatening than mere printed words. *Education* (1919) noted:

The tendency of children to imitate the daring deeds seen upon the screen has been illustrated in nearly every court in the land. Train wrecks, robberies, murders, thefts, runaways, and other forms of juvenile delinquency have been traced to some particular film. The imitation is not confined to young boys and girls but extends even through adolescence and to adults.[7]

The *Christian Century* (1930) commented:

The movies are so occupied with crime and sex stuff and are so saturating the minds of children the world over with social sewage that they have become a menace to the mental and moral life of the coming generation.[8]

The comic strips of the Sunday supplements and the comic books they spawned were no less heartily condemned. John Mason Brown led the attack on comic books, which appeared in the *Saturday Review of Literature* (1948):

> The comic books, however, as they are nowadays perpetually on tap, seem to me to be, not only trash, but the lowest, most despicable, and most harmful form of trash. As a rule, their word selection is as wretched as their drawing, or the paper on which they are printed. They are designed for readers who are too lazy to read, and increase both their unwillingness and inability to do so . . . most comics, as I see them, are the marijuana of the nursery; the bane of the bassinet; the horror of the house; the curse of the kids; and a threat to the future.[9]

Television, of course, eventually came to occupy a special niche in the hearts of media critics. Marie Winn took aim at the tube in *The Plug-In Drug* (1977):

> Not unlike drugs or alcohol, the television experience allows the participant to blot out the real world and enter into a pleasurable and passive mental state. The worries and anxieties of reality are as effectively deferred by becoming absorbed in a television program as by going on a "trip" induced by drugs or alcohol . . . it is the adverse effect of television viewing on the lives of so many people that defines it as a serious addiction.[10]

Still more recently, the computer age brought with it novel opportunities for evil influence:

> I think there are strong possibilities that the video games contribute to the problem of violence in society . . . teaching the children that violence is somehow an acceptable thing and is a legitimate way of expressing your anger . . . There's nothing constructive in the games. Everything is eliminate, kill, destroy, let's get up and do it fast.[11]

> Wherever computer centers have been established . . . bright young men of disheveled appearance, often with sunken glowing eyes, can be seen sitting at computer consoles . . . They work until they nearly drop, twenty, thirty hours at a time . . . Their rumpled clothes, their unwashed and unshaven faces, and their uncombed hair all testify that they are oblivious to the world in which they move. They exist, at least when so engaged, only through and for the computers. These are computer bums, compulsive programmers. They are an international phenomenon.[12]

Simple Theories

At one time, Italian forensic psychiatrist Cesare Lombroso (1836–1909) propounded a scientific theory that criminals invariably were born with certain stigmata of degeneracy. These included such features as the low forehead, large protruding ears, funny nose, low pain sensitivity, and so on. All such criminal traits were explained in terms of reversion to a more primitive, savage biological state involving physical and nervous deterioration. The predisposition to crime was said to be built in to such individuals, both physically and mentally. Lombroso and his colleagues had empirical evidence for their assertions, having carefully studied the inmates in institutions for the criminally insane. Hence they considered their theory to be scientifically derived and validated, elegant in its simplicity. Their new science was called criminal anthropology.

Those dissatisfied with the Lombroso theory, however, noted that the Italian researchers had failed to study either a noninstitutionalized group of criminals or a group of noncriminals. It might be that the "criminal stigmata" in question were present only in the institutionalized criminally insane, a small subsample of criminals, and therefore did not really predict or determine criminal behavior in general. Or, the identical traits might prove to be commonly found among the general populace, totally invalidating the theory. In fact, when researchers studied a representative sample of unincarcerated persons, they found that the so-called stigmata occurred no more frequently among prisoners than among other people.

Many other well-meaning and sincere individuals have, like Lombroso, formulated overly simple and comprehensive explanations of human problems. Such theories generally are based upon considerable experience with a limited and biased sample of individuals from whom gross generalizations are drawn. The tendency to heap the blame for all antisocial behavior variously upon comic books, trashy novels, or crime movies, for example, usually is linked to the observation that certain misfits, unfortunates, or criminals have admitted to liking them. This becomes the "scientific proof" of the new theory of evil influence. In retrospect, such "proofs" appear quite flimsy. (Of the many media forms that have been the focus of controversy, only television has generated a reasonably large and respectable research base, and this is primarily focused upon the singular issue of television violence.)

Simple theories of evil media influence have been applied again and again. In the 1920s, for example, the motion picture came under attack for its evil influence upon American audiences. Certain members of

Congress, for example, introduced bills to prohibit the shipment of motion pictures that showed or simulated the acts of outlaws, bandits, bank robbers, train robbers, and other undesirables. Such films, they reasoned, would undermine morality and cause criminal behaviors in viewers. Their goal was an America safe from Westerns or mysteries, where John Wayne, Humphrey Bogart, Edward G. Robinson, and their ilk should have remained unknown.

In 1940, Sterling North, book reviewer of the *Chicago Daily News*, wrote an article on the comic book menace, describing the comics as a "violent stimulant" and "sadistic drivel," providing audiences a "hypodermic injection of sex and murder." Psychiatrist Fredric Wertham took up the crusade, launching an all-out attack on the comics as a mental health menace and reporting them to be "definitely and completely harmful." His views were presented in a 1948 *Colliers* article by Judith Crist, "Horror in the Nursery," and later in his classic book *Seduction of the Innocent*.

In 1953, at the behest of Senator Joseph McCarthy, United States libraries removed and banned over 100 books that he considered subversive to the American way of life. There were also several public book-burning ceremonies before President Eisenhower came out strongly in opposition to such activities. A 1981 national survey of libraries, principals and school superintendents revealed that 20 percent of U.S. schools were being pressured to ban certain books from classrooms and libraries. Among the works found objectionable were *Huckleberry Finn, Brave New World, The Merchant of Venice, 1984,* and many other widely celebrated books.

More recently, media critics have focused most of their attention upon television, describing it as a "plug-in drug," "a form of hypnosis," and "a form of sensory deprivation." Video games, computers, and music television have each drawn their share of fire as well. As I write this chapter, for example, the pressure to censor/regulate rock video productions is growing, as parents and teachers once again rally to the banner of moral indignation. Of course, many of these crusading parents and educators were themselves the first "victims" of the evil influence of rock-and-roll via radio, records, and movies. They once battled against their own parents and teachers, who denounced this new, outrageous form of music as detrimental to mental, physical, and moral health.

The simple theory that turns up, again and again, in these attacks upon the media is sometimes known as the "hypodermic needle" theory:

> Thus the mass media were pictured as a giant hypodermic needle, pecking
> and plunging at a passive audience . . . Conceived of as an all-powerful
> influence on human behavior, the mass media were pictured as sending forth
> messages to atomized masses waiting to receive them, with nothing inter-
> vening.[13]

The hypodermic needle theory of media influence, in its most blatant
form, views audiences as the passive receptors of virulent "viruses"
produced by the media. These pass directly into our brains, there to
bring about the destruction of rational thought, the undermining of
moral strictures, and the generation of impulsive and/or criminal behaviors. Of course, most contemporary critics of the media are too
sophisticated to offer the theory in quite this form. For all the increased
sophistication of the rhetoric, however, this simple and emotional theory has been resurrected repeatedly in the assault upon mass media.
Its very simplicity has assured its attractiveness to a large group of
anxious Americans. It makes absolutely clear just what the problem
is, where the responsibility lies, and how the situation may be cor-
rected. It provides a blueprint for community action by concerned
citizens, a war-cry for aspiring politicians, a focal point for outraged
morality.

The hypodermic needle theory postulates an insidious, well-nigh irresistible force inherent in the media, which attacks our minds, morals,
children, families, and our entire society. Critic Jerry Mander, in an
article on "Television: The Evil Eye," wrote that television involves
". . . a steady stream of mesmerizing images placed in our heads by
the people who control the media. It occupies our minds like an in-
vading army." Little wonder that this view of the malevolent media
generates so much determined resistance.

> While the 'hypodermic needle' theory was abandoned long ago by com-
> munications researchers, the public continues to feel that the media have
> direct, usually menacing, effects on their audiences.[14]

Although contemporary media researchers work with considerably
more complex and sophisticated models, their work is all too readily
seized upon by moralizers, popularizers, and politicians to be offered
up to the public in a highly simplified form. Moreover, the reaction
against new media forms usually consolidates well in advance of the
relevant research findings, as in the case of video games and televised
rock videos.

Fruits of the Mass Media

An important by-product of mass media is mass culture, or popular ("pop") culture. This refers to such phenomena as best-selling novels, blockbuster movies, "hip" fashions, hit tunes (and/or rock videos), mass-marketed toys, the leading TV sit-coms, the latest diet-book craze, and other cultural artifacts which reach millions of people through the aid of print or electronic media. Those who deem mass media an evil influence condemn mass culture as one of the fruits of such influence. The very term "mass culture" harbors negative connotations and has been applied pejoratively for some two hundred years. Critic Dwight Macdonald, for example, preferred the term "mass" culture to the kinder "popular" culture because ". . . its distinctive mark is that it is solely and directly an article for mass consumption, like chewing gum." In a similar vein, scholar P. A. Sorokin wrote, "I rarely trouble myself with reading a best seller: its being such is a sufficient evidence of its commonplace character." The words "popular," "successful," "mass market," "best seller," and "celebrity" have all been used as terms of disparagement by the intellectual critics of mass culture.

Dwight Macdonald noted that the output of such media as the radio, television, and the movies is almost entirely "Masscult"—his term for mass culture. He found Masscult a "vulgarized reflection of the arts and a cultural nightmare." Its uniform product was said to be providing nothing more than brief distraction, making no demands upon an audience but merely pandering to its taste:

> Masscult is bad in a new way: it doesn't even have the theoretical possibility of being good. Up to the eighteenth century, bad art was of the same nature as good art, produced for the same audience, accepting the same standards. The difference was simply one of individual talent. But Masscult is something else. It is not just unsuccessful art. It is non-art. It is even anti-art.[15]

Some of the earliest criticisms of mass culture were directed toward the emergence of eighteenth-century popular literature; the critics have never since been stilled. Today, they are particularly concerned with the effects of television programming upon popular taste and loudly decry its devastation of artistic integrity and creativity, its apparent devotion to mediocrity. According to Bernard Rosenberg, prominent critic of mass culture, for example, "At its worst, mass culture threatens not merely to cretinize our taste but to brutalize our senses, while paving the way to totalitarianism."

Contemporary criticisms of mass culture are scarcely original. That is, the critique of mass culture is a litany that has been chanted again and again, with minor variations, for two centuries or more. According to sociologist Herbert J. Gans, the critique typically emphasizes four themes:

1. *The Profit Motive*—Popular culture creations are mass produced by profit-motivated entrepreneurs for the express purpose of generating income by gratifying consumers.
2. *Corruption of True Art*—Popular culture borrows elements of high culture and thereby debases it. Moreover, it lures talented artists with the promise of wealth and tempts them to abandon their own aesthetic standards in favor of marketplace standards.
3. *Corruption of the Audience*—Mass culture consumers are receiving only superficial gratifications, and possibly are being emotionally harmed. A vast and passive audience, they also become more vulnerable to totalitarianism.
4. *Corruption of Society*—Mass culture reduces the overall quality of the arts, and the taste of the entire culture, to the lowest common denominator.

The critique of mass culture is strikingly similar to that of the mass media: the two go hand-in-hand. The critic of mass media or mass communications, however, may choose to emphasize the media "form," while the critic of mass culture targets the "content," products, or overt messages of the media. The former may be more concerned with the effects of rapidly shifting television images upon our eyes and brains, while the latter condemns the violence and sexuality of popular television shows.

Marshall McLuhan drew considerable attention to the distinction between media "form" and "content" with his well-known phrase "The medium is the message." That is, he set down a firm opinion to the effect that media form, rather than content, has the most profound effect upon society. He was not particularly concerned with what movies or novels or television programs were *about,* or whether they were overly sexy or inappropriately violent. "Our conventional response to all media, namely that it is how they are used that counts, is the numb stance of the technological idiot" (*Understanding Media,* 1964). What is important, he asserted, is the medium itself.

McLuhan presented evidence that the print medium, which superseded oral communication, revolutionized human consciousness. It profoundly shaped both the way in which people thought and the kinds of things they thought about. The electronic media, he argued, particularly television (and increasingly computers), were proceeding to do the same. Television, as a remarkable extension of the human senses and nervous system, had heightened immediate awareness of the entire world, reducing it to a "global village." Our ability to withstand and usefully process the resulting massive influx of information, however, remained to be determined.

McLuhan's ideas and contributions were many and complex, and we will be returning to them. For the moment, however, McLuhan serves as an example of a scholar who resisted the temptation to attack the *content* of mass media and mass culture in order to struggle with the impact of the various media, "per se," on humanity. That many strongly disagree with this perspective may be correctly surmised from Dwight Macdonald's review of McLuhan's seminal book *Understanding Media,* which he described in *Book Week* (June 7, 1964) as "impure nonsense, nonsense adulterated by sense."

Putting aside questions of whether media form or content is preeminent in influencing consciousness and society, we may simply note that there exist two related but discriminable routes by which mass media's purported evil influence may be disseminated. That is, if the message doesn't corrupt you, the medium will! If we are to further our understanding of the psychological threat or threats posed by the mass media, then, we will need to consider both of these dimensions.

Argument and Plan

The central argument of this book, briefly stated, is that attacks and dire predictions historically have accompanied each development of the mass media. Although couched in logic and scientific theory, such reactions have been based partly on fear: fear of change, fear of human violence and sensuality, fear of imagination and fantasy. Hostility, in individuals and groups, frequently may be traced to fear—whatever the apparent provocation. I am proposing that various forms and applications of mass media repeatedly have frightened and threatened many, thereby becoming choice targets for attack and scapegoats for the evils of society. Just how and why the media have challenged and threatened us, and continue to do so, has been little explored; this critical information has all but gotten lost amid the ruckus.

The old hypodermic needle theory is not so much an explanation of our fears as a caricature of the threat. It is time to attempt some greater perspective on our relation to the media. This requires that we explore, with hindsight, public reaction to several important media developments. We need to see how and why the various media advances have upset and unsettled so many people, so often. We need to consider the social and psychological factors that may be driving or amplifying the anti-media response. By collecting, in one place, reactions to diverse media developments we can hope to transcend the singular and gain an overview of these issues. Such is the plan of this book. We will be examining public response to the inception of newspapers, novels, radio, movies, comics, television, video games, computers, and so on. This approach, I believe, will help us to understand current controversies regarding the media and prepare us for the inevitable arrival of new media forms, applications, and their associated threats.

The coming chapter will provide some necessary background regarding the impact of writing and printing on human thought and civilization. Before proceeding, however, I should emphasize that the intent of this work is not to declare the media totally free of all wrongdoing and negative effect. Such a position would be insupportable and naive. Rather, I am proposing that the multitude and magnitude of evils attributed to the media have been frequently exaggerated in the service of managing human fears, and that a reexamination of the issue is in order.

Notes

1. Neil Postman, *Amusing Ourselves To Death* (New York: Viking, 1985), pp. 3–4.
2. Donald N. Wood, *Mass Media and the Individual* (St. Paul, Minnesota: West, 1983), p. 5.
3. Plato, *The Dialogues of Plato* (New York: Random House, 1937), Vol. 1, "Phaedrus," translated by B. Jowett.
4. Samuel Taylor Coleridge, *Lectures in Shakespeare and Milton,* cited in Q. D. Leavis, *Fiction and The Reading Public* (London: Chatto & Windus, 1932), p. 137.
5. O. S. Fowler, *Sexual Science* (1875) cited in Robert Hendrickson, *The Literary Life and Other Curiosities* (New York: Penguin, 1982), p. 211.
6. George M. Beard, *American Nervousness* (New York: G. P. Putnam's Sons, 1881), pp. 133–34.
7. Article in *Education,* 1919, cited by D. Thomas Miller in R. J. Glessing and W. P. White, *Mass Media: The Invisible Environment* (Chicago: Science Research Associates, 1973), p. 13.
8. Article in *Christian Century,* 1930, cited by Miller, Ibid., p. 13.
9. John Mason Brown, *Saturday Review of Literature,* March 20, 1948, pp. 31–32.
10. Marie Winn, *The Plug-In Drug* (New York: Bantam, 1978), pp. 24–25.
11. Alvin Poussaint, *Jet,* November 29, 1982, p. 12.
12. Joseph Weizenbaum, *Computer Power and Human Reason* (San Francisco: W. H. Freeman, 1976), cited in Sherry Turkle, *The Second Self* (New York: Simon and Schuster, 1984), p. 205.
13. Everett M. Rogers, "Mass Media and Interpersonal Communication," in

Gary Gumpart and Robert Cathcart, *Inter/Media* (New York: Oxford University Press, 1979), pp. 194–95.

14. S. J. Ball-Rokeach and Melvin Defleur, "A Dependency Model of Mass Media Effects," Ibid, p. 229.
15. Dwight Macdonald, *Against The American Grain* (New York: Random House, 1962), p. 4.

2

Writing, Printing, and Thinking

We are immersed in a vast sea of written words and printed documents. These are as natural to us, today, as air and water, a part of our human ecology. Birth and death are marked by certificates, marriages legitimized by them; employment and business transactions are defined and controlled by contracts and regulations. The process of education is mediated by mountains of books, millions of printed words, and vast quantities of sharpened pencils. While literacy is not universal, contemporary Western culture is highly literate by any reasonable standards. Nonliterate individuals are considered severely handicapped; they can scarcely navigate their way through our reading-oriented society. Even the most literate among us are intimidated by the "revised and simplified" income tax regulations and forms that are a required part of our lives. It is difficult for us, therefore, to imagine a world without the written word or one in which documentation of any kind was scarce. Nevertheless, such a time existed.

The ability to store and communicate information via the written word undoubtedly made possible the rapid advance of civilization. At the same time, however, it profoundly influenced human thinking processes and set the stage for our later preoccupation with evil media influences. It is necessary, therefore, to look back and reflect upon such historical events as the invention of writing and the spread of literacy and to consider the world thereby created. In particular, we must take note of the transition from a pre-literate, oral tradition to a literate one and later from a manuscript-oriented to a print-oriented culture. These two developments, and the human responses to them, provide an essential context for understanding more recent media events.

In Songs and Pictures

Before writing, people depended upon the spoken word, aided by gestures, to communicate with one another. The business of preserving important information was delegated to the storyteller. Communities generally had their own designated storytellers who, in some place of assembly, would recite the ancient lore to gathered adults and children. As an aid to memory, stories often were in the form of verse and song, and all learned to recall and recite at least a part of their group's history and traditions.

Oral history is temporary history; it passes rapidly into oblivion. Of the many songs, stories, and poems of this era, relatively little remains. Even while oral history flourished, moreover, it bore little resemblance to actual happenings. Accuracy in recitation was not as important as *drama,* which served to hold the audience and to aid the memorization. Hence the importance of events, such as natural disasters or battles, regularly was exaggerated in the telling and re-telling. The workings of nature and chance became the interventions of powerful gods and spirits, and human heroes assumed godlike proportions. The net result was the creation of a rich mythology, passed from parent to child, storyteller to storyteller, mouth to mouth. The kernels of historical truth rapidly became overlaid with a tapestry of mythology and poetry. For want of writing, however, much of this ancient heritage has been lost.

The earliest known books are the inscribed, baked-clay tablets of Mesopotamia and the papyrus rolls of ancient Egypt; these are believed to date back some 3000 years B.C. Of course, one might consider the very earliest cave drawings to be attempts at recording information, but these do not appear to represent a *system* of communication. By the time of the Mesopotamian tablets, however, pictures had been systematized into a form of pictographic writing. The early pictographs further evolved into pictorial symbols, which were more easily written on the moist clay medium. Eventually, a system of pictorial writing emerged which we know as cuneiform writing, and which is generally attributed to the ancient Sumerians (early conquerors of Mesopotamia). The Egyptians, during roughly the same period, developed their own method of pictorial writing, called hieroglyphic writing. Other early civilizations appear also to have followed the route from pictorial representation to pictographic scripts, recording these on clay tablets. Consequently, the surviving literature of clay-tablet books is considerable, including both poetry and prose, prayers and myths, history and commercial records. They have preserved for us some of the songs of Omar Khayyam, the epic of Gilgamesh, and Hammurabi's Code of Laws.

Pictographs inscribed upon clay tablets, wooden tables, pottery, or upon bronze or lead objects, were rather limited forms of media. Picture scripts, moreover, with their hundreds or thousands of individual symbols, were not readily learned; few had the necessary time or patience to become literate. The physical process of inscription was slow and exacting, and the resulting tablets or metal artifacts were not very portable. In much of the ancient world, consequently, reading and writing fell to the province and control of the priesthood, whose temples housed large collections of inscribed tablets. Literacy was rare enough to be transformed into a profession by the scribes of ancient Egypt, a small group of educated individuals whose ability to read and write made them valuable as government employees. As a medium of communication, then, pictographic script was available only to a limited audience, hardly an ideal "mass" medium. Nevertheless, cuneiform writing and the clay tablet remained a viable form of record keeping for some 3000 years.

The world of songs and pictures, characteristic of earliest civilization, gradually was undermined by increasingly symbolic forms of writing, and eventually was destroyed by the ascendancy of the phonetic alphabet. In ancient Greece, the oral tradition of Homer had been largely replaced by the written word in Plato's day. Such epic works as the *Odyssey* and *Iliad* apparently were composed and recited without the aid of an alphabet, but certainly would have been lost to the world had they not been subsequently preserved in writing. By the seventh century B.C. literary writing was already established in Greece, although oral recitation certainly continued. In the fifth century B.C., the time of Aeschylus, Euripides, Aristophanes, Herodotus, and other luminary figures, Greek civilization reached a new cultural peak, and a book trade was already established. The virtual explosion of cultural accomplishment at this time probably would not have been possible without two preceding developments: adaptation of the phonetic alphabet, and the increased use of papyrus for writing material.

In Words and Logic

The origins of the alphabet are not precisely known. It is believed to have originated between 1700 B.C. and 1500 B.C. in the lands along the eastern Mediterranean. Even the Greeks and the Romans, much closer to the problem than ourselves, were not entirely sure where the alphabet had originated. They considered the Phoenicians, Egyptians, Assyrians, Cretians, and Hebrews among the possible inventors. While the nationality of the inventor(s) is unknown, it is clear that the alphabet originated with the North Semitic peoples. It was the Phoenician version of the North Semitic alphabet that eventually was adopted by the

Greeks, who then went on to make some changes of their own. The alphabets in use today throughout Western civilization are derived from this Greek alphabet.

The great innovation of the alphabet was not the use of signs and symbols for communication; this much had been accomplished by the pictographic scripts. Rather, it was the principle of representing each sound of human speech by its own symbol. A pictograph represented a picture, a scene, a slice of human experience; a written word in the Greek alphabet instead represented a spoken word. As to the advantage of this approach, alphabet scholar David Diringer (1948) wrote:

> The alphabet is the last, the most highly developed, the most convenient and the most easily adaptable system of writing. Alphabetic writing is now universally employed by civilized peoples; its use is acquired in childhood with ease. There is an enormous advantage, obviously, in the use of letters which represent single sounds rather than ideas or syllables; no sinologist knows all the 80,000 or so Chinese symbols, but it is also far from easy to master the 9000 or so symbols actually employed by Chinese scholars. How far simpler it is to use 22 or 24 or 26 signs only![1]

The simplicity of the alphabet freed reading and writing from the domination of the priests and ruling classes, making mass literacy a real possibility. Moreover, by the fifth century B.C. papyrus rolls, made from the stem of the papyrus plant, became the chief writing material of civilized peoples. This made the task of writing far less arduous and greatly increased the availability of written materials. The Greeks were among the first to profit from this new technology and soon found themselves in a period of unparalleled literary, philosophic, and scientific accomplishment. This cultural leap forward was not simply the cumulative effect of more citizens reading and writing. The new alphabet, the new way of taking in, organizing, and expressing information had also transformed the Greek mind. The phonetic alphabet required a new way of processing and manipulating information, a new mode of thought. It demanded the Greeks transcend the realm of sensory experience, the world of song and picture, and focus instead on abstractions. Unlike pictograms, the individual letters of the alphabet were meaningless, referring only to equally meaningless sounds. These, however, could be manipulated and arranged such that meaningful sentences and thoughts emerged. The processes involved were far removed from the content of the thought or communication. (The written word "cow," and the sound it refers to, for example, are not at all cowlike, yet no such similarity is required for communication.) Before long, the Greeks had taken a mental step away from the sensory world of everyday experience into the world of abstraction. Their ability to abstract soon led them to new concepts, powerful perspectives, and important discoveries.

It was not accidental that the arrival of Greek literacy coincided with the flowering of Greek civilization. In committing themselves to the phonetic alphabet, the Greeks had begun to train themselves and their children in linear, sequential thinking in order that letters and words might properly be organized to create meanings. From this type of thinking it was but a small step to the discovery of logic and the concern with order, themes which came to dominate Greek intellectual life. Similarly, the thinking tool we call "analysis," the breaking apart of wholes into small, manageable parts, was implicit in alphabetic literacy. Words, sentences, and thoughts could be taken apart, manipulated, and put back together. Even time itself succumbed to the new talent for analysis, with the Greeks developing a heightened sense of chronological order, of the movement of events through time, of cause and effect relations.

At about this time, the Greeks came to view the entire universe as logical and orderly rather than irrational or dominated by the whims of various gods. Once this perspective was established, the Greeks were able to begin systematic inquiry into the natural laws. In a span of a hundred years, the Greek scientist/philosophers opened up investigations into mathematics, biology, physics, medicine, and so on. Rational thought began to displace myth and superstition. Even Greek art reflected an increasing dissection of the world, and an effort to represent it as it truly existed, free from myth or exaggeration. Literature gravitated away from the poetic toward a more realistic and orderly prose. Rationalism became the basis of Greek intellectual life, and the abstract became increasingly valued over the concrete and the sensory. Plato, in fact, concluded that abstract ideas constituted the *only* reality, with the sensory world revealing only pale reflections or shadows of these. Direct experience, the evidence of the senses, was drastically devalued, considered illusory and untrustworthy. This split between the worlds of mind and body was set firmly into history by Plato, and remains an influential perspective even today. Both Plato, and his student Aristotle, became bulwarks of the rationalism that came to dominate Western thought.

In the span of a few hundred years, then, humankind left the world of song and picture, a world of sensory experience and gestalt configurations (wholes), for the world of phonetic words, logic, reason, linear and analytic thought, and deified abstraction. Along the way was gained a wealth of practical and scientific knowledge, a treasure trove of art and philosophy. Still, nothing is gained without price, and the price for such advances was the alienation of individuals from the world of direct sensory experience and emotionality. Hence McLuhan's comment that ". . . literate man, when we meet him in the Greek world, is a split man, a schizophrenic, as all literate men have been since the invention of the phonetic alphabet." The word "schizophrenic" is not intended in the clinical sense, of course, but in the more literal meaning of a "split-head."

The profound effects of the alphabet on the Greeks may be one of the best examples of how media influences mind. This was undoubtedly one of the sources of McLuhan's controversial thesis that "the medium is the message." That is, it was not *what* was written with the alphabet, but the very fact of reading and writing, which had so far-reaching an effect upon human consciousness. The rationalist tradition that emerged in ancient Greece, with its mind–body split and tendency toward abstraction, became central to Western thought. Emotionality, save for the spiritual variety, was by and large relegated to the realm of the primitive and the bestial, while logical/analytic thinking became the machinery of everyday life. Sensation, intuition, imagic thinking, daydreaming, and such were relegated to the esoteric (at the least) or the pathological (at the extreme). The spoken word, with its inevitable emotional overtones and its immediate, personal qualities was trivialized, while the written word, more abstract and impersonal, affectively neutral, but enduring, was relied upon to knit together the fabric of Western civilization.

There may have been those among the ancient peoples who eschewed the new alphabet technology, considering it an evil influence, but their views are long since lost. Oral criticism, like oral history, was temporary; only the written word endured. We know that Socrates, among the greatest of the Greek philosophers, chose not to put his thoughts into writing. He preferred the immediate verbal dialogue of face-to-face encounters. Had Plato not preserved his teachings, Socrates might be unknown to us today. Even Socrates, however, was a product of the alphabetic age. His method of teaching through questioning was quite analytical, intended to tear down belief systems in a step-by-step fashion until some ultimate, abstract truths might be revealed. This sort of determined inquiry embarrassed and irritated those responsible for defending the established belief system of his day, and he eventually was declared to be an evil influence and removed from society. It is a tragic irony that Socrates, who denied the written word, nevertheless was martyred for expressing forcefully the rationalistic, analytic, and abstract mode of thought it had fostered.

The view that alphabetic literacy was the key to rationalistic, abstract thought has been confirmed through contemporary studies of nonliterate peoples. Katherine Scherman (1956), for example, studied the nonliterate Eskimos inhabiting the islands of northern Canada. Examining their language and customs, she noted:

> There are no abstract words and all verbs are verbs of action. The Eskimos, though extraordinarily quick and alert mentally, are not thinkers in our sense—and their language is a reflection of their life and their racial character. It is a language of people whose lives are lived in their bodies and not in their minds.[2]

Anthropologist Ashley Montagu, on the basis of his studies of primitive peoples, expressed a similar sentiment:

> Most nonliterate peoples are extreme realists . . . identify themselves very much more closely with the world in which they live than do literate peoples of the world. The more "literate" people become, the more they tend to become detached from the world in which they live.[3]

In Type and Print

Word and logic endured, but the papyrus scroll gave way, eventually, to a new writing material called "parchment." This consisted of animal skins (sheep, goats, pigs, cattle) which had been washed and divested of hair or wool, soaked in a limepit, stretched on a frame, scraped clean, moistened, and then covered with pounded chalk and allowed to dry. The finest quality parchment, called "vellum," was produced from calfskin. The Romans used parchment extensively, and the Christian Church followed the Hebrew practice by choosing it over papyrus for its sacred writings. The scroll was replaced by the "codex," an arrangement of folded leaves bound along one side and protected by wooden covers. Handwritten parchment books, or "codices manuscripti" in Latin, have survived from the third or fourth centuries A.D., and this medium remained dominant through the Middle Ages.

The Roman or Latin book eventually reached all parts of Europe, bringing religion, culture, and the Latin language to diverse peoples. Papal Rome, after the fall of the Roman Empire, continued to send missionaries everywhere, and their books accompanied them. The abbeys they built became centers of learning in an era sometimes referred to as the "Dark Ages." Book production in the Middle Ages was largely within the province of these Christian monasteries. In a designated writing room, or "scriptorium," monks functioning as scribes spent their days copying and illuminating sacred and secular works. Their work was restricted to the daylight hours because artificial illumination posed a fire hazard and was not permitted. The task of copying a book was long and exacting and readily subject to errors of the eye, hand, and mind. In order to limit interruption and distraction, speech was not allowed in the scriptorium; essential communication was limited to gestures. Umberto Eco's novel *The Name of the Rose* provides readers with a fascinating portrayal of life and intrigue in just such a monastic scriptorium.

Despite the scribal labors of a thousand years, the average European of the thirteenth century had little regular contact with the written word. Books were expensive and largely reserved for the clergy, secular scholars, government workers, and the educated aristocracy. The art of papermaking, however, imported from China, soon set the stage for the next part of the media revolution. With paper, inexpensive books became a possibility. It was the labor involved in copying that remained the significant obstacle. The concept of printing, also imported from the Orient, provided the germ of a solution.

The Chinese, still wedded to a pictographic script, had devised wood block printing techniques as early as the sixth or seventh century A.D. They went on to invent movable types fashioned from several materials, including baked clay, tin, copper, and lead. The complexity of Chinese writing, however, required thousands of separate characters, making the process of printing both expensive and cumbersome. On the other hand, the European alphabet had very few letters and could take advantage of printing technology. While a number of Europeans attempted to perfect a method for printing multiple copies of a book using movable type, it was Johann Gutenberg who devised the first practical printing press (circa 1450).

The invention of the printing press meant that for the first time reading materials would be available to all. The large scale production of books and other documents became a reality. No longer were readers compelled to decipher handwritten works, which provided little in the way of punctuation and frequently lacked clear separation of words. The slow, laborious business of manuscript reading, usually done out loud, otherwise in a low mutter, was replaced by a more rapid and silent scanning of perfectly formed and spaced letters and words. No longer were educators forced to dictate texts to their students, who otherwise could not obtain them. The invention and subsequent development of printing marked a turning point in the history of civilization, the beginning of an educated and literate public. McLuhan noted: "Printing from movable type created a quite unexpected new environment—it created the PUBLIC." The transition from media to mass media was at hand.

Like alphabetic writing, printing also had profound psychological consequences. Specifically, it enhanced greatly all of the effects of alphabetic literacy. For this reason, McLuhan referred to print as "the extreme phase of alphabet culture" and considered the invention of printing to be as significant for civilization as that of writing. Print acquainted readers with the properties of uniformity, homogeneity, and repeatability. These have little to do with sensory or emotional experience but much to do with logic, abstraction, and rationality. Such properties also presaged the arrival of the assembly line and mass production techniques. Printing, after all, was the assembly line version of writing, cranking out unit after unit of uniform, invariable product.

Communications scholar Neil Postman recently (1984) summarized the psychological effects of print upon readers:

> . . . almost every scholar who has grappled with the question of what reading does to one's habits of mind has concluded that the process encourages rationality . . . To engage the written word means to follow a line of thought, which requires considerable powers of classifying, inference-making and reasoning. It means to uncover lies, confusions, and overgeneralizations, to detect abuses of logic and common sense. It also means to weigh ideas, to compare and contrast assertions, to connect one generalization to another. To accomplish this, one must achieve a certain distance from the words themselves, which is, in fact, encouraged by the isolated and impersonal text . . . print put forward a definition of intelligence that gave priority to the objective, rational use of the mind and at the same time encouraged forms of public discourse with serious, logically ordered content.[4]

The age of typography, of the printed word, powerfully reinforced the habits of analytic thought, abstraction, and rationality, and these soon were carried to new heights. Just as cultural progress had accelerated in response to alphabetic literacy, it accelerated once again in response to print literacy. The printing press in fact proved to be a major force in the demise of the Middle Ages and the stimulus for an intellectual and cultural Renaissance that transformed the Western world.

Petrarch, a fourteenth-century poet and scholar, called for a determined study of the writing and thought of ancient Greece and Rome. Indeed, it was Petrarch who first labeled the period from late Roman times until his own day as an age of "darkness." This Renaissance idea that the revival of culture depended upon revival of classical learning became central to fifteenth and sixteenth century intellectual life. Initially, the leaders of this movement were a group of lay scholars known as the Humanists, who succeeded in freeing scholarship and education from the total control of the clergy and established the tradition of a literate laity.

Medieval textbooks were unwelcome in Humanist schools, and the demand for classical texts markedly increased. If the new educational/cultural thrust had had to rely solely upon hand-copied manuscripts, the Renaissance might have ground to a halt. Fortunately, the mid-fifteenth century brought the invention of the printing press, which could supply the growing need for educational materials. The new invention spread quickly throughout Europe, and in the span of only fifty years it resulted in the production of some six million printed books. The Humanists, therefore, were successful in creating a vast scholarly literature based upon their studies of classical literature and culture and in stimulating the rise of a literate urban laity. That the printed word had unique effects upon the psychological processes of its readers was little noticed.

The Humanists, more interested in the humanities than the sciences, nevertheless saw to the translation and availability of the ancient Greek scientific works. From this foundation, and the analytical/abstract habits of thought furnished by alphabetic and print literacy, philosophers soon formulated the rules of inductive and deductive reasoning that constitute the "technology" of scientific discovery. Arithmetic, geometry, and algebra were also a regular feature of the Humanist educational program. While the Scientific Revolution was a product of the seventeenth century, all of the groundwork was laid by Renaissance scholars supported by the availability of printing.

The seventeenth and eighteenth centuries were a period of Enlightenment, bringing to fruition the cultural advances of the Renaissance. This era was characterized by the strenuous application of reason to all matters, physical and spiritual. The empirical, scientific method of investigation was demonstrated by Galileo, and Newton offered mathematical demonstrations of natural law. Even traditional religious practices came under rational scrutiny. The Deists, for example, postulated a rational Creation and a rational God, while denouncing such irrationalities as biblical prophecies and miracles. Their God was an impersonal, abstract one embodied in natural laws. Another group, the Atheists, took the more extreme rational–materialist position that humanity manifested no spiritual quality whatever, but consisted merely of complex biological machinery.

We may conclude this abbreviated historical overview with two observations. First, both Deist attacks upon religion, and the resulting defense, were conveyed by means of printed books. Works by Voltaire and Rousseau, for example, extolled reason as the only appropriate test of religious truth. Persuasive argument—by way of the book—became an established intellectual tradition, even among those who challenged the supremacy of reason. Second, there were some books that simply could not be tolerated by the Church. These were characterized as corrupting, heretical, evil influences. Thus was born the *Index Librorum Prohibitorum,* the *Index of Forbidden Books,* and organized censorship. More extreme forms of censorship aimed at stifling corrupting thought included book burning, and the dreaded Inquisition.

In Thought and Mind

The history of Western civilization is not our primary interest here, but it provides an essential context for the study of evil media influences. It is already clear that the media are capable of instituting massive psychosocial changes. The alphabet and the printed word each contributed to powerful modifications in the way people lived and thought. That media constitute an INFLUENCE can no longer be doubted. Why that influence has appeared, over the last few hundred years, to be more evil than otherwise remains to be determined.

The key elements in our historical excursion, thus far, are these:

- The alphabet replaced the image and the song as the primary vehicle for communcation in Western civilization.
- Alphabetic literacy promoted rational, linear, analytical, and abstract thought.
- Printing vastly amplified the psychosocial effects of the alphabet.
- Each of these developments stimulated powerful cultural changes.
- A marked separation from and devaluation of sensory and emotional experience accompanied these changes.
- A tradition of media censorship by the Church was established.

Other psychological aspects of alphabetic and print literacy have been postulated. The most important of these is the tendency of literacy to support "individualism." This is the philosophy that views the rights, interests, and freedoms of the individual as paramount in society. Prior to the dominance of the written word, cultural identity and basic education were embedded in and transmitted through the tribal unit. These were passed with ceremony from old to young, in song and story, helping to reinforce powerful group ties among the listeners. Once alphabetic writing became common, however, all vital information could be recorded upon an impersonal medium to be read by any literate person at any time. The educational function had been cleaved from tribal life, and the literate individual became relatively free of community. Moreover, the analytical, abstract mode of thinking encouraged by literacy also fostered "introspection." That is, it became easy and natural for individuals to take some distance from sensation and situation in order to examine these in abstract thought. Greek literature and drama, for example, became increasingly psychological and introspective as the effects of alphabetic literacy became manifest. The struggles, choices, and trials of the individual became a matter of immediate concern to Greek audiences and of enduring concern to Western peoples.

To the extent that books became available and literacy widespread, individual readers found that they could transcend personal experience and parochial concerns to share the knowledge and experience of hundreds of learned people. The printed word was a portal into other worlds: the past, the mythic, the geographically distant, the abstract, the theoretical, and the merely possible. The determined individual no longer could be bound by tradition and taboo, nor denied access to the greater universe of ideas. As Lewis Mumford wrote: "More than any other device, the printed book released people from the domination of the immediate and the local."

The habits of the mind we have identified—rationality, abstraction, linearity, analysis, individualism—proved to be an important part of the American heritage. This is particularly so because the early Americans were a highly literate group. They brought the Bible to the New World and the determination that everyone be able to read it. They quickly passed laws requiring children to be educated in the matter of reading and writing, so that all might know the Gospel. Reading was not to be left to a ruling aristocracy in America; it was to be the right and responsibility of all. Neil Postman wrote:

> Whatever else may be said of those immigrants who came to settle in New England, it is a paramount fact that they and their heirs were dedicated and skillful readers whose religious sensibilities, political ideas and social life were embedded in the medium of typography.[5]

Once largely reserved for the clergy and the aristocracy, reading and writing became increasingly accessible to all. The printed word, the first truly "mass" medium, rapidly and thoroughly permeated European and American cultures. Government and education became completely dependent upon it, with little controversy or opposition. The turmoil in human affairs, after all, was generated more by the clash of ideas and motives than by the media involved in their expression. Of course, it did not take long for a new generation of media applications and forms to appear and for these to engender suspicion and fear. We will get to these shortly.

Were the alphabet and the printed word evil influences? The answer probably rests with a moral judgment of Enlightenment cultural values, particularly the extremely high valuation of logic and reason. It has been suggested, by some, that Western civilization became overly rational, logical, abstract, and analytical; that it overspecialized. Mc-Luhan, while acknowledging that such specialization made possible Western science, technology, power, and efficiency, also noted the detached, disinterested, fragmented mentalities thereby produced.

A group of American psychologists in the 1960s and 1970s became fascinated with the idea that our predominantly logical, analytical thought processes had blinded us to alternate, equally valid states of consciousness that were better known to Eastern cultures. Some considered this state of affairs tied to an overdevelopment of the left hemisphere of the cerebral cortex, the "left brain," at the expense of the right. A search for intuitive and holistic modes of perception and thought ensued, with many individuals seeking these through psychedelic drugs, Yoga, and/or various forms of meditation. Psychologist Robert Ornstein, writing on the quality of consciousness in Western society, warned:

> . . . the development of a hyperanalytical, "rational" science, unbalanced by a holistic perspective born of intuition, can proceed, if unchecked, to a point close to self-destruction.[6]

Such protests regarding the rational/analytic bias in Western thought are congruent with the view of history offered above. Some have called for a reintegration of picture, emotion, and intuition into our culture; a better synthesis of mental functions for better mental balance. However, as we look at media developments of the past few hundred years, we will find that attempts in this direction have met with a highly ambivalent reception. In fact, any media violations of the well-established modes of abstract, rational, intellectual thought have met with the cry of "evil influence" from a significant sector of society.

Notes

1. David Diringer, *The Alphabet* (New York: Philosophic Library, 1948), p. 37.
2. Katherine Scherman, *Spring on an Arctic Island,* cited in J. C. Carothers, "Culture, Psychiatry, and the Written Word," *Psychiatry,* 1959, 22, p. 314.

3. Ashley Montagu, *Man: His First Million Years,* cited in Marshall McLuhan, *The Gutenberg Galaxy* (Toronto: University of Toronto, 1962), p. 96.
4. Neil Postman, op. cit., p. 51.
5. Ibid, p. 31.
6. Robert Ornstein, *The Psychology of Consciousness* (New York: Harcourt Brace Jovanovich, 1977), p. 119.

Part II

The Response to Innovation

3

Pressure on the Press: Journalism

*If newspapers are useful in overthrowing
tyrants, it is only to establish a tyranny of
their own. The press tyrannizes over publick
men, letters, the arts, the stage, and even
over private life. Under the pretense of
protecting public morals, it is corrupting them
to the core, and under the semblance of
maintaining liberty, it is gradually
establishing a despotism as ruthless, as
grasping, and one that is quite as vulgar as
that of any Christian state known.*
—James Fenimore Cooper,
in *Discovering the News*

At the dawn of the Renaissance, news of important events travelled
either informally, by word of mouth, or formally, by means of a town
crier, posted proclamations, or privately circulated handwritten letters.
The systematic gathering of information, however, was seen as the
legitimate business only of government, religious authorities, and large
commercial enterprises. These agencies held and used information to
advance their particular interests, releasing whatever they chose to a
wider audience. The notion that information could, or should, circulate
freely had yet to emerge. Knowledge was a carefully hoarded com-
modity, a source of power and profit. Too much knowledge, in the
hands and heads of the masses, might very well become a source of
evil influence. Sir Roger L'Estrange, in the mid-seventeenth century,
forcefully condemned the concept of a public newspaper on the grounds
that too much information gives the multitudes "not only an Itch but
a Colourable Right to be Meddling with the Government."

In an age of royalty and aristocracy, the common man and woman
was not thought to require very much information. Royal decrees and
taxes had to be made known, certainly, but happenings at Court or in
foreign lands were the business of the ruling class. The world of the
commoner was confined to the needs of day-to-day existence and the

religious beliefs/responsibilities imparted by the Church. The merchant class necessarily had a broader perspective by virtue of personal travels and contact with the travelled. The happenings of the world, after all, might directly influence the ability to import and export various goods. It is not surprising, therefore, that merchants provided much of the impetus toward the development of the newspaper. The *idea* of the newspaper was a powerful one, however, and ultimately the daily news made its way to the masses. Predictions of dire consequences were not long in coming.

Struggling to Birth

The forerunners of the press were several and extend back as far as ancient Rome. The *Acta Diurna,* written by hand and daily posted in public places, was a Roman gazette, which recorded important social and political events. It announced births, deaths, treaties, trial verdicts, edicts, and so on, as these were released by the appropriate authorities. The *Acta Senatus* was a similar vehicle recording the proceedings of the Roman Senate.

The Chinese developed a Court newsletter during the T'ang dynasty (A.D. 618–907), and the late Middle Ages found manuscript newsletters circulating among branches of the larger European trading companies. In sixteenth century Venice, the government issued manuscript newsletters to be read aloud in public. With the price of admission fixed at one "gazetta," the newssheets soon became known by this name. News pamphlets, which took advantage of printing technology, became frequent toward the latter part of the sixteenth century; some 450 of them were published in England between 1590 and 1610. A news booklet containing summaries of the year's news, the *Mercurius Gallobelgicus,* was issued yearly from 1594 to 1635. This was the first of many news publications named for Mercury, messenger of the gods.

By the seventeenth century, commercial bulletins became increasingly common, with a focus upon shipping-related events. These papers, known as "corontos," brought the "currents" of the news. The London stationer who published the first of these in England, in 1621, was imprisoned for his efforts; he had not obtained a license to publish. Another stationer, Nathaniel Butter, obtained the necessary license and continued publication of corontos, thereby establishing himself as the father of English journalism. Between 1621 and 1641, Butter and others published a stream of newsletters. The *Weekley Newes,* a numbered and dated series of letters, began publication in 1622. Domestic news, however, was censored heavily by the authorities. The latter also responded harshly to the reporting of politically sensitive foreign events. In 1632, the Star Chamber issued a decree that suppressed all news books for several years. News and newspapers were already perceived as threatening in government circles.

Censorship was the general rule in England and the Continent during the seventeenth century, although it waxed and waned. Historian of journalism Harold Herd wrote that the dislike of journalism at this time was "violent and unconcealed," with repressive measures including censorship, fines, suppression of publication, and imprisonment. In 1680, English judges affirmed that:

> . . . his Majesty may by law prohibit the printing of all newsbooks and pamphlets of news whatsoever not licensed by his Majesty's authority as manifestly tending to the breach of the peace and disturbance of the kingdom.[1]

The abolition of the Star Chamber, in 1641, brought a flurry of news publication activities, but these were soon restrained by the Licensing Act of 1662, which remained in effect more than 30 years. Thereafter, another period of expansion began. By 1711, newspapers had emerged in England that addressed not only commercial and political happenings but the social, artistic, and entertainment needs of readers. The *Tatler* and the *Spectator,* for example, attempted a more literary and sophisticated format. Each was sold for one penny. Censorship soon was reinstated, however, in the form of a Stamp Act (1712), which imposed a duty on each periodical according to length. Related taxes upon advertisements and paper were also created. These taxes on knowledge had the predictable effect of destroying many newspapers, including the *Spectator,* but not permanently. Newspapers were soon on the increase once again, with editors and publishers accepting the risk of arrest and seizure of type under England's severe libel laws. Such influential English newspapers as *The Daily Advertiser* (1730), *Morning Post* (1772), and *The Times* (1788) soon were firmly established.

The idea and fact of the newspaper struggled for life in Europe despite the climate of censorship and repression. Religious and secular authorities had recognized the profound influence this new institution might wield and desperately sought to keep it contained. This proved not to be possible. Publications continued to multiply, bearing such titles as the *Courant, Newes, Post, Mercury, Gazette,* and so on. The following accounts of criminal misdeeds provide some flavor of these early publications:

NATURES CRUELL STEP-DAMES; or, Matchless Monsters of the Female Sex, Elizabeth Barnes and Anne Willis, who were executed 26 April, 1637, at Tyburn, for the unnaturall murthering of their owne children. (1637)

NEWS FROM FLEETSTREET; or, The Last Speech and Confession of the Two Persons Hanged there for Murther. With an exact Account of all the Circumstances of their Murthering the Knight for which they Dyed. (1675)[2]

The contents of these early news publications combined the elements of fact, speculation, and sensationalism. Given the difficulties and delays in collecting information during this era, the actual news content was somewhat meager. Spelling and style were inconsistent, along with veracity. Published criticism of the government, however, proved sufficiently persistent and formidable to require the founding of loyal journals by the Royalists. The first issue of the *Mercurius Aulicus,* printed at Oxford, proclaimed:

> The world hath long enough beene abused with falsehoods: And there's a weekly cheat put out to nourish the abuse amongst the people, and make them pay for their seducement. And that the world may see that the Court is neither so barren of intelligence, as it is conceived; nor the affaires thereof in so unprosperous a condition, as these Pamplets make them . . . we now go into business; whereas we shall proceed with all truth and candor.[3]

If the printing of sensational news, sensitive political information, and questionable facts were insufficient to stir controversy, there was also the matter of advertising. Newspapers, booklets, and pamphlets were recognized by merchants as marvelous vehicles for reaching the consuming public. As early as 1657, an all-advertisement weekly, the *Publick Advisor,* went to press. It included such matters as houses sought, or available for purchase, individuals seeking employment, and goods for sale. The following is an early example of printed advertising copy:

> In Bartholomew Lane on the back side of the Old Exchange, the drink called Coffee (which is a very wholsome and physical drink, having many excellent vertues, closes the Oriface of the Stomack, fortifies the heat within, helpeth Digestion, quickneth the Spirits, maketh the heart lightsom, is good against Eye-sores, Coughs, or Colds, Rhumes, Consumption, Head-ach, Dropsie, Gout, Scurvy, Kings Evil, and many others) is to be sold both in the morning, and at three o'clock in the afternoon.[4]

The birth and infancy of the press were marked by unceasing controversy, with a few critical themes beginning to emerge. One of these had to do with press accuracy. The earliest papers delighted in printing stories about the discovery of strange new lands, horrible sea monsters, and distant disasters. These were based solely upon rumor, and validation (or invalidation) was impossible because of the distances involved. Critics urged that such reports cease in favor of printing more local news. The editor of one publication, the *True Briton,* in 1723 wrote:

> The *True Briton* has already done some Service to the Publick, since he has provok'd the Mercenary and Hackney Scribblers of an abandon'd Faction to entertain the Town with *Domestic Abuses,* and to shorten the *Foreign Intelligence,* which generally used to fill their Papers. What they now seem to attempt, Every-Body can disprove, but their former Method of Entertaining us with Lyes from Abroad, could not so easily be confuted.[5]

Related to the issue of accuracy was the charge of sensationalism. In events both foreign and domestic, the press was found to focus upon the scandalous, the brutal, and the sexual aspects of the news. Rape and murder proved most popular with printers, editors, and readers, to the chagrin of authorities and sophisticates. A third realm of criticism focused upon the veracity of the advertising appearing alongside the news, particularly the ads for miracle tonics and cures. All in all, the earliest versions of the newspaper offended the sensibilities of those who considered themselves the guardians of an orderly and rational society. It threatened to undermine legitimate authority by exposing and criticizing its activities, and to weaken the rule of law by publicizing and sensationalizing criminal activities. Bombardment of the masses with unnecessary, inaccurate, and sensational news matter was regarded not merely as a nuisance, but a menace to social well-being.

The Menace in America

Sir William Berkeley, governor of Virginia in 1671, wrote home to Charles II regarding difficulties in the administration of the colony. On the brighter side, he noted:

> I thank God, there are no free schools nor printing, and I hope we shall not have these hundred years; for learning has brought disobedience, and heresy, and sects into the world, and printing has divulged them, and libels against the best government. God keep us from both.[6]

In the colonies, as in Europe, authoritarian government maintained its power not only by force of arms, but by the control of education and information. Political and religious leaders everywhere had come to understand that the technology of printing had powerful social implications. Consequently, both church and state were invested in firm control of printing in the American colonies. Colonial authorities forbade anyone to own or operate a press without license, and they parceled out approved church and government printing jobs only to the most loyal.

Benjamin Harris, a Boston bookseller and coffeehouse proprietor, is credited with printing the first newspaper in the colonies. On September 25, 1690, he published *Publick Occurrences both Foreign and Domestick*. After only a single issue, this newspaper was suppressed; Harris had neglected to obtain a proper license. Moreover, in a single issue he had criticized the mistreatment of captured Mohawk Indians by the authorities and reported an embarrassing rumor concerning the sexual behavior of the French monarch. Most copies of the paper's only edition were destroyed, and Harris quit news publishing in favor of printing books.

The business of news publication in Boston eventually was assigned to its postmaster, John Campbell, a loyal and otherwise conservative civil servant. The Boston *News-Letter,* which appeared in 1704, was "Published by Authority." This meant that all of its content had been duly approved for printing; it also insured that much of it was stale and dull. The *News-Letter* was not a very profitable venture; it attracted few readers and little advertising. Within a span of 20 years, however, it found itself competing with two rival Boston papers, the *Gazette* and the *New-England Courant*. Boston had become a three-newspaper city, and a newspaper industry had taken root in the New World.

The *New-England Courant* was founded by James Franklin and his apprenticed younger brother, Ben, along with the help of some local political dissidents. The dissidents hoped to use the newspaper to challenge the enormous power of congregationalist minister Cotton Mather and his allies in civil government. An early encounter with Mather led him to respond forcefully to the *Courant:*

> . . . the practice of supporting and publishing every week a libel of purpose to lessen and blacken and burlesque the virtuous and principal ministers of religion in a country, and render the services of their ministry despicable, even detestable, to the people, is a wickedness that was never known before in any country, Christian, Turkish, or Pagan, on the face of the earth.[7]

Despite the hue and cry, authorities did not immediately act to suppress the *Courant*. It was allowed to continue publishing its single sheet (both sides) of news, which combined reports of shipping, local gossip, letters from Europe, and letters to the editor from Boston readers. The letters took some liberties in their satiric comments on local happenings and personalities, and generally were signed with pseudonyms. Several of these secretly were contributed by brother Ben, who slipped his anonymous contributions under the print shop door. All went well at the *Courant* until James Franklin attempted more open criticism of the authorities. In 1723, the colonial government responded by forbidding him to publish the *Courant* or any other newspaper. The elder Franklin and his supporters countered by releasing young Ben Franklin from apprenticeship and promoting him to publisher.

Benjamin Franklin's talents were quickly revealed as dwarfing those of his older brother, leading to nasty quarrels. Before long, Ben Franklin fled Boston in secrecy, bound for Philadelphia and his own print shop. Nevertheless, the Franklins' activities at the *Courant* already had made their mark on the colonies. It had become clear that a newspaper could survive official censure providing it had a determined group of supporters willing to step in and provide continuity when necessary. The press could not readily be silenced.

The ability of a newspaper to withstand official censure soon was tested more severely in New York City, which was then ruled by an oppressive colonial administrator, Governor William Cosby. A poor, refugee printer named John Peter Zenger had been helped to establish a new newspaper, the *Weekly Journal*. His benefactors were a group of political dissidents, outspoken opponents of the governor. Their essays for the *Journal* objected to the tyrannical form of rule, calling for the establishment of representative government. Cosby soon responded by jailing Zenger on a charge of criminal libel, a serious offense, and refusing him reasonable bail. Zenger, who had not authored but merely printed the dissident opinions, was to be the scapegoat of inflamed authority.

With the help of Ben Franklin, Philadelphia lawyer Andrew Hamilton, then in his eighties, was persuaded to ride to New York (on horseback) to appear for Zenger's defense. Hamilton shocked the court by freely admitting Zenger had printed the materials in question, yet insisting that no crime had been committed. He argued that a charge of libel additionally required proof that the printed matter was, in fact, false, malicious, and seditious. Proof of sedition was not then required by law, but Hamilton was attempting to set a precedent. He addressed his comments to the jury, rather than the judge, arguing persuasively that jurors had the power to see justice done and need not support the unjust legal technicalities. Despite direction to the contrary by the presiding judge, the jury brought in a unanimous verdict of not guilty.

Andrew Hamilton had saved the day, successfully defending the role of the newspaper as critic of political events and related personalities.

Newspapers and news pamphlets eventually became important forces in supporting the American Revolution. By 1750 there were at least fourteen weeklies in the colonies, some quite successful. The imposition of a Stamp Act, in 1765, transformed many into organs of political ideology. This legislation imposed heavy taxes not only on tea (as is widely believed) but also on newspapers and legal documents. The tax would have been sufficient to destroy many papers, but publishers chose to evade the Stamp Act and argue for its abolition. As colonial opposition to the Crown attempted to rally support, the newspaper became a primary vehicle for political argument and propaganda. In the process, of course, accuracy sometimes suffered in the name of patriotism.

The potential of the newspaper to mobilize public opinion, to stimulate opposition to government authority, was realized on the eve of the American Revolution. Earliest establishment fears regarding the evil social and political influence of the print medium had proven justified. The Royalists, unable to suppress this new force, could resort only to publishing competing newspapers. War in the press preceded revolution in the streets.

The contributions of the press in stirring and supporting the revolt against English rule were confirmed and legitimized through the subsequent creation of the Bill of Rights, and particularly the First Amendment to the Constitution. That is, citizens who had just rebelled against oppressive authority were well aware that the press had provided vital information and communication during their struggles. The power of the printed word had been demonstrated, and many expressed grave reservations about ratifying a new constitution unless it guaranteed continued freedom of the press. Unwilling to risk a new tyranny, they required a free press to guard their new liberties and serve as watchdog against abuse of authority by the new government. As a result, the Constitution was amended as follows:

> Congress shall make no law representing an establishment of religion, or prohibiting the free exercise thereof; or abridging the freedom of speech, or of the press; or the right of the people peaceably to assemble, and to petition the government for a redress of grievances.

Freedom of the press, as provided for by the first amendment, was unique to the United States. British law, for example, had clearly subordinated the press to government. Consequently, the Founding

Fathers could not have predicted the profound consequences of their bold experiment. The first amendment, regarded by some as the great protector of American freedoms, has since been attacked repeatedly as a standing invitation to irresponsibility, immorality, profanity, and other evil influences. The question of whether government retains some right and responsibility to regulate a "free" press, and how this ought to be accomplished, has remained a central issue in the unending battle against a perceived media menace.

Taking Liberties

The initial response of the press to its new freedom was lacking in restraint, largely because such latter-day notions as fairness and objectivity in reporting had yet to be devised. During this period, the primary concern of a newspaper was the support of whatever faction financed and controlled it. Post-Revolutionary issues about how the new Republic ought to be governed, particularly with regard to states' rights versus centralized power, were the subject of diatribes by the various competing publications and the cause for rabid journalistic attacks upon George Washington and other notables. The editor of the *Gazette of the United States,* loyal to President Washington, in 1799, characterized American newspapers as "the most base, false, servile, and venal publications, that ever polluted the fountains of society." Another critic, in the same year, noted "Many of our American papers are not so valuable after being blackened and defiled by stupid printers and editors, as when immediately from the paper mill." Reviewing this period, media historian John Tebbel remarked on:

> . . . unprecedented vitriol pouring out from both sides of the politically controlled press, so vicious and unrestrained that the period between 1789 and 1808 has often been called by journalism historians the 'dark ages' of the American newspaper.[8]

Prior to the 1830s, the American press consisted of political papers, controlled by candidates or parties, and commercial papers, serving the interests of the business community. Both types of papers were relatively expensive, costing about six cents an issue, and were sold primarily by subscription; circulation was limited to a few thousand each. Most had the terms "advertiser," "mercantile," or "commercial" in their names. Although the press constituted a "mass medium," of sorts, it did not yet serve the masses. All of this was to change dramatically in subsequent decades, a period characterized by democratization of many aspects of American life and the rise of an urban middle-class.

During the 1830s a group of newspapers broke with tradition to establish a radically new model of journalism. These were the "penny papers," inexpensive newspapers that were sold in the streets, by newsboys, rather than by annual subscription. The first of these, the *New York Sun,* appeared in 1833 and quickly achieved new heights in circulation. In 1835, it was emulated by two other penny papers, the *Evening Transcript* and the *New York Herald.* Soon the concept spread from New York City to other urban centers, and a new era in journalism had begun. Instead of serving the interests of political and mercantile leaders, the penny papers were addressed to middle-class readers. The need to reach these people, to achieve broader circulation, became the dominant motive of the new industry. The newspaper was on the verge of becoming a true mass medium.

The need to attract and maintain readership required many changes from traditional newspaper practices. Some of these were foreshadowed in a statement by James Gordon Bennett, founder of the *New York Herald:*

> Our only guide shall be good sound practical common sense, applicable to the business and bosoms of men engaged in everyday life. We shall support no party, be the organ of no faction or coterie, and care nothing for any election or any candidate from President down to constable. We shall endeavor to record facts, on every public and proper subject, stripped of verbiage and coloring, with comments suitable, just, independent, fearless and goodtempered . . .[9]

Not only did Bennett announce his independence from politics, but he set as a journalistic goal the accurate presentation of facts. This is not to say that he was successful in achieving such objectivity, but he did succeed in establishing a new set of goals for the newspaper industry. He attempted to report the news in a blunt, straightforward style, eschewing the polite euphemisms of the day. He dared to print the word "leg" instead of "limb," and "shirt" instead of "linen." Moreover, the crime, sin and corruption of city life were routinely exposed; murder became daily newspaper fare. Editorials were used to satirize the foibles of politicians, businessmen, clergy, and the establishment in general—to the delight of readers. Bennett's *Herald* soon became one of the most important New York City papers of its era.

The new type of newspaper was not without its critics, particularly among the established six-penny papers. The *Boston Spectator,* in

1836, stated that the new penny papers were "doing infinitely more to promote licentiousness and corrupt our youth, then they were doing good." In 1840, the establishment press declared a "Moral War" designed to put the *Herald* out of business, charging its editor with lies, libel, indecency, blasphemy, and evil influence. A group of newspapers regularly attacked Bennett and the *Herald* by name in their editorials, and some refused to accept ads for establishments that advertised in the *Herald*. Respectable men and women, it was said, would not buy or read the *Herald*, and hotels, clubs, and reading rooms were urged to ban Bennett's "dirty sheet." Bennett was variously labelled an "obscene vagabond," "a polluted wretch," and a "venomous reptile"; he was accused of "reckless depravity" and "moral leprosy." The *Herald*, and the new form of journalism, survived.

Some of the criticism aimed at the penny papers was clearly justified. In 1835, for example, the *Sun* published a series of articles on astronomical discoveries made by means of a new telescope. After a few days of introductory comments, the details of flora and fauna observed on the moon were reported. The most sensational of the articles described the activities of man-bat creatures discovered to inhabit the satellite. These sensational reports sold many thousands of newspapers and excited the entire nation. A final article in the series told of an unfortunate problem with the telescope that prevented further observations. Eventually, of course, the series was exposed as a hoax, perpetrated by *Sun* writer Richard Adams Locke. Several years later, Edgar Allan Poe contributed his own hoax, reporting upon a "steering balloon," which completed an ocean crossing in three days. Such stunts enraged the more straight-laced, "respectable" newspapers, but they succeeded in attracting still more readers to the penny papers.

In general, criticisms of the penny press were similar to the early charges against the English press. Sensationalism, the exploitation of criminal activities, inaccuracy, and misleading advertising were all cited as sins of the new newspapers. Such sins were only compounded by their popularity. In 1836 the *Public Ledger* noted:

> In the cities of New York and Brooklyn, containing a population of 300,000, the daily circulation of the penny papers is not less than 70,000. This is nearly sufficient to place a newspaper in the hands of every man in the two cities, and even of every boy old enough to read. These papers are to be found in every street, lane, and alley; in every hotel, tavern, counting-house, shop, etc.[10]

The establishment press had concerned itself with presenting important political and commercial events to a small, respectable audience. The penny press, however, introduced a revolutionary set of goals and policies. It asserted that ordinary people were entitled to the news of the day, reported in a straightforward manner, free of censorship or social taboos. A newspaper was said to be responsible to its readers, rather than any political or commercial interests. Readers were entitled to know the facts of crime and scandal occurring in their communities, as well as other happenings of "human-interest." The result was a reframing of the entire business of news publishing, such that the general public became the object of its attentions.

The new approach to journalism was further advanced by Horace Greeley, who founded the New York *Tribune* in 1841. Greeley devoted special efforts to the matter of influencing public opinion through editorial examination of current issues. Where Bennett's *Herald* emphasized news gathering, the strength of the *Tribune* lay in editorial opinion and debate. Greeley was particularly concerned with massive social changes occurring during this period, and their effects upon the poor; he also pressed Lincoln for the immediate emancipation of the slaves. A few decades later, Samuel Clemens (Mark Twain) indicated that he was less than impressed with the role of the newspaper in influencing public opinion. In 1873 he noted:

> That awful power, the public opinion of this nation, is formed and molded by a horde of ignorant self-complacent simpletons who failed at ditching and shoemaking and fetched up in journalism on their way to the poorhouse.[11]

Despite the considerable changes in journalism that occurred during the 1830s and 1840s, many historians place the birth of the New Journalism in the post-Civil War era. The years between 1865 and 1900 were characterized by a host of social, cultural, and political changes linked to the industrial revolution and the urbanization of America. In this period of time the population of the country doubled, manufacturing increased sevenfold, and electricity was harnessed for light and power; telegraph and telephone lines made their way across the nation. Increased national wealth also created significant progress in mass education and culture. Amidst all of this change, the newspaper experienced a considerable evolution of its own. The development of the newspaper, in this era, is best traced through the activities of journalists Joseph Pulitzer and William Randolph Hearst.

Pulitzer founded the St. Louis *Post-Dispatch* in 1878 and quickly built it into that city's leading newspaper. He was, from the first, a crusader, using the newspaper to attack corruption in all quarters. He insisted upon a relentless search for the facts related to such stories. Consequently, he succeeded in establishing the *Post-Dispatch* as a model of courage and integrity in journalism. A champion for the common man, Pulitzer willingly tackled the evils of big business and crooked politics. More, he offered a vision of what a newspaper ought to be:

> An institution that should always fight for progress and reform, never tolerate injustice or corruption, always fight demagogues of all parties, never belong to any party, always oppose privileged classes and public plunderers, never lack sympathy with the poor, always remain devoted to the public welfare, never be satisfied with merely printing news, always be drastically independent, never be afraid to attack wrong, whether by predatory plutocracy or predatory poverty.[12]

In 1883, Pulitzer went to New York City to purchase the *World,* and he developed it into the nation's leading newspaper. He attracted 250,000 readers by combining thorough news coverage, aggressive editorials, eye-catching headlines, and human interest stories. Low priced, popularized, and entertaining, the *World* was attracting a new audience— the rapidly increasing urban working class, the burgeoning immigrant population of the cities. The front page of the *World,* of course, was objectionable to some; its headlines were filled with sex, scandal, and corruption. Aimed at the working class, it was damned by intellectuals as blatant sensationalism. The editorial page, on the other hand, contained well-written and informed discussion of the issues of the day. Pulitzer attempted to be all things to all people, hoping to capture the widest possible readership without abandoning his editorial idealism. His chief rival, William Randolph Hearst, displayed no such ambivalence.

Hearst first used the San Francisco *Examiner* to emulate Pulitzer's techniques for attracting readership, developing it into a more sensationalized version of the *World.* It took him only a year to double that newspaper's circulation. Like Bennett and Pulitzer before him, Hearst filled the front page with sensational headlines of sex, crime, and scandal. He initiated his own crusades, although some doubted the depth of his convictions. In 1896, Hearst arrived in New York City to found the *Journal* and to take on Pulitzer in direct competition. Hearst adopted and developed many of Pulitzer's own innovations and used his vast financial resources to hire away some of the best *World* staff. He found new causes to champion and new corruptions to expose; he introduced a new style of editorial, written in simple words and short sentences. Moreover, the *Journal* concentrated on developing its art department; it pioneered in the use of color printing, the creation of comic strips, and the application of photography to news reporting. In sum, Hearst perfected a powerful formula for reaching the working class, for taking the medium to the masses. The resulting formula, however, was anathema to the American intellectual community, and it quickly came to be viewed as a primary source of evil influence.

Press and Mind

The printing press originally entered a European society composed of medieval monarchies. It was a time of rigidly stratified, authoritarian governments, whose leaders proclaimed their divine right to rule. The powerful Roman Church claimed responsibility for the spiritual guidance of humanity, based upon divine revelations. Both secular and religious realms were provided for by authoritarian hierarchies. The individual, particularly the peasant, had relatively few decisions to make about his actions and beliefs. State and church created powerful legal and moral doctrines, which bound the common folk and effectively defined their universe. Information was rigidly controlled, as the authorities took full responsibility for deciding what was good for people to know.

The Renaissance began a series of profound social and intellectual changes in European society, many of which were furthered by the Enlightenment of the seventeenth and eighteenth centuries (chapter 2). The eighteenth century was marked by the rapid growth of science, industry, and an ethic of rationality. The conviction grew that humanity might be capable of understanding the universe without recourse to the supernatural and that such understanding would lead to increasing mastery of nature. This emphasis upon logic and rationality severely challenged and undermined the traditional authority of both church and state. Where previously the individual human being was thought to be weak, flawed, and dependent upon church and state for guidance, a new philosophy suggested that people were rational, independent, and able to choose intelligently between right and wrong. The press, by making more information available to greater numbers of people, played a part in reinforcing the new philosophy. Inevitably, this earned for newspapers and journalists the harshest forms of censure and retaliation from established authorities. In the eyes of those concerned with preserving the status quo, the press was undeniably a source of evil influence.

In America, Thomas Jefferson took note of the new philosophy and the role of the press, as follows:

No experiment can be more interesting than what we are now trying, and which we trust will end in establishing the fact, that man may be governed by reason and truth. Our first object should therefore be, to leave open to him all the avenues of truth. The most effectual hitherto found, is freedom of the press. It is therefore the first to be shut up by those who fear the investigation of their actions.[13]

This noble experiment, however, was directed toward the educated, propertied, white males of the newly created country. The poor, the female, and the black were never considered in this context, and the working class urban masses had yet to congregate. The landed intellectuals who helped to frame the Constitution and provide for freedom of the press naturally had in mind the existing press and its existing audience. When the industrial revolution and rapid urbanization of America created a new kind of press for a new kind of reader, the notion of a "free press" began to look less desirable to the wealthy and the educated. They noted the war for supremacy between Hearst and Pulitzer, and the new heights of journalistic sensationalism thereby generated, and wondered whether the working class really ought to be reading such things. Was it necessary or helpful to anyone? Was it, rather, a source of evil influence and corruption loosed upon a naive and intellectually limited mass audience?

Edwin Godkin, in 1894, complained of a "villainous" press that appealed to a "childish" public, adding:

I know of no good influence now which is acting on the masses, and the practice of reading trivial newspapers begets, even among men of some education, a puerile habit of mind.[14]

In 1896 a movement to ban both the *World* (Pulitzer) and the *Journal* (Hearst) was initiated by those who deemed them a public menace. Clergymen spoke against them in sermons, clubs and libraries canceled subscriptions, and so on. All of this had little effect upon their circulation or success. Sex-and-crime sensationalism remained much in evidence, with artists at the *Journal* adding illustrations designed to produce still greater emotional impact. Headlines grew bigger and blacker; full-width "banner" headlines regularly appeared on the front pages. If the newspaper was about to destroy American minds and morals, there seemed little way to stop it.

It seems clear, in retrospect, that much of the fear and moral outrage generated by the newspapers was stimulated by their "sensationalism," their determination to arouse an emotional response in the reader. The formula for accomplishing this required detailed descriptions of sexual scandals and violent crimes, large and shocking headlines, and numerous illustrations. News hoaxes, provocative advertising, color printing, and comic strips were also helpful. Such appeal to the emotions was antithetical to the logical, rational mode of thought that was the ideal of the Enlightenment. The great experiment in reason, as proposed by Jefferson, seemed little related to the reality of the daily newspaper at the turn of the twentieth century. The vision of the nation's masses being daily assaulted and manipulated by the newspapers was frightening to many; where might it lead? Society surely required protection from such evil influence; the masses surely required protection from an unscrupulous press.

Freedom of the press in the United States had created a unique social situation. In place of governmental or religious controls on the distribution of information, there was created a free marketplace of ideas. These ideas might differ not only in content but also in the manner of their presentation and their intended audience. Consequently, individuals of vastly differing backgrounds, outlooks, and capabilities could shop freely for those sources of information that appealed to them. The right of each individual to choose from competing offerings was made paramount in America, even where it appeared to threaten society as a whole. The question remained, however, whether this was a suitable or practical system for the poor, the immigrants, the workers, the masses. Even educated, middle-class individuals might find themselves overwhelmed and confused by a multitude of competing ideas, sensationalized accounts of the news, irresponsible advertising, and manipulation of the emotions.

Were the newspapers destroying minds? A prominent New York City physician and expert on neurasthenia (nervous exhaustion), George M. Beard, in 1881, cited the newspaper as one of the causative agents in an epidemic of "nervousness." His popular book *American Nervousness, Its Causes and Consequences* defined nervousness as a deficiency of nerve-force. Already epidemic in the urban centers of the East Coast, neurasthenia was said to be a disease of modern (nineteenth-century) civilization. The role of mass communication, via telegraph and newspaper, was particularly important, as it carried the sorrows and horrors of all parts of the globe directly to millions of homes and minds. The result was a massive draining of nervous energy, leading to the deficiency state known as neurasthenia (see Beard quotation, chapter 1).

Beard was concerned that Americans were suffering from an overload of information and overly taxed emotional resources as a partial result of reading the daily newspaper. Other culprits included steam power, travel by railroad, and "the mental activity of women." Beard also pointed out that the liberty allowed Americans in making choices for themselves was responsible for considerable nervous strain. Apparently, a free market place of ideas was hazardous to one's health.

Not only were newspaper readers bombarded by bad news from all parts of the world, they were also exposed daily to the strange mosaic patterns of unrelated items that composed the news page. Unlike books, newspapers did not offer a clear, linear, rational organization of information. Rather, they presented a smorgasbord of serious news, features, ads, games, puzzles, comics, fiction, and so on. These were soon joined by the "interview," a new form of news. A report in *The Nation* (1869) complained: "The interview as at present managed, is generally the joint product of some humbug of a hack politician and another humbug of a reporter." The interview, to critics, was merely another form of "nonnews," along with comics, puzzles, and other light entertainment. The juxtaposition of "news" and "nonnews," sorrows and puzzles, murders and comics, in the same documents encouraged a curious new kind of mental activity on the part of readers. Rapid shifts in attention and mood were required and engendered; emotional involvement might be quite intense and yet abruptly terminated by turning to the comics. Critics perceived this as a potentially dangerous mental and emotional development.

While the development of the newspaper as a medium was to continue, the basic outline of the media controversy had already taken shape by the beginning of the twentieth century. That is, a medium offering sensational/emotional appeal, and/or a nonlinear, nonrational mode of presentation, must pose a threat to the mental, emotional, and moral health of vulnerable Americans.

In retrospect, of course, early controversy regarding the newspaper strikes a somewhat quaint historical note. Today, the "menace" has been invested in newer forms of media, leaving the newspaper an old and widely accepted institution. There are trashy newspapers, to be sure, but most believe that there are excellent ones as well. More important to our concerns, there is little feeling today that daily newspaper reading is ruining the mental health of millions. Our entire population has grown up with dailies, weeklies, and huge Sunday supplements, and few have found them a serious source of mental confusion or moral corruption. "Newspaper reading" is nowhere to be found among the published lists of etiological factors in psychiatric illness. The dire predictions and grave concerns of the critics, it seems, were exaggerated with regard to the adverse psychological impact of the medium.

The cries of "evil influence" arose largely from the fears of well-intentioned citizens in response to the introduction by newspapers of sensational/emotional elements into their carefully ordered world views. Illustrations, photographs, bold headlines, and "graphic" descriptions were particularly threatening in this regard. The powerful images promoted by newspapers possessed a menacing quality that was objectionable to many. Book-oriented worshippers of the rational word were particularly affected. We will find further evidence for this thesis as we examine, in coming chapters, some closely related media developments.

Notes

1. Cited in Harold Herd, *The March of Journalism* (London: George Allen and Unwin, 1952), p. 11.
2. Ibid, pp. 19–20.
3. Ibid, pp. 19–20.
4. Ibid, p. 21.
5. Cited in Lee Brown, *The Reluctant Reformation* (New York: David McKay, 1974), p. 22.
6. Cited in John Tebbel, *The Media in America* (New York: Thomas Cromwell, 1974), p. 4.
7. Ibid, p. 22.
8. Ibid, p. 71.
9. Ibid, p. 167.
10. Cited in Frank Luther Mott, *American Journalism* (New York: Macmillan, 1962), p. 241.
11. Samuel Clemens, cited by Melvin L. Defleur in Wilbur Schramm and Donald Roberts, *The Process and Effects of Mass Communication* (Urbana, IL: University of Illinois Press, 1974), p. 66.
12. Cited in Tebbel, op. cit., p. 264.
13. Thomas Jefferson, cited in William L. Rivers and Wilbur Schramm, *Responsibility in Mass Communication* (New York: Harper and Row, 1969), p. 38.
14. Cited in Brown, op. cit., p. 28.

4

Fear of Fiction: The Novel

> . . . *it may, with confidence, be pronounced,*
> *that no one was ever an extensive and*
> *habitual reader of novels, even supposing*
> *them all to be well selected, without suffering*
> *both intellectual and moral injury and of*
> *course incurring a diminution of happiness.*
> —Reverend Samuel Miller, 1803

Although the sensationalism of early newspapers was widely declared both vulgar and evil, it nevertheless found a receptive audience. In fact, the greater the emotional impact and sensational appeal of any newspaper, the more successful it was in gaining and maintaining circulation. The eventual reaction against sensationalism was related directly to the strength of its appeal to the masses. That is, the greater the audience, the greater the presumed threat to individual health and to social order. A similar situation evolved in the public's reaction to fiction and the novel. Powerful attraction to the more emotional/sensational aspects of fiction inevitably was met by powerful opposition to such literature. Early prose fiction, as serialized in periodicals or published in book form, soon was denounced and damned as an evil influence. Before we examine this development, however, a bit of background is in order.

Approaching the Novel

Sensationalism did not begin with fiction or the newspaper; it appeared even in earlier religious literature. In this context, of course, it was more acceptable to establishment observers. The power to create intense imagery, to stimulate emotional responses, and to transcend the rational was perfectly appropriate to religious practices and writings. The first American best seller, for example, was the Rev. Michael Wigglesworth's *The Day of Doom* (1662). Popular in New England for a century, it presented in verse a Calvinist vision of judgment day and its horrors for the sinful:

> Its presentation had an emotional drive, a vividness of imagery, and a compelling narrative movement all combined in great effectiveness. Here were verses far more sensational than the ballads about murders and hangings that were sold on the street, and Wigglesworth's influence over generations of New Englanders came largely from his shocking sensationalism.[1]

Another popular religious work marked by powerful sensational/emotional elements was *The Practice of Piety* (1665) by Lewis Bayle. Composed of meditations and prayers for all occasions, it included powerful representations of the consequences of original sin. "O Wretched Man! where shall I begin to describe thine endless Misery?" The specific miseries of youth, adulthood, aging, and death were then delineated in detail, and these were mere prelude to the tortures of Hell, with its "ghastly Spirits," "howling Devils," "noisome stench," and so on.

Another religious work, John Bunyan's *The Pilgrim's Progress* (1678), was so widely read and enjoyed in England that it was dismissed by intellectuals of its era as mere popular fare. A religious allegory which read somewhat like a novel, it went through 160 editions by 1792; some 120 American editions are recorded. The work is said to have been as widely circulated in England as the Bible. It concerned the pilgrimage of a man named Christian through sundry dangers and distractions on his journey to the Celestial City. Bunyan's personal experiences and feelings were translated into Christian's encounters with such characters as Obstinate, Pliable, Ignorance, Worldly Wiseman, and such. More important to our considerations, Christian encountered significant hazards and enemies on his journey, including Giant Despair and the demon Apollyon. Hence his passage was marked by many dramatic situations and adventures. Simply written and cheaply published, Christian's adventures soon were available to all. The remarkable success of this work, later recognized as a classic, provides early evidence of the public's interest in a literature of excitement and adventure.

A form of literature popular in Colonial America was the "captivity" book. This involved a personal account of being captured and tortured by Indians. One such work detailed the slaughter of friends and neighbors, near starvation, enforced nakedness, and other trials of its female author. It was called *The Sovereignty and Goodness of GOD, Together With the Faithfulness of His Promises Displayed; Being a Narrative Of the Captivity and Restauration of Mrs. Mary Rowlandson* (1682).

Another captivity work was *Jonathan Dickinson's Journal; or, God's Protecting Providence* (1699), the story of a Quaker missionary. The book documented his shipwreck, capture by naked savages, tortures, and his struggles to escape. It was, therefore, a tale of high adventure despite its diary format and religious overtones.

There also existed a realm of adventure literature outside the province of religion. Stories of Alexander the Great, Charlemagne, King Arthur and the Knights of the Round Table, the fall of Troy, and so on, were embedded in the English cultural and literary heritage. Such "romances" generally were in verse, intended for recitation at court, but many eventually appeared in prose. The *History of the British Kings* (circa 1139 A.D.), written in Latin by Geoffrey of Monmouth, included the story of King Arthur's origins, coronation, conquests, and eventual passage to Avalon. Many years later, the adventures of Arthur and his knights were rendered in a prose romance entitled *Le Morte d'Arthur* (1485) by Sir Thomas Mallory. It was one of the first prose romances to be generally available in English. Not only did the Arthur stories offer battles between gallant knights, fights with dragons and monsters, powerful magicians and enchanted swords, but also considerable discourse on the nature and conduct of love. The problems of lovers, such as Lancelot and Guinevere, early established their literary niche by way of these romances.

Exactly where and when the first true "novel" appeared, and which previous literature most contributed to its conception, is not critical to our concerns. For many, however, Daniel Defoe's *Robinson Crusoe* (1719) is considered the first English novel of incident. (A novel of incident is one in which the story line and its action takes precedence over the characters. In the novel of character, the portrayal of human beings is more important than the action of the plot.) Writers before Defoe had produced stories of adventure and fantasy, but the storytelling art reached a new level with his work. Unlike his predecessors, Defoe struggled to create a sense of reality in his story. Rather than invent fantastic monsters and heroes, he placed Crusoe in a desperate but realistic situation in which he had to learn novel ways to house, feed, and clothe himself. Readers were able to identify with an ordinary human being struggling to survive an extraordinary—but not fantastic—situation. A moral and religious message was included concerning trust in God and the merits of patience and industry, but much of the religious material was edited out in subsequent editions.

Robinson Crusoe was an immediate and great success; it became a permanent part of English literature. Widely read in America even before its Colonial publication (1774), it was translated eventually into almost all languages. Written for a popular audience, *Robinson Crusoe* was also the first work of fiction to appear as a newspaper serial (in 1719). Its success may be attributed to its realistic style and attention to detail, an adventure theme, and its powerful appeal for ordinary, middle-class readers. Through the device of telling the story in the first person, Defoe made it easy for readers to identify with Crusoe and thereby become personally involved in his trials and triumphs.

Although he authored a tale of adventure, Defoe did not attempt to tamper directly with the emotions of his audience. His style remained cool and matter-of-fact; there were no sensational episodes or emotional appeals. Even the death of Crusoe's companion, Friday, was dealt with in a brief and matter-of-fact manner. The moral message of the work was intended to supercede its emotional impact. The preface, moreover, indicated that the editor (Defoe) believed this material to be a true history rather than a fiction and stressed the religious and moral lessons of the work. The "novel," as such, had not yet taken on a mature form; it remained relatively innocent, hardly a cause for serious censure or concern. Still, Defoe had produced the first lengthy prose fiction which deliberately created the illusion of reality, and this was a critical development.

While Defoe provided the public with a new kind of realistic adventure, a few authors attempted the same realism in the realm of romance. Titles such as *Love in Excess* (1719) and the *Secret History of Cleomira* (1722), by Mrs. Haywood, seemed to promise passion and sensation, but these were nowhere to be found within their contents. Such works were akin to the writings of Defoe in that they dealt with realistic happenings while carefully avoiding the emotional/sensational aspects of life. Although they concerned romantic relationships, they were intent upon providing a moral message regarding the importance of virtue and did so in a rather rational and abstract style. Even the "love scenes" were cool and rational: "After this a considerable time was passed in all those mutual endearments which honour and modesty would permit" (*The History of Miss Betsy Thoughtless*). These early novels adhered to a cultural code that required rational behavior, good taste, and common sense in all matters, love and sex included.

Enter Pamela

On November 6, 1740, a little known but well-to-do London printer, Samuel Richardson, published anonymously a book called *Pamela: or, Virtue Rewarded*. The work was an immediate and overwhelming success. Only a few months later the London *Daily Advertiser* carried this announcement:

> This Day is published (Price bound 6s) In two neat Pocket Volumes The Second Edition (to which are prefix'd Extracts from several curious Letters written to the Editor on the Subject) of Pamela: or, Virtue rewarded. In a Series of Familiar Letters From A Beautiful Young Damsel, To Her Parents. Now first Published In order to cultivate the Principles of Virtue and Religion in the Minds of the Youth of Both Sexes. A Narrative which has its Foundation in Truth and Nature; and at the same time that it agreeably entertains, by a Variety of curious and affecting Incidents, is entirely divested of all those Images, which, in too many Pieces calculated for Amusement only, tend to inflame the Minds they should instruct.[2]

In Richardson's story, Pamela Andrews, a poor-but-virtuous servant girl in a wealthy household faced severe moral and physical trials following the death of her mistress. Suddenly she was subjected to the determined advances of the young master of the house, initially through seduction and later through attempted rape. All the while, Pamela struggled to maintain virtue and virginity and, in the end, was rewarded by a proposal of marriage (which she accepted). Readers followed these events by means of a series of letters written by Pamela at critical moments (or immediately thereafter), rather than by way of any story-telling narrative. The plot was less than challenging, as noted by Samuel Johnson: "Why Sir, if you were to read Richardson for the story, your impatience would be so much fretted that you would hang yourself. But you must read him for the sentiment."

Considered by some to be the first "true" novel, *Pamela* is primarily a novel of character. Substituting correspondence for narrative, Richardson immersed his readers in the moment-to-moment inner experience of his characters, each of whom was acutely self-aware. Instead of being told a story, readers were encouraged to experience firsthand the characters' lives and struggles. With a little imagination, one could take residence in Pamela's mind and perceive the world through her senses. Richardson called his technique "writing to the moment," a method of describing emotions/sensations as they arose rather than in cool recollection. The focus of the entire novel was upon the emotional tensions created by characters in their dealings with one another. Clearly, this sort of "sentimental" novel represented a break from the flat, rational, matter-of-fact prose narratives that had preceded it.

Like Defoe, Richardson chose to publish his novel as an edited set of "authentic" documents. Both authors attempted thereby to underscore the realism of their work and avoid religious objections to "fiction" (sometimes interpreted by the pious as "lies"). Richardson was not able to maintain his pose for long, however, in the face of *Pamela*'s astounding popularity. Within a year, five editions had been published and several translations were under way. It became "must" reading for fashionable ladies, and many purchased decorated fans that reproduced scenes from the book (an early "media tie-in"). By 1742, three versions of the story had appeared on the English stage. A wax-work representation of Pamela and her adventures appeared on a London street corner. Alexander Pope, who sat up all night reading it, remarked that *Pamela* "will do more good than a great many of the new sermons." Another Pope felt otherwise, and the work soon appeared on the Papal index of banned books. Nevertheless, Benjamin Franklin elected to reprint *Pamela* for the colonies, and it became thereby the first English novel to be produced in America.

Pamela was far too successful to be ignored. Reaction was swift and took two distinct forms; there were those who ridiculed the work and those who imitated it. The latter penned such titles as *Pamela's Conduct in High Life, Life of Pamela,* and *Pamela The Second,* while the former offered somewhat more creative titles including *Anti-Pamela, or Feigned Innocence Detected* and *Shamela.* The subtitle of *Shamela,* written by Henry Fielding, read as follows:

> An Apology For The Life of Mrs. Pamela Andrews In which the many notorious Falsehoods and Misrepresentations of a Book called Pamela are exposed and refuted; and all the matchless Arts of that young Politician set in a true and a just light. Together with a full Account of all that passed between her and Parson Arthur Williams; whose Character is represented in a manner something different from that which he bears in Pamela. The whole being exact Copies of authentick Papers delivered to the editor. Necessary to be had in all families.

Fielding's *Shamela* satirized the story, morality, and sentiment of *Pamela.* Using a parallel story line, he completely reversed the motives of the characters such that Pamela was really the scheming seductress. Not yet satisfied, Fielding next published *Joseph Andrews* (1742), which renewed the attack and became the most famous of the Anti-Pamela works. In this book, Pamela's brother, Joseph, is the household servant whose virtue is constantly assaulted by aggressive females. Bernard Kreissman, in his study *Pamela-Shamela* (1960), offered this view of Fielding's two efforts to depose *Pamela:*

> In these two works, Fielding sounded most of the notes which were to be amplified by later critics of *Pamela. Shamela* by its open bawdiness was a

condemnation of the concealed eroticism of *Pamela,* though in the main it was an attack on Pamela's business view of morality. *Joseph Andrews,* on a far higher level, continued the assault by a dissection of the personality of such views. It centered in its charge on the hypocrisy, the vanity, the affectation, and the snobbery of Pamela's ethical outlook, though it too criticized the hints of lechery lurking between the lines of Pamela's letters.[3]

Fielding was not the only observer to question the effects of reading *Pamela* upon minds and morals. In 1741, an Anti-*Pamela* pamphlet was published, anonymously, whose primary objections appeared upon its title page:

Pamela Censored: In A Letter To The Editor. Showing That under the Specious Pretence of Cultivating the Principles of Virtue in the Minds of the Youth of both sexes, the Most Artful and Alluring Amorous Ideas are convey'd. And that, instead of being divested of all Images that tend to inflame, Her letters abound with Incidents, which must necessarily raise in the unwary Youth that read them, Emotions far distant from the Principles of Virtue.

The author of *Pamela Censored* went on to express the concern that young men reading Richardson's book would be tempted into repeating the seduction/rape scenes with "some other Pamelas." Moreover, the work might fill innocent readers with "lewd ideas." All of this begins to sound very familiar, as it is simply an early expression of the standard anti-media critique. *Pamela,* and the new form of realistic fiction, stood accused as an evil influence.

The pens of Richardson, Sterne, Smollett, Fielding, and others produced an outpouring of realistic, sentimental prose fiction in the years following the appearance of *Pamela.* Richardson's *History of Clarissa Harlowe* (1747-48) and Fielding's *Tom Jones* (1749) were major landmarks in the maturation of the realistic, dramatic novel. Conversational dialogue appeared for the first time, so that readers could directly witness crucial encounters rather than hear of them retrospectively. In *Tom Jones,* an omniscient, omnipresent narrator replaced the fictive "editor" of bundles of letters or chance-found manuscripts. Laurence Sterne took the novel to new levels of emotionalism, as the mere experience and/or expression of emotion increasingly was glorified without reference to its morality. Soon it became fashionable to write novels in which even melancholia and suicide had prominent roles.

Horace Walpole, in 1764, took the step of adding a mysterious Gothic setting and supernatural terror to the novel of sentiment, publishing *The Castle of Otranto.* The original preface declared the work to be an old manuscript found in the library of a long-established English family, translated from an Italian original. In a second edition, Walpole confessed his authorship and his intention to blend the ancient and the modern types of romance in his work. He wished to maintain the achievements of realism with regard to character, while placing people in more interesting, even extraordinary, situations. Walpole's much imitated work soon yielded a new popular genre, the Gothic novel. Others authors were experimenting with historical and Oriental novels. The floodgates had been opened.

As it gained in popularity, the novel eventually created a hue and cry worthy of being labelled "social crisis." Although considered sinful or merely worthless in educated circles, by the dawn of the nineteenth century prose fiction had become extremely popular. The primary audience for the novel was not among upper-class intellectuals but among the increasingly visible middle class. Innovations in writing technique had made it possible for the novel reader to become intensely involved in realistic situations of great variety, to identify with characters, to visualize highly detailed scenes, and to experience intense emotions. One could share the most intimate experiences, in complete privacy, with little apparent risk. This was too delicious an opportunity for most to miss. At the same time, this situation raised the hackles of intellectuals, educators, and clergy everywhere. Such figures were certain that the novel reader risked much, and they set out to warn society of its peril. A world of morality and rationality was threatened by the romanticism, sensationalism, and emotionality of the novel. At special risk were young women, who had become a major part of the novel-reading audience. An English article entitled "Novel Reading a Cause of Female Depravity" (1797) was reprinted in America several times in the service of warning.

Denouncing the Novel

Critics in the late eighteenth and early nineteenth centuries expressed their considerable alarm at the popularity of novels and novel reading. An article in *The Christian Spectator* (1822) noted:

> Till lately, it was well settled, in most pious families, what books were, and what books were not admissable. Fiction in nearly all its forms was prohibited, not merely on account of its moral blemishes and unreal pictures of human life, but as tending in its very nature to enervate the youthful mind, and give it a disrelish for substantial and profitable reading.[4]

Along similar lines, a retrospective article in the *American Monthly*

Magazine (1824) noted that novel reading was once considered about as disreputable as betting at a cockfight or gaming table. It went on to say:

> Those who had sons would have supposed them forever incapacitated for any useful pursuit in life, if they exhibited any inclination for novel reading; and those who had daughters who exhibited such an inclination would have considered them as totally unfitted for ever becoming good wives or mothers; and if they found, after due attempts at correction, that the evil was incurable, lest the report of it should ruin the young lady's marriage proposals, they uniformly endeavored to keep it as profoundly secret . . .[5]

In the 1806 Phi Beta Kappa address at Yale University, Samuel P. Jarvis warned that the taste for novels had reached an astounding and alarming level. He added that "The evil consequences attendant upon novel reading are much greater than has generally been imagined."

What exactly was it about novels and novel reading that was so shameful and evil? Opinions varied, but Carl Van Doren has offered the following summation:

> The dullest critics contended that novels were lies; the pious that they served no virtuous purpose; the strenuous, that they softened sturdy minds; the utilitarian, that they crowded out more useful books; the realistic, that they painted adventure too romantic and love too vehement; the patriotic, that dealing with European manners, they tended to confuse and dissatisfy republican youth.[6]

In "The Progress of Error" (1780), William Cowper provided a memorable and poetic critique of fiction and the novel, including an opinion regarding the motives of both writers and readers:

> Ye writers of what none with safety reads,
> Footing it in the dance that fancy leads:
> Ye novelists, who mar what ye would mend,
> Snivelling and drivelling folly without end;
> Whose corresponding misses fill the ream
> With sentimental frippery and dream,
> Caught in a delicate soft silken net
> By some lewd earl or rake-hell baronet:
> Ye pimps, who, under Virtue's fair pretense,
> Steal to the closet of young Innocence,
> And teach her, inexperienced yet and green,
> To scribble as you scribbled at fifteen;
> Who, kindling a combustion of desire,
> With some cold moral think to quench the fire;
> Though all your engineering proves in vain,
> The dribbling stream ne'er puts it out again.

Oh that a verse had power, and could command
Far, far away, those flesh-flies of the land,
Who fasten without mercy on the fair,
And suck, and leave a craving maggot there.
Howe'er disguised th'inflammatory tale,
And covered with a fine-spun specious veil,
Such writers, and such readers, owe the gust
And relish of their pleasure all to lust.[7]

Another prominent observer, Samuel Johnson, was particularly concerned about the consequences of identification with realistically portrayed fictional characters. The characters in question were those endowed with both positive and negative qualities. Our participation in their adventures, he argued, would lead us gradually to "lose the abhorrence of their faults" and "regard them with some kindness." It was necessary, therefore, to create characters that were clearly drawn as Good or Evil. Only in this manner might readers be spared the moral corruption implicit in the realistic novel.

Still other observers contended that novels contributed to an overstimulation of the imagination at the expense of appropriate orientation to reality. Among these were Thomas Jefferson:

> When this poison infects the mind, it destroys its tone and revolts it against wholesome reading . . . The result is a bloated imagination, sickly judgement, and disgust towards all the real businesses of life.[8]

A similar sentiment was expressed by the Rev. Samuel Miller, who wrote that novel reading:

> . . . has a tendency to dissipate the mind, to beget a dislike to more solid and instructive reading, and in general, to excite a greater fondness for the production of imagination and fancy than for sober reasoning and the practical investigations of wisdom.[9]

According to an article in *Weekly Magazine* (1798), the dangers of an overactive imagination applied particularly to the young female of the species:

> Novels not only pollute the imaginations of young women, but likewise give them false ideas of life, which too often make them act improperly; owing to the romantic turn of thinking they imbibe from their favorite studies. They read of characters which never existed, and never can exist . . . it requires more discernment than is to be found in youth to separate the evil from the good . . . the evil steals imperceptibly into her heart, while she thinks she is reading sterling morality.[10]

A similar opinion was offered by the *Monthly Mirror* (1797):

> . . . those who first made novel reading an indispensible branch in forming the minds of young women have a great deal to answer for. Without this poison instilled, as it were, into the blood females in ordinary life could never have been so much the slaves of vice.[11]

Connecticut minister and poet Timothy Dwight also warned that the reading of novels, in time, led females to lose contact with reality. Both mind and morality, then, were said to be at risk as a result of reading novels. Upon careful study of a great number of such early critiques of the novel, scholar G. Harrison Orians (1937) concluded:

> . . . there must have been a considerable audience to whom novelists and novel-reading were anathema, and who held that indulgence in romances enervated the strength, enfeebled the mental powers, instilled erroneous and corrupt ideas, and was an ill preparation of a serious life in a workaday world. Novels, it was maintained, were subversive of the highest moral principles or, in short, were the primer of the Devil.[12]

Menace Multiplied

If a single novel constituted an evil influence, what might be the impact upon society of a large aggregate of novels? The guardians of morality and sanity soon took note of yet another threat to civilization, and many spoke out against that insidious institution known as the "circulating library."

The first circulating library in London dates back to 1740, the very year of *Pamela*'s publication. By the end of the eighteenth century, there were about 1,000 such libraries operating in England. These were not free, public libraries, but more like "clubs" that charged an annual subscription fee. In the colonies, Benjamin Franklin established his Library Company in 1731, which he later claimed as "mother of all the North American subscription libraries." In the 1760s, subscription and rental libraries of various kinds became quite popular in the colonies, and they inevitably offered the latest novels from Europe. Initially viewed with some suspicion by booksellers, the library soon was recognized as an important new market and a source of advertising and publicity for new works. By 1785, the catalogue of the American Circulating Library in Philadelphia listed 100 novels; more than a third of the titles available in 1796 from W. P. Blake, Boston, were novels and romances. Caritat's, the most famous of New York's circulating libraries, listed over a thousand titles of fiction in 1799. Works such as

Delicate Embarrassments, Venial Trespasses, Misplaced Confidence, Female Frailties, and *Excessive Sensibility* became readily available.

The success of the library reflected, in part, the success of the novel. It also reflected a considerable increase in the size of the reading audience. Illiteracy remained, to be sure, yet reading was finally making inroads even among the poor. Bookseller James Lackington, in 1791, offered the following well-known (if somewhat exaggerated) comments of the state of English literacy:

> I cannot help observing, that the sale of books in general has increased prodigiously within the last twenty years. According to the best estimation I have been able to make, I suppose that more than four times the number of books are sold now than were sold twenty years since. The poorer sort of farmers, and even the poor country people in general, who before that period spent their winter evenings in relating stories of witches, ghosts, hobgoblins, etc. now shorten the winter nights by hearing their sons and daughters read tales, romances, etc., and on entering their houses, you may see *Tom Jones, Roderick Random,* and other entertaining books stuck up on their bacon racks, etc. If John goes to town with a load of hay, he is charged to be sure not to forget to bring home *Peregrine Pickle's Adventures;* and when Dolly is sent to market to sell her eggs, she is commissioned to purchase *The History of Pamela Andrews.* In short all ranks and degrees now READ.[13]

There is little doubt that the circulating libraries permitted the general public to gain access to far more reading matter, particularly novels, than ever before; subscription and rental fees were within the reach of most families. This provoked some to label the library "slop-shops in literature," responsible for corrupting the minds of "every butcher and baker, cobbler and tinker . . . ," along with farmers, servants, and schoolchildren. Coleridge, in *Biographia Literaria* (1817), took aim at both the libraries and their most popular wares:

> For as to the devotees of the circulating libraries, I dare not compliment their pass-time, or rather kill-time, with the name of reading. Call it rather a sort of beggarly daydreaming, during which the mind of the dreamer furnishes for itself nothing but laziness, and a little mawkish sensibility; while the whole material and imagery of the doze is . . . manufactured at the printing office, which pro tempore fixes, reflects, and transmits the moving phantasms of one man's delirium, so as to people the barrenness of a hundred other brains afflicted with the same trance or suspension of common sense and all definite purpose.[14]

The circulating library succeeded in creating a significant new market for fiction, one requiring constant supply. There were not yet enough accomplished writers of the novel to meet the increased demand, however, A group of so-called literary "hacks" found this a favorable situation for the introduction of quick imitations of their favorite works. Seducers, threatened virgins, and sentimentality became stock elements in a new "formula fiction" whose representatives took up residence in all the circulating libraries. Authors and publishers alike were soon condemned for the increasingly commercial aspects of their efforts. The reputation of the circulating libraries as evil influences only increased as their shelves grew heavy with less-than-inspired works. The most vociferous complaints of the era, however, did not concern the lack of talented authors or brilliant novels so much as the potential for social and psychological harm inherent in the dissemination of popular works of fiction. In Sheridan's comedy, *The Rivals* (1775), for example, a female character was portrayed as highly overinvolved in her fiction reading habit. Another remarked:

> A circulating library in a town is as an evergreen tree of diabolical knowledge! It blossoms through the year! And depend on it, Mrs. Malaprop, that they who are so fond of handling the leaves will long for the fruit at last.[15]

Through the eighteenth century the high cost of books severely restricted the size of the reading public, and the circulating libraries represented early attempts to deal with this problem. Novels were not among the most expensive of books, but neither were they cheap. The original edition of *Robinson Crusoe,* for example, sold at 5 shillings a copy when the average laborer was making only 10 shillings per week. For many, library membership was the only practical route to the latest reading matter. Q. D. Leavis remarked, "What saved the lower-middle-class public for some time from a drug addiction to fiction was the simple fact of the exorbitant price of novels."

In England, relatively inexpensive reading matter became available to the less privileged through little paperbound volumes known as "chapbooks," which were sold by peddlers, and also by way of the newspapers. The latter, however, were not intended primarily as vehicles for fiction, and were rather heavily taxed by the government. Nevertheless, they made available occasional short stories and serializations of novels. *Robinson Crusoe,* for example, was reprinted in the *Original London Post* and again in chapbooks. It was in the nineteenth century, however, that improvements in printing press technology made possible vast quantities of inexpensive printed materials. The menace that was fiction was then fully unleashed upon an eager public, to the chagrin of literary critics, moralists, educators, and clergy.

The serial publication of novels in very cheap editions became a popular practice in mid-nineteenth century London. Edward Lloyd, in 1841, began to publish large quantities of very cheap fiction, including serialized novels in penny parts. These soon became known to the disapproving as "penny dreadfuls." A typical work of this kind was *Vice and its Victim; or, Phoebe, the Peasant's Daughter* by Thomas P. Prest. It involved the trials of a young innocent, Phoebe, who had been persuaded to run away with a wicked aristocrat, Lord Shelbourne. Upon discovering this shameful circumstance, Phoebe's mother died of shock while her father became insane. Phoebe then went on to endure a series of misadventures involving robbers, duels, revenge, murder, and so on, while fainting a total of twenty-eight times. On the final page, of course, she settled down to marital bliss. The story is representative of the genre in its use of stock situations and characters, its focus upon arousing emotions, and its "virtue-triumphant" conclusion; the text abounds with ornate expressions and cliches. Modern readers would find it all very tedious, or perhaps hilarious. Of course, the work of Charles Dickens frequently appeared in the same serial format, and his stories, too, were condemned by critics as crude and given to emotional excess. In 1846, Charles Knight, publisher of *Knight's Penny Magazine,* in a final issue lashed out at the all-fiction penny dreadfuls:

> . . . are carrying out the principle of cheap weekly sheets to the disgrace of the system, and who appear to have got some considerable hold upon the less informed of the working people, and especially upon the young . . . such writers, if they deserve the name of writers, are scavengers. All the garbage that belongs to the history of crime and misery is raked together, to diffuse a moral miasma through the land, in the shape of the most vulgar and brutal fiction.[16]

Hepworth Dixon attacked the penny dreadfuls in a series of articles for the *Daily News* of 1847. His aim was to expose the immorality and evil influence of the new body of very cheap literature that was reaching the poorest and least educated citizens. According to Dixon, their stories:

> . . . poison the very fountains of human life, by confounding conscience, confusing the sense of right and wrong, and by corrupting and inflaming those passions whose regulation and coordination with duty constitute the basis of morals, and offer the only guarantee for the peace and well-being of the social body.[17]

The works of Prest, Dickens, and their serialized contemporaries soon were branded as "sensation novels" and taken to task for their

"violent incident, stagey dialogue and melodramatic use of coinci-
dence." Nevertheless, the public proved eager to read them, and soon
it was possible to acquire bound versions of popular serials. A deluge
of cheap novels began to appear, bound in yellow covers, and widely
known as "Yellow Backs." Another set of cheap editions, sold at all
the railway stations, was the popular Railway Library. The availability
of such fiction in cheap editions soon enhanced the split between the
educated, who condemned them, and the general public. An 1863 article
in the *Quarterly Review* on "The Sensation Novel" attempted to alert
the public to the new menace:

> A class of literature has grown up around us, usurping in many respects,
> intentionally or unintentionally, a portion of the preacher's office, playing
> no inconsiderable part in moulding the minds and forming the habits and
> tastes of its generation; and doing so principally, we had almost said ex-
> clusively, by 'preaching to the nerves.' . . . Excitement, and excitement
> alone, seems to be the great end at which they aim . . .[18]

Free of the tax burden imposed by the English upon their newspaper
industry, the American press of the nineteenth century flourished. In
fact, special mailing rates for newspapers in the United States made
this format particularly appealing to publishers. There soon developed
a specialized form of newspaper that had little or nothing to do with
the news. This was the "family story paper," a new vehicle for fiction
that developed in conjunction with cheap pamphlet-novels (the original
"dime novels").

Beginning in the 1830s, weekly story papers devoted to fiction began
sprouting up all over the country, carrying serializations of one or more
novels. They freely "borrowed" material from one another and from
publications in England and France. Dependent upon a steady flow of
stories, they held innumerable writing contests as a means of collecting
as many free or nearly-free contributions as possible. They competed
with the somewhat more "respectable" magazines, which were also
growing more numerous, and often succeeded in beating the magazines
in circulation. Among the better known story papers were the *Philadelphia Saturday Courier*, the *Uncle Sam*, the *Flag*, the *New York
Ledger*, *Brother Jonathan*, and the *New World*.

Not satisfied merely with printing weekly installments of "pirated"
fiction, the story papers soon issued longer, pamphlet-like "supplements" or "extras." Initially, these were printed on newspaper presses
and sold on the street, unbound, by newsboys. In New York City,
such "extras" eventually acquired brightly colored paper covers, although thousands were mailed coverless in order to take advantage of

the newspaper postage rates. Soon, storybook publishers across the nation were issuing supplements and extras on a regular basis. This created a major problem for "legitimate" book publishers, whose well-manufactured and handsomely bound editions remained too expensive for many consumers. Harper and Brothers soon found it necessary to begin publishing novels in brown paper covers, with prices reduced, to compete with the storybook supplements. Other publishers followed suit, and the revolution in "cheap books" was in full flower.

In 1858, Erastus F. Beadle arrived in New York City from Buffalo, where his *Dime Song Book* had proven a popular and profitable success. Two years later, he published a dozen cheap, pamphlet novels dealing with pioneer life, Indian attacks, and related adventures. There was considerable demand for these little novels; many were shipped to soldiers in the Union army camps and hospitals. The first novel of the series, *Malaeska, the Indian Wife of the White Hunter,* by Ann S. Stephens, was immediately successful (it has sold nearly half a million copies over the years). By 1865, Beadle and Company had published some four million "dime novels" (some actually sold for a nickel). The publishing house went on to exploit its early success by producing additional series pamphlet books featuring new formats and authors: Beadle's New Dime Novels, Beadle's Pocket Novels, and Frank Starr's American Novels.

Good commercial ideas engender competition, and various Beadle rivals, such as DeWitt's Ten-Cent Romances, and Ten-Cent Novelettes, soon appeared. In the 1870s, whole "libraries" of cheap books were born: Lakeside Library, Fireside Library, People's Library, Home Library, Seaside Library, and so on. The dime novels of America, however successful, inevitably shared the unsavory reputation of their English "cousins," the Railway novels. They were characterized by concerned citizens as sensation-oriented, lacking in both literary merit and morality, and intended for the commercial exploitation of the poor. They were, in short, evil and corrupting influences, which compounded the sins of fiction by making it so widely available at such low prices. One New York Assemblyman went so far as to introduce a bill to prohibit their sale to anyone under sixteen years of age lacking the written consent of a parent.

The evidence that unsavory dime novels damaged or ruined a generation of Americans remains elusive. More definite, by far, is the evidence of the rapid demise of the pamphlet-novel. Did it fall victim to a new, more durable, 50-cent book format? Was it killed off by changes in the postal rates and regulations? Had publishers simply glutted the market? Whatever the reason(s), the dime novel, like the dinosaur, abruptly disappeared. However, if one were to search for the origins of the much maligned "pulp" magazine, the earlier dime novel would be found in its family tree. The spirit of the dime novel, moreover, was resurrected still later, in the mid-twentieth century, in the form of a new generation of western, detective, romance, and Gothic paperback books.

The Threat of Fiction

The arrival on the literary scene of realistic prose fiction, in the mid-eighteenth century, and its dissemination to the masses in the mid-nineteenth century, created consternation within certain strata of society. The educated, the privileged, the pious, the guardians of social welfare, all tended to view these developments in the most negative manner. The novel, like the newspaper, brought the external world into every household, along with an emphasis upon the sensational and the emotional. The newspaper had threatened to overload vulnerable nervous systems with unnecessary and overstimulating information, to expose innocents to the existence of immoral characters and happenings. The threat of the novel was even greater. Instead of merely reading reports of the misbehavior of others, consumers of the novel could visualize and experience the sensations and emotions of the wicked and immoral. Authors willingly provided enough vivid details regarding scenes and sentiments so that readers might construct the entire story in their inflamed imaginations. The little not provided directly by the author was readily supplied by readers' fantasies. Here was the ultimate corruption: the direct undermining of reason by imagination, the glorification of emotion and sensuality, the compromise of social reality in favor of silent, solitary, self-gratification.

The rise of the sensation novel represented a betrayal of the rationalistic ideals of the Enlightenment, which had called for order, logic, and reason to prevail in human affairs. Literacy, long the vehicle of religion and education, had itself been compromised into something common and distasteful. It had devolved into a vehicle for mere entertainment, dalliance, fancy, escapism, or kill-time. Readers of cheap literature would undoubtedly find themselves drifting away from the real world, becoming pathologically immersed in and addicted to their dime fantasies. Morality would suffer first, as storybook sexuality, crime, and violence became part of daily life, and sanity itself would thereafter be in question.

The critics, of course, seemed little concerned about their own potential corruption or loss of sanity. It was tacitly assumed that worldly, educated, and accomplished men could view such materials with impunity, while the young, the female, and the lower-middle class could not. The protection of the "vulnerable" was, and remains, the rallying cry of all anti-media campaigns, along with the call to preserve the social order. Considering the number and kind of novels routinely devoured by Americans in the twentieth century, it seems unlikely that any degree of rational thought or social order has survived. Moreover, we have yet to take into account additional sources of evil media influence, manifest early in the present century, which also are claimed to have assailed our moral and mental faculties. This constitutes our next task.

Notes

1. Frank Luther Mott, *Golden Multitudes: The Story of Best Sellers in the United States* (New York: R. R. Bowker, 1947), p. 14.
2. Announcement in London *Daily Advertiser* (1741) cited in Bernard Kreissman, *Pamela-Shamela* (Lincoln, NE: University of Nebraska, 1960), p. 3.
3. Ibid., p. 22.
4. Article in *The Christian Spectator* (1822), cited in Orians, op. cit., p. 197.
5. Article in *American Monthly Magazine* (1824), cited in Orians, Ibid.
6. Carl Van Doren (1921), cited in Orians, Ibid, p. 195.
7. Poem by William Cowper, "The Progress of Error" (1780), cited in Lionel Stevenson, *The English Novel* (Boston: Houghton Mifflin, 1960), p. 149.
8. Thomas Jefferson, cited in Herbert Ross Brown, *The Sentimental Novel in America* (Durham, N.C.: Duke University, 1940), p. 4.
9. Reverend Samuel Miller (1803), cited in Orians, op. cit., p. 200.
10. Article in *Weekly Magazine* (1798), Ibid., p. 199.
11. Article in *Monthly Mirror* (1797), Ibid., p. 200.
12. G. Harrison Orians, Ibid., p. 210–11.
13. James Lackington (1791), cited in Q. D. Leavis, *Fiction and The Reading Public* (London: Chatto and Windus, 1932), p. 132.
14. Samuel Taylor Coleridge (1817), cited in Leavis, Ibid., p. 137.
15. Richard B. Sheridan (1775), cited in Stevenson, op. cit., p. 149.
16. Charles Knight, in *Knight's Penny Magazine* (1846), cited in Margaret Dalziel, *Popular Fiction 100 Years Ago* (London: Cohen and West, 1957), p. 47.
17. Hepworth Dixon, *Daily News* (1847), cited in Dalziel, Ibid., p. 49.
18. Article in *Quarterly Review,* "The Sensation Novel" (1863), cited in Leavis, op. cit., p. 159–60.

5

Infamous Images: The Comics

Images, we know, are far older than written words; drawing and painting preceded the alphabet. For over 2,000 years, nevertheless, the written word reigned supreme in the realms of human communication and education. Its ascendancy, we have noted, greatly enhanced the development of abstraction and logic, skills which became central to Western civilization. Reinforced by the technology of printing, the culture of the alphabet gradually led humanity away from immediate sensory involvement with the world. People could learn much of happenings in distant times and places, but this information increasingly was received and processed in abstract form through the medium of written language. The ability to read, manipulate, and produce abstract symbols eventually came to define the terms "intelligent" and "educated."

Although they remained with us, images occupied a more specialized niche in the new culture. For example, they retained their place at the heart of religious experience. In the visions of the divines, and in the works of inspired artists, the ability of imagery to evoke powerful emotional reactions was honored and revered. Images from the old and new testaments filled the churches, castles, and public buildings. In this context, the image was reassuring and comforting, its evocative properties bound to a spiritual message. Once imagery reappeared in a secular context, however, to become an aspect of the mass media, it was soon indicted as a particularly potent source of evil influence.

It is noteworthy that when the Congress of the United States was first pressured to pass antiobscenity legislation (1842), the bill which emerged addressed itself to images, rather than words. That is, the new invention of photography quickly was identified as a threat to society that had to be contained. Years later, the imagery of the cartoon, the comic strip, and the comic book also became anathema in certain quarters. The image had returned, and its welcome was not certain.

71

A Graphic Revolution

During the nineteenth century, a vastly improved ability to reproduce images mechanically brought about a "graphic revolution." Photographs, drawings, and cartoons began to appear with great frequency in popular reading matter. Newspapers, magazines, and billboards became increasingly illustrated, as publishers and advertisers began to shift their efforts from rational/intellectual argument to emotional impact and appeal. According to Postman (*Amusing Ourselves to Death*), " . . . the picture forced exposition into the background, and in some instances obliterated it altogether."

As early as 1825, American periodicals began routinely to incorporate illustrations taken from wood engravings. By the time of the Civil War, *Harper's Weekly* magazine was able to provide excellent pictorial coverage of the conflict, drawing heavily upon the work of artist Thomas Nast. The circulation of the *Weekly* exceeded 100,000 during the war, and reached 160,000 shortly thereafter. Tebbel (*The Media in America*) noted: "Pictures held the most fascination for its readers—illustrations and cartoons of contemporary life, particularly Nast's political cartoons, which reached their climax in the seventies."

In the latter part of the nineteenth century a new form of magazine appeared—the picture magazine. *Frank Leslie's Illustrated Newspaper* (1855) was among the first to make liberal use of pictures in the reporting of news, with a decided emphasis on the sensational. "Frank Leslie" was, in fact, a London-born engraver named Henry Carter. The success of his initial effort soon led to the birth of *Frank Leslie's New Family Magazine* (1857), *Frank Leslie's Budget of Fun* (1858), and *Frank Leslie's Ladies Magazine* (1871). Through his publications, Carter forcefully demonstrated the special power of the image in mass media. In a journalistic attack upon unsanitary practices in the New York dairy industry, for example, he provided readers with vivid pictures of dying cows in filthy dairies, producing a powerful public reaction. Before long, the New York legislature was forced to take action and institute reforms of the dairy business.

The appearance of photography upon the mass media scene, and the use of the halftone photo-engraving process, soon revolutionized newspaper illustration. The *New York Daily Graphic*, founded in 1873, relied heavily upon news drawings, cartoons, and photographs. The *New York World* dazzled readers with pictures in its Sunday edition, and soon it was in competition with the *Herald* as to photography and illustration. Entire magazines devoted to photography appeared, and by 1905 these numbered in the hundreds. Meanwhile, the American comic weeklies *Puck* (1877), *Life* (1883), and *Judge* (1881) remained filled with satirical drawings and cartoons reminiscent of England's *Punch* (1841).

Life caught the attention of the public in 1887 with the drawings of Charles Dana Gibson. The Gibson Girl, drawn as a slim, serene, self-reliant American female became a popular symbol of the times. Other publishers took note of the public's positive reaction to pictures, and there emerged in the 1890s a new generation of highly illustrated ten-cent magazines. These included *McClures, Cosmopolitan, Peterson's, Godey's,* and *Argosy.* The success of these graphic periodicals soon threatened such higher priced and more traditional competitors as *Harper's, Scribner's,* and the *Century.*

The ability of the visual image to capture and influence an audience was not lost upon publisher William Randolph Hearst. His San Francisco *Examiner,* a flamboyant and sensational paper, was quick to make extensive use of the new technology. When he purchased New York's *Journal,* he quickly hired a staff of top cartoonists and illustrators to liven up its pages. The massive reaction against the sensation-oriented *Journal,* on the part of clergy, educators, librarians, and others, was in large measure a response to its liberal use of photos, illustrations, and other graphic innovations.

Noting the popularity of the *World's* Sunday edition, with its color supplement and comic section, Hearst set out to win over the Sunday reader. In 1896 he issued an eight-page comic section, all in color, called the *American Humorist.* Comic "strips" were not yet in vogue, and much of the comic section consisted merely of individual cartoons. Hearst observed that Richard F. Outcault's "Yellow Kid" had been sufficiently popular to turn up in a series of individual drawings in the *World.* He promptly hired Outcault away from the *World,* making the "Yellow Kid" a regular feature of the *Sunday Journal.* The name and appearance of this comic character rapidly became well known throughout New York. A bald, silly-looking fellow with large ears and a toothless grin, sporting a bright yellow nightshirt, he soon became the symbol of Hearst-type journalism. Critics would thereafter condemn Hearst and other sensation-oriented journalists as representing the "yellow press" or practicing "yellow journalism," epithets originating with the "Yellow Kid." According to journalism scholar Frank Luther Mott (*American Journalism*): "Yellow journalism brought more pictures than ever before into the daily papers."

Early newspaper cartoons were not always funny to public figures, particularly when they satirized politicians and current happenings. In 1899, members of the California legislature, favorite targets of the cartoonists, succeeded in passing an anti-cartoon law which forbade caricatures reflecting on character. Attempts were made to pass similar laws in other states, including New York. Enforcement was lacking, however, and the movement to ban caricature eventually was abandoned.

The first American comic strip in the modern sense of the term was drawn by *Journal* staffer Rudolph Dirks in 1897. Consisting of several color panels, it concerned the mischievous pranks of the "Katzenjammer Kids," Hans and Fritz, "unbearably cruel, soulless little brats." The concept was provided by an earlier, German strip, "Max and Moritz." A variety of new strips followed, including "Foxy Grandpa," by Charles E. Schultz and "Buster Brown," by Richard Outcault. Over the next two decades such classics as "Bringing Up Father" (George McManus), "Alphonse and Gaston" (F. B. Opper), and "Mutt and Jeff" (H. C. Fisher) were born. The comic strip quickly became a permanent part of the American scene; imagery had found a new home.

The first generation of American comic strips aimed at simple humor rather than storytelling; their artwork was simple and sometimes crude. Nevertheless, they attracted a significant audience and therefore were commercially successful. According to Stephen Becker (*Comic Art in America*) the Yellow Kid evoked:

> " . . . that first, gentle wave of mass hysteria which accompanies the birth of popular art forms. The Yellow Kid was soon on buttons, cracker tins, cigarette packs and ladies' fans; eventually he was a character in a Broadway play.[1]

The Yellow Kid and his friends cavorted in Hogan's Alley, an urban slum. They were poor street urchins, abandoned by the adult world, left to their own devices. According to Asa Berger (*The Comic-Stripped American*), they represented a world of " . . . tough, dirty little immigrant kids," and the humor "masked a sense of despair." It's narrative was written in misspelled gutter-language, the better to capture the flavor of life among the urban poor. "The Katzenjammer Kids," Hans and Fritz, spoke a Germanic Pidgin English and devoted all of their considerable energies to the thwarting and/or destruction of all authority. Their pranks were aggressive and physical, likewise their punishments. Mr. Mutt, of "Mutt and Jeff" fame, was a compulsive gambler and schemer, willing to do almost anything to raise the price of another bet. Jeff was his foil and victim. Characters such as these were hardly aimed at a genteel, educated audience. The latter found them coarse and offensive, an evil influence, while the lower and lower-middle classes readily recognized and related to them.

According to comics scholar Coulton Waugh (*The Comics*):

> . . . the leveling process of democracy was at work to bring the ideas of the simple people into the light, to give them their place in the sun. It was an inevitable process. A great flow of simple gaiety and humor roared over the dam from which the flood gates of respectability had suddenly been released.[2]

Newspapers earlier had reflected the interests of the upper and upper-middle classes. When the circulation wars demanded a broader base of readership, comics were introduced to provide a powerful lure to less sophisticated readers. Their graphic representation of slapstick violence, however, was repellent to some of the original readership. Opposition to the comics soon was heard from the pulpit and found in the conservative press. David F. McCord, in a retrospective article on "The Social Rise of the Comics" (1935), noted: "We have had some real menaces in this country: as a nation we dote on alarm . . . But seldom have we exceeded the big peril of 1910—the comic supplement." Even the first generation strips, considered quite innocent by today's standards, were then viewed by some as constituting a public menace.

The comics were first indicted for their use of slang and subversion of good manners, both considered important offenses circa 1910. They were also said to promote disrespect for the law, for married life, and for adults. Critic Mary G. Pedrick (*Good Housekeeping,* 1910), having spread the comic sections out on her floor for study, found herself confronted by:

> . . . a carpet of hideous caricatures, crude art, and poverty of invention, perverted humor, obvious vulgarity, and the rudest coloring . . . which makes for lawlessness, debauched fancy, irreverence.[3]

An article in *The Outlook* offered an even stronger attack upon the comic supplement:

> Its stock-in-trade . . . consists chiefly in making fun of old people, deriding parents by representing them in ridiculous attitudes, and of vulgar presentations of the lowest kind of marital relations between the cheapest sort of people . . . We are permitting the vulgarization of our children on a great scale . . . We are teaching them lawlessness; we are cultivating lack of reverence in them; we are doing everything we can, by cheapening life, to destroy the American homes of the future.[4]

In 1907, an editorial on "Cultivating Dreamfulness" in the *Independent* charged that the Sunday comics "cannot help but vitiate taste and deprave intelligence." It went on to emphasize the " . . . pathological effect of the nervous erethism, which results from the cultivation of the imagination to a high degree . . ." The goal of the piece was to alert parents to the mental health risks inherent in the "vicious colored supplement."

The following year, the Boston *Herald* grandly announced that it was abandoning its comic supplement, indicating that "Parents and teachers object to them." *Current Literature* (1908) suggested that the death of the comics surely was at hand: "A tide of protest is rising all over the land." New York's *Evening Post* noted: "It is a reproach to our civilization that they should have been allowed to swarm over the land." *The Ladies' Home Journal* (1909) charged that the Sunday comic supplement constituted "A Crime Against American Children" and found parents to be "criminally negligent" for allowing children to read them. Noting that scores of educators had written to the magazine on the "baneful influence" of the comic supplements, they urged readers not to purchase newspapers which printed them. In 1911, however, seeing that the strips had not yet died, a group of concerned individuals formed The League for the Improvement of the Children's Comic Supplement. The group had little noticeable impact upon the genre. In 1920, Elizabeth R. Pennell, writing for *North American Review,* observed that the comics continued "to cling to the hen-pecked husband, the wrangling wife, the meddling mother-in-law" and that they had reduced American humor "to its lowest, most primitive form."

Gershom Legman, prominent opponent of violence in later comic books, also had some critical comments for the strips:

> Children are not allowed to fantasy themselves as actually revolting against authority—as actually killing their fathers—nor a wife as actually killing her husband. A literature frankly offering images for such fantasies would be outlawed overnight. But, in the identifications available in comic-strips— in the character of the Katzenjammer Kids, in the kewpie-doll character of Blondie—both father and husband can be thoroughly beaten up, harassed, humiliated, and degraded daily.[5]

During the 1930s, the number of pictures, illustrations, and comics in the metropolitan daily newspapers increased considerably. The tabloids (small-page newspapers) were particularly active in this regard, an important factor in causing the term "tabloid" to assume derogatory connotations. The more graphic the periodical, the more scorn it received from religious and intellectual quarters. Still, the Graphics Revolution continued, and photography became the central feature of a new generation of picture magazines. *Life* appeared in 1936, followed one year later by *Look*. As for the comics, very early public opinion polls confirmed that they had acquired higher reader interest than any other newspaper feature, and frequently they surpassed the news content in this regard as well.

The popularity of the comics soon was reinforced by the appearance of a second generation of strips, many of them involving serious and dramatic adventures. This was the era of "Tarzan" (1929), "Buck Rogers" (1929), "Dick Tracy" (1931), "Flash Gordon" (1933), and so on. In 1938, "Superman" made his appearance, followed a year later by "Batman." Strips that told serialized adventure stories were supplementing or replacing the older "gag" strips. By 1944, an article in the Journal of Educational Sociology noted that comic strips were read by well over half the nation's adults and by two-thirds of all children over six. Every Sunday morning, some forty million children were reading the Sunday comic supplements. The overall audience of the comic strips was estimated at between sixty and seventy million. Both in content and popularity, the comic strips were now to be taken seriously. Moreover, they provided the basis for another media form which was to stir still greater controversy—the comic book.

The Graphic Revolution had taken the nation by storm, upsetting the long-established supremacy of linear, logical, abstract words and thoughts in the media. Emotion, sensation, sensuality, and violence had, according to some, hopelessly corrupted American reading matter and the minds of the vulnerable. The Katzenjammer Kids had played their greatest prank, but not all Americans were laughing.

Seduction of the Innocent

It is difficult, and probably unnecessary, to say exactly when the first American comic book was published. Certainly, early experiments with this media form bore little resemblance to the more familiar comics of the mid-1930s and thereafter. In 1897, for example, a collection of "The Yellow Kid" cartoons was reprinted in a five-cent comic book. In 1902, the Hearst papers announced the availability of comic books based upon their popular comic strip characters, including "The Katzenjammer Kids" and "Alphonse and Gaston." Although that marked the first nationwide marketing of comics, these were merely collections of reprinted strips, bound and sold at fifty cents each. The well-known ten-cent comics did not appear until 1934, with "Famous Funnies." It, too, was merely a collection of old strips. By this time, the strips had become firmly enmeshed in American culture, and critics were not taken too seriously. Collecting strips into a booklet format did not significantly enhance their "threat."

The era of the "modern" comic book probably began with the publications of George Delacorte (Dell). In 1937 he published the first comic book containing original stories, called "Detective Comics." Regarded by many as the first "true" comic book, its initials (DC) were the basis of the famous "DC-Comics" imprint. Gradually, the all-original comics began to take over the market. "Action Comics" appeared in 1938, featuring a character called Superman, and "Detective Comics," in 1939, offered its own caped hero, Batman. By 1940 there were some sixty different comic book series; just a few years later this figure had more than doubled. About 300 series existed by 1950, peaking at 650 in 1954. The comic book had thrust itself upon the American scene in a manner that could not long be ignored.

What were the new comics offering in the way of content? The earliest generation of comic books consisted of the burlesque, slapstick humor of the strips; they were "the funnies." They involved the pranks of youngsters, the squabbles of family life, the trials of the "fall guy" or underdog. In the late 1930s, following changes in the character of the newspaper strips, comic books incorporated adventure themes. By the 1940s, the adventures of "superheroes" took center stage, and Disney-style animal comics also began to appear.

While some critics rejected the comics in all their varieties, three types of comic books created the most controversy. In order of increasing evil influence these were: superhero, crime, and horror comics. The superhero comics really began with Superman. While Tarzan, Flash Gordon, and Buck Rogers were clearly superior types of human beings, Superman was more of a godlike, invulnerable, invincible creature. (In the tradition of a much earlier superhero, Achilles, he did have a single, well-defined weakness—the substance kryptonite.) Born on the eve of the Second World War, Superman's mission was to fight for Truth, Justice, and the American Way. In his early adventures, before the invention of super-villains, Superman battled with Nazi beasts and heinous Japanese. Writing of the birth of the superheroes, Reitberger and Fuchs (*Comics: Anatomy of a Mass Medium*) noted:

> They mirrored the spirit of the era and America's attitude towards political problems; they expressed the idea that America was the savior and preserver of all true social values, guardian of democracy, deliverer of the oppressed from the bondage of Fascism and National Socialism.[6]

In their various adventures, figures like Superman, Batman and Robin, Green Lantern, Captain Marvel, and their ilk were always concerned with the defense of good against evil. Rarely did they destroy the villains in their stories, preferring capture, humiliation, and imprisonment. Nevertheless, determined critics found many objectionable aspects to such works. For one thing, the stories were violent, and the exercise of superpowers was a study in the application of violence to problem solving. Children might be learning from these stories that "might makes right," and that it was appropriate to take the law into their own hands. Gershom Legman (*Love and Death*) charged that Superman and his imitators:

> . . . invest violence with righteousness and prestige . . . the Superman formula is essentially lynching . . . Fists crashing into faces become the court of highest appeal . . . really peddling a philosophy of 'hooded justice' in no way distinguishable from that of Hitler and the Ku Klux Klan.[7]

The superhero comics, to Legman, were a training ground in fascism, a "complete course in paranoid megalomania." This included a worship of uniforms and insignias, and an "undercurrent of homosexuality and sado-masochism." He noted their overinvolvement with powerful masculine bodies in tightly fitting costumes, and that the heroes lacked normal social relationships. As for Wonder Woman, " . . . strictly Lesbianism." While some critics merely raised their eyebrows regarding the cohabitation of Batman and his young ward, Robin, Legman strongly condemned "the two comic-book companies staffed entirely by homosexuals and operating out of our most phalliform skyscraper." Fredric Wertham (*Seduction of the Innocent*) agreed that superheroes clearly were homosexual, and complained that Robin " . . . often stands with his legs spread, the genital region discreetly evident." His idyllic relationship with Batman was described as " . . . a wish dream of two homosexuals living together."

Wertham, in *A Sign for Cain,* later returned to his assault of Superman, emphasizing the charge of racism:

> Superman is the embodiment of racial superiority, race pride, race prejudice. He explicitly belongs to a "super race." No dark-skinned or dark-complexioned or not-so-tall-or-so-full-chested youngster, whoever he is or whatever he achieves, can measure up to the white Superman. To the people of the East and of Africa, whose feelings we ignore, the Superman whom we teach to our children has become the symbol of the arrogance of the West.[8]

There is a final aspect of the superheroes that critics found objectionable: they were "unrealistic." This is important in relation to the common attack upon mass media as inimical to mental health. By concerning audiences with such fantasy constructions as Superman and Captain Marvel, the lines between fantasy and reality were said to be weakened. James D. Landsdowne, writing in the *Journal of Education* (1944) on the "The Viciousness of the Comic Book" noted that "The comic book removes the reader from the land of reality to the land of wish-fulfillment." The effects of the fantastic characters and story line were said to be compounded by the use of "over-stimulating" colors in the illustrations. As for the effects of such exposure, Landsdowne warned that a child might well become " . . . either a daydreamer or a loafer," a passive "dead weight" upon society. In a similar vein, John Mason Brown, of the *Saturday Review of Literature* referred to comic books as "the marijuana of the nursery," noting their singular utility as " . . . knockout drops for unruly children, as sedatives." For all of their exciting qualities, then, superhero comic books were viewed by critics as highly addictive "drugs," which might produce passive/schizoid children unprepared to recognize and deal with real life.

Despite all the presumed "sins" of Superman and his cohorts, they failed to generate the same degree of public fear and concern as did the "crime comics." A report prepared for the United States Conference of Mayors, on the comic book menace, indicated: "Emphasis on murder, mayhem, sex, and glorification of crime constitute the 'new look' in comics . . . " It also noted that some 50 cities had initiated some action to ban the sale of objectionable comic books.

Norbert Muhlen, writing in *Commentary* (1949), attacked crime comics in his article "Comic Books and Other Horrors." He criticized detective/mystery novels and radio shows, but indicated that "the newest, widest-circulated, least inhibited, and least understood carrier of horror and destruction is the comic book." American children, he noted, " . . . take their daily lethal dose of crime and cruelty, torture and terror as regularly as their daily vitamin-enriched breakfast food." The crime comics, in particular, were condemned as "murderous mass entertainment," with the message "to kill rather than be killed, to destroy rather than to be destroyed."

Public reaction to crime comics reached a peak in response to the writings and public appearances of Dr. Wertham, and articles about his work. Judith Christ wrote an article for *Colliers* (1948) called "Horror in the Nursery," which introduced many parents and educators to Wertham's opinions. It was accompanied by a large photo showing two children holding down a third and jabbing her arm with a fountain pen "hypodermic." This was said to be a reenactment of an actual case, stimulated by reading the crime comics. The photo and title, ironically, were as sensational as some of the works objected to in the text of the article. Nevertheless, they had the desired effect of mobilizing public opinion. Wertham was quoted as having extensively studied the impact of comic books on children, finding "the effect is definitely and completely harmful." He went on to claim that " . . . comic book reading was a distinct influencing factor in the case of every single delinquent or disturbed child we studied." This rather startling and clearcut finding was supported only by a review of case material. Such a procedure could not impress the scientific community, but certainly could and did have immense impact upon the general public.

Wertham was a master of the vignette; his articles and books were filled with brief references to dramatic cases. The following sample comes from his article in *The Saturday Review of Literature* (1948):

> A thirteen-year-old boy in Chicago has just murdered a young playmate. He told his lawyer, Samuel J. Andalman, that he reads all the crime comic books he can get hold of. He has evidently not kept up with the theories that comic book readers never imitate what they read. He has just been sentenced to twenty-two years in jail; while the comic book publishers who killed his mind with thoughts and methods of murder . . . continue as before.[9]

In the same article, Wertham claimed (without documentation) that 75 percent of parents were against crime comic books. The remaining 25 percent, he noted, were "either indifferent or misled by propaganda and 'research.' " The use of quotation marks around "research" was to let readers know that any negative findings on this issue by social scientists were to be disregarded. Comic books caused juvenile crime, and he would not tolerate information to the contrary. A precocious 14-year-old reader, in a subsequent issue of the magazine, challenged Wertham to explain the horrible Leopold–Loeb murder case, which took place well before the era of comic books, and charged him with "fanatic hatred and prejudice toward comic books."

According to Wertham, most comic books were crime comic books. The "Superman-Batman-Wonder Woman group is a special form of crime comics" he noted in his most influential book, *Seduction of the Innocent* (1954). The same was said of Western, jungle, horror, and interplanetary comics. By virtue of depicting crime, all were said to lead to a marked blunting of conscience, mercy, sympathy, and respect for others. By providing the details of crimes, moreover, they were said to be offering children blueprints for delinquency and encouragements to sadism.

Wertham summarized the effects of the comics as follows:

1. The comic-book format is an invitation to illiteracy.
2. Crime comic books create an atmosphere of cruelty and deceit.
3. They create a readiness for temptation.
4. They stimulate unwholesome fantasies.
5. They suggest criminal or sexually abnormal ideas.
6. They furnish the rationalization for them, which may be ethically even more harmful than the impulse.
7. They suggest the forms a delinquent impulse may take and supply details of technique.
8. They may tip the scales toward maladjustment or delinquency.[10]

Wertham's crusade against the comics found support among both antiviolence liberals and morality conscious conservatives; educators concerned about literacy and school behavior problems also found the cause worthwhile. Moreover, American society as a whole, in the late 1940s to mid-1950s, was highly concerned, if not obsessed, with the problem of juvenile delinquency. Articles in magazines and newspapers daily examined the cause(s) of the post World War II delinquency problem. In 1954 alone, the staid *New York Times* published some fifty articles on possible links between mass media and juvenile crime. Wertham's work on the crime comics offered all concerned parties a simple, straightforward "cause" for juvenile delinquency and suggested simple remedies. For many, this was enough. McLuhan commented:

> The elders of the tribe, who had never noticed that the ordinary newspaper was as frantic as a surrealist art exhibition, could hardly be expected to notice that comic books were as exotic as eighth-century illuminations . . . The mayhem and violence were all they noted. Therefore, with naive literary logic, they waited for violence to flood the world. Or, alternatively, they attributed existing crime to the comics. The dimmest-witted convict learned to moan, "It wuz comic books done this to me."[11]

The American Bar Association's section on criminal law created a special subcommittee to investigate the possible links between crime and mass media. These lawyers heard the following explanation as to the urgency of the matter:

> Large metropolitan cities to small hamlets have passed local laws censoring or banning crime comics; state laws are under consideration; groups have been formed, both national and local, to remove crime comics from places of sale and we are currently witnessing in many localities what almost

amounts to an hysteria, evidenced by the mass burning of crime comics by parents' and childrens' groups.[12]

The final straw in the comic book question was the appearance of the horror comics. In 1949, E.C. comics first experimented with a few horror stories in their "Crime Patrol" comics. By April, 1950, E.C. had transformed this comic into "The Crypt of Terror," and it was soon thereafter renamed "Tales From the Crypt." Another comic was transformed into "The Vault of Horror," while a third became "The Haunt of Fear." All were billed as "Illustrated Suspenstories We Dare You To Read!" Stories were narrated by such characters as the Crypt Keeper, the Vault Keeper, and the Old Witch. According to comics historian Les Daniels (*Comix: A History of Comic Books in America*): "It may be said without qualification that the new trend at E.C. . . . created reactions more intense than anything that comic books ever produced."

The emphasis in the horror comics was on particularly gruesome varieties of death, with readers spared no details in the illustrations. The tone of the narrative, however, was strictly satire and sarcasm, creating "black humor" out of the most bloodcurdling situations. The combination of horror and humor seemed to delight many young readers but to genuinely frighten any parent who happened upon such comics among their children's possessions. Youngsters flocked to join the E.C. Fan-Addict Club. This was simply too much for the adult world to endure. Denis Gifford (*The International Book of Comics*) noted:

> But the rising tide of illustrated evil reached unspeakable peaks as publishers, editors, artists and writers sought to outdo one another in their greed for sales, and what had begun as the most creative era in comic-books crashed in nationwide, even global, shockwaves that brought the entire industry tumbling down."[13]

In 1954 a subcommittee on Juvenile Delinquency of the U.S. Senate, initiated by Senators Robert Hendrickson and Estes Kefauver, investigated the comics, paying special attention to the E.C. horror products. Senator Kefauver questioned E.C.'s publisher regarding the cover illustration of a comic book: "This seems to be a man with a bloody ax holding a woman's head up which has been severed from her body. Do you think that is in good taste?" And so on. As a result, the entire horror line at E.C. was cancelled.

Results of Congessional pressure were not limited to horror comics, particularly when the Senators heard so much about the crime comics from Wertham and his supporters. The entire industry soon found itself forced to adopt a highly restrictive publishing "Code." The "Code of the Comics Magazine Association of America, Inc." included a section devoted to crime comics, another to horror, and another concerned with sex, religion, dress, and dialogue. Some excerpts from the code follow:

In every instance good shall triumph over evil and the criminal punished for his misdeeds.

No comics shall explicitly present the unique details and methods of a crime.

No comic magazine shall use the word horror or terror in its title.

All lurid, unsavory, gruesome illustrations shall be eliminated.

Suggestive and salacious illustration or suggestive posture is unacceptable.

Censorship had come to the comics. The fears of parents, teachers, lawyers, clergy, and psychiatrists led, at last, to an oppressive system of censorship in the form of the Code. This document prohibited not merely "explicit" illustrations, but "suggestive" illustration, a term which might mean anything. Details of crimes, although readily available in the daily newspapers, could not be referred to in the comics. A panicked public had traded the presumed evil influence of the comics for the social evils of censorship. In a short time, twenty-four of twenty-nine crime comics publishers were out of business. Los Angeles passed an anti-comics ordinance in 1955 (soon found unconstitutional), and similar statutes appeared in England and Canada. When the smoke had cleared, the comic book industry emerged badly battered but not destroyed. Predictably, Superman survived. As for the E.C. horror staff, they soon turned their energies toward a new, and highly successful project—MAD magazine.

It is interesting to note that the Senate subcommittee, after hearing much testimony and reviewing reams of documents, eventually rejected the notion that crime and/or horror comics were the sole or primary cause of increased juvenile delinquency. Senator Kefauver ultimately decided that delinquency was a more complex issue related to moral breakdown in the home and community, parental apathy, the effects of war upon the American family, and other imperfections within society. This conclusion, of course, did little to reverse the damage done by the investigation and attendant anti-comics publicity. It is also apparent, in retrospect, that the emergence of a post-baby-boom youth culture in the 1950s panicked many by virtue of its alien fashion, fads, music, and norms. Comic books were simply a convenient target for such concerns.

Decades later, in 1985, an article in *Publishers Weekly* reported on the complete recovery of the comics industry, estimating that some 3,000 comics specialty shops had been opened in the preceding five years. Comics of all kinds were not only produced and read, but they had become collectibles, with early issues bringing hundreds or thousands of dollars. Moreover, the comics were now welcome in such major bookstore chains as Waldenbooks and B. Dalton. The "repressed" had returned.

Impact and Images

In the first decade of this century, and again in the 1950s, debate regarding the impact of images upon the innocent and the vulnerable reached a level approaching hysteria. First the comic strip, and later the comic book, were found to be significant sources of evil influence, threatening the mental health and morality of our young and the very fabric of American society. In the era of the comic strip debate, the newspaper and the novel had already become accepted media forms. By the time comic books came under attack, the strips were also widely accepted. While the specific media form changed, then, the nature of the attack did not. Educators, clergy, and physicians took leading roles in public denouncements of the "graphic" aspects of each media development, proclaiming these to be inimical to mental health and conventional morality. Such charges succeeded in frightening large numbers of parents, thereby generating "grass-roots" support for the attacks and interesting the politicians. The sensual/sensational aspects of each media form, whether presented graphically (as in the comics) or yielding graphic fantasies (as in the novel) were the specific focus of attack. Any content that produced emotional reactions was immediately suspect. Critics longed for a return to the rational, linear, abstract mode of media presentation and thought that characterized the period of the Enlightenment but will not come again. They looked to censorship for simple solutions and inevitably failed. Newspapers, novels, comic strips, and comic books remained firmly entrenched in American life.

A new element in the mass media debate, before mid-century, was the involvement of the social scientists and the application of scientific methods. It is noteworthy, for example, that the era of the comic book "menace" led to two special issues of the *Journal of Educational Sociology*. In 1944, and again in 1949, the journal published a collection of relevant research papers on the comic book, in the hope of offering an "objective" perspective. Editor Harvey Zorbaugh noted the "emotional excesses generated by the current controversy" and expressed alarm regarding "unreasoning condemnation, the setting up of scapegoats, the burning of books and cries for censorship."

A paper by Frederic M. Thrasher, Professor of Education at NYU and a member of the Attorney General's Conference on Juvenile Delinquency, indicated that Wertham's opinions, while presented as definite conclusions, had not been substantiated by any scientific research. Wertham had studied only the criminal and disturbed, not the normal, and had also selected extreme examples to convince readers. No statistical summary of his investigations was offered, no comparison of comic book readers with nonreaders. Moreover, no safeguards against bias in data collection or interpretation were described. In sum:

> Wertham's dark picture of the influence of comics is more forensic than it is scientific and illustrates a dangerous habit of projecting our social frustrations upon some specific trait of our culture, which becomes a sort of "whipping boy" for our failure to control the whole gamut of social breakdown . . . The current alarm over the evil effects of comic books rests upon nothing more substantial than the opinion and conjecture of a number of psychiatrists, lawyers, and judges.[14]

Another prominent contributor to this literature was Dr. Lauretta Bender, a psychiatric authority on childhood. Rather than condemn the comics, she regarded them as the modern equivalent of folklore, serving to stimulate fantasies that ultimately helped children to deal with the problems of living. Both superheroes and villains, she argued, were necessary ingredients to childhood fantasy and always had been. From the myths of ancient Greece to those of the American West, children have always immersed themselves in dramas of violent conflict between the forces of good and evil. From her perspective, the comics were in no way inherently evil and might well be helpful to the normal developmental processes of childhood.

Despite the reasoned skepticism of the social scientists and the alternative theoretical perspective offered by Bender, Wertham's forces temporarily won the day. The restrained voices of science and reason could not compete with the powers of published horror images and the evocative power of Wertham's anecdotes. In this respect Wertham and his supporters were correct: Visual and fantasy images were indeed powerful vehicles of experience. Sensational images could exert an influence upon human behavior. Whether this usually or necessarily led to illiteracy, crime, mental illness, and immorality, however, remained very much a matter of inflamed opinion. This issue was to be replayed many times in the twentieth century, with little resolution, as concerned citizens sought out one or another form of mass media as a focus for their frustrations, failures, and fears.

Notes

1. Stephen Becker, *Comic Art in America* (New York: Simon and Schuster, 1959), p. 10.
2. Coulton Waugh, *The Comics* (New York: Macmillan, 1947), p. 8.
3. Mary G. Pedrick, "The Sunday Comic Supplement," *Good Housekeeping*, May, 1910, p. 625.
4. Cited in David F. McCord, "The Social Rise of the Comics," *American Mercury*, July, 1935, p. 362.
5. Gershom Legman, *Love and Death* (New York: Hacker Art Books, 1963), p. 28.
6. Reinhold Reitberger and Wolfgang Fuchs, *Comics: Anatomy of a Mass Medium* (Boston: Little, Brown, 1972), p. 117.
7. Gershom Legman, op. cit., pp. 39–40.
8. Fredric Wertham, *A Sign for Cain* (New York: Macmillan, 1966), p. 213.
9. Fredric Wertham, "The Comics . . . Very Funny!", *The Saturday Review of Literature*, May 29, 1948, p. 27.
10. Fredric Wertham, *Seduction of the Innocent* (New York: Rinehart, 1954), p. 118.
11. Marshall McLuhan, *Understanding Media* (New York: New American Library, 1964), p. 154.
12. Cited in James Gilbert, *A Cycle of Outrage* (New York: Oxford University Press, 1986), p. 85.
13. Denis Gifford, *The International Book of Comics* (New York: Crescent Books, 1984), p. 184.
14. Frederic M. Thrasher, "The Comics and Delinquency: Cause or Scapegoat," *Journal of Educational Sociology*, 1949, 23, pp. 195, 200.

6

The Sin in Cinema: Movies

The first half of the twentieth century was a trying period for those concerned with evil media influences. The call-to-arms with regard to comic strips in the first decade and the flap over comic books some forty years later were only small parts of the overall picture. As the forces of urbanization and industrialization proceeded to create a new America and as the pace of technological advance accelerated, media threats appeared with increasing regularity.

The family at the turn of the century found itself adrift in a sea of inexpensive, readily available commercial entertainment—dime novels, pulps, newspapers, comics—with much more yet to come. This intrusion of mass media into daily family life was bitterly resented and feared by those holding traditional values; they felt entitled to govern family members' access to information, to retain strict control over moral education, and to structure and supervise "wholesome" leisure time activities. Commercial mass entertainment was perceived as a challenge to parental, religious, and educational authority and control, an opportunity for the world to impinge upon family members in a direct and unregulated manner. No longer could women and children be protected from the sensual and the sensational. Where would it all lead?

This situation was further aggravated by the arrival of yet another form of cheap entertainment—the motion picture. Dime novels had entranced readers merely by suggesting graphic and emotional mental images; the newspapers had filled their pages, and readers' senses, with photography and illustrations; the comics had lured people away from the printed word with their crudely drawn images and strips. Now there appeared a medium with the awesome power of *moving* images. Its potential for evil influence was early recognized to be enormous, and its popularity only amplified the threat. A bit of movie history is required, however, before exploring the content of such concerns.

Peep-Shows and Movie-Palaces

W. K. L. Dickson, working at the Edison Laboratories, in 1892 developed a moving picture device called the Kinetoscope. It lacked a projector mechanism and required that viewers peep into a box-like structure in order to see its moving images. Nevertheless, it was a notable innovation. Ten such Edison Kinetoscope peep-show machines were exhibited in New York City in 1894. For a 25-cent admission fee, patrons could view an entire row of 5 such machines, taking their turns at the peepholes. As primitive as it sounds today, this was the cutting edge of phototechnology, and customers eagerly lined up to await their turn. Soon the Edison Kinetoscope was being distributed throughout the country, offering short films of vaudeville acts and boxing matches. The addition of nickel coin boxes on each machine permitted patrons to choose only those films they wished to see. According to Benjamin Hampton (*A History of the Movies*), the early movie devotees were the customers of the arcades, parlors, and dime museums: " . . . they could not see them often enough, and they wandered from one place to another, searching for films they had not seen before."

The projection of a Kinetoscope film upon an external viewing screen was accomplished in 1895 by the addition of another new device, the Vitascope. This Vitascope/Kinetoscope combination was to evolve into the modern motion picture projector. In the following year, a public exhibition of "Thomas A. Edison's Latest Marvel" took place in New York City, Paris, and London. These successful demonstrations, combined with the Edison name, ensured the popularity of the new medium. Vaudeville shows began adding movies as yet another type of act, while some theaters used them simply as "fillers" between live shows. Arcade owners created impromptu "theaters" by hanging a sheet for a screen and putting out some chairs. By the turn of the century, Edison and several competitors were manufacturing and selling improved and less expensive projectors. Any playhouse, and many peep-show arcades, could afford to acquire one.

It was a strike of New York City vaudeville performers, in 1901, that suggested to theater managers that films might be substituted for live acts. They soon discovered that projected movies could simplify their business practices and reduce their expenses while continuing to attract large audiences. Needless to say, the news spread quickly to playhouses throughout the country.

The first true "nickelodeon" opened its doors in 1905, offering some 200 seats and a movie called "The Great Train Robbery." Rather than a converted playhouse, storefront, or arcade, this was a business operation conceived solely for the purpose of bringing movies to the public—and vice versa. Within a year of its opening, about a thousand more appeared; in five years the total was closer to ten thousand. A movie "craze" spread throughout the country, and *Variety* reported that it was "boom time" for the motion picture industry. Marcus Loew, who operated a string of penny arcades, had the foresight to dismantle them and turn them into motion picture theaters. Soon he converted a group of New York City playhouses to the same end, putting together the first movie "empire." No longer in the province of vaudeville, or restricted to the back rooms of arcades, the motion picture had found a home of its own.

The audience for the movies was drawn, in part, from those who previously attended the live stage melodramas and/or the vaudeville shows. The motion picture offered these viewers a degree of realism that could not be approached on stage. Outdoor scenes, crowds, chases, and exotic locations, difficult or impossible to capture on stage, were readily and accurately portrayed in the cinema. Movies were also far more accessible than legitimate theater, particularly in smaller cities and towns. Moreover, while a ticket to the legitimate theater might cost one dollar and a vaudeville show a half dollar, admission to the movies could be obtained for a nickel or a dime.

The largest part of the audience, however, consisted of those who had rarely or never attended commercial entertainment. These were urban working-class individuals, many of them immigrants. The movies offered them affordable relief from the fatigue and boredom of a long day's shift in the factories, providing stimulation and excitement to enrich otherwise burdensome lives. Moreover, the silent screen offered no language barriers. An article in the *American Magazine* (1913) noted: "For a mere nickel, the wasted man, whose life hitherto has been toil and sleep, is kindled with wonder."

Many of the early movie theaters, particularly in working-class areas, were small, uncomfortable, and less than clean. The audience would see a series of 15-minute silent films and perhaps participate in a slide-show "sing-along." Vendors walked up and down the aisles selling a variety of candies and soft drinks. From time to time, shows would be interrupted while the film was repaired, to the accompaniment of much whistling, clapping, and foot-stomping. Picture-content aside, this type of atmosphere, along with the notion of sharing a darkened room with strangers of all sorts, inevitably proved threatening to some serious-minded and conservative citizens.

The world's first motion picture production studio was built by Thomas Edison in 1893. It was from this New Jersey location that Kinetoscope films were made for distribution throughout the country. When the projected motion picture made its debut in 1896, audiences viewed such productions as *Burlesque Boxing, Venice, Kaiser Wilhelm Reviewing His Troops,* and *Umbrella Dance.* Many early films were based upon vaudeville and burlesque skits. In an attempt to maintain a monopoly on film production, Edison refused to sell or rent his motion picture cameras. After a few years, however, competitors appeared with their own cameras, and the field of film production was open to all.

The first American "story" films came from the Edison studios. Edwin Porter, in 1903, produced *The Life of an American Fireman, Uncle Tom's Cabin,* and *The Great Train Robbery,* the last of which was a particularly great success, earning the "Western" a permanent place in American film and culture. On the basis of audience reaction to Porter's work, other producers turned to the story film. Plots were melodramatic or sentimental, tending to focus upon the exploits of police and criminals, cowboys and Indians, bosses and workers, or villains and waifs. Popular demand for new films was insatiable, and producers turned for ideas to successful novels, stories, and plays. Early film works included *Ben Hur, Dr. Jekyll and Mr. Hyde,* and *The Scarlet Letter.* With the growth of the industry, motion picture plots soon became more "formula" oriented, using tried-and-true techniques of crowd pleasing and aiming for mass attendance.

Initially, the one-reel movie had been standard fare. The vaudeville model of entertainment dictated that audiences would not sit still for acts that ran for more than fifteen minutes. It came as a considerable surprise, therefore, when the 1912 four-reel French import, *Queen Elizabeth,* starring Sarah Bernhardt, earned huge profits despite its incredible hour-and-a-half duration. The following year a lengthy Italian film, *Quo Vadis,* ran for twenty-two weeks in a Broadway theater. The American film industry certainly got the message. In 1915, Paramount alone produced over 100 feature-length films. Producers began scrambling to acquire film rights to novels and plays and were willing to pay impressive sums if necessary.

The movie "serials" arrived in 1912 and soon became a major attraction. Producers simply transformed the old stage melodramas and dime novels to the movie screen, emphasizing adventure, suspense, and the sensual. Each episode offered new thrills and outrageous cliffhanger endings, both designed to keep audiences coming back. Evil villains contended regularly with heroes and heroines in such sagas as *The Adventures of Kathlyn* (1913), *The Exploits of Elaine* (1914), *Perils of Pauline* (1914), *The Hazards of Helen* (1914), and so on.

By 1915, the movies had thoroughly infiltrated American life. They had moved in an incredibly short time from the arcades to the theaters. Film quality had been improved, and theaters were becoming more commodious and respectable. The new movie theater was clean and carpeted, provided unholstered seats, ushers, and decent bathrooms. This was important, because it succeeded in attracting a new group of patrons. That is, the middle class finally joined the urban working class in its infatuation with cinema. Some theaters went far beyond the necessities of middle-class standards, attempting to become luxury movie "palaces." The drama critic for the *New York Times,* attending the opening of the posh Strand theater, in 1914, found the affair to be " . . . very much like going to a Presidential reception." The Strand boasted thick rugs, paintings, chandeliers, a 30-piece orchestra, and a small army of uniformed ushers.

The era of the movie "star" began in 1910, after initial attempts by film producers to keep actors' identities from becoming widely known. (A popular figure, after all, might demand a greater salary.) Nevertheless, producer Carl Laemmle decided to create a star of actress of Florence Lawrence via a deliberate publicity campaign. Both the press and the public, it turned out, were hungry for news about movie performers, making the star system both inevitable and profitable. As a marketing tool, it was simply too powerful to be ignored. Consequently, by 1915, movie star Charles Chaplin was reported to be earning some $10,000 a week. The first fan magazine, *Motion Picture Story Magazine,* appeared in 1911, achieving a quarter-million circulation in only a few years. It was soon joined on the racks by *Photoplay Magazine* (1912), and *Motion Picture Stories* (1913). These new publications provided plot outlines of films and, increasingly, information on the stars. Before long, even the major newspapers were featuring long articles on the movies.

Between 1914 and 1922 some 4,000 new theaters opened, causing many of the older nickelodeons to shut down. Many of the new theaters, moreover, were built in residential areas. These were the "neighborhood" theaters, a new concept in the industry. Some suburban communities were reluctant to accept movie theaters, perceiving them as purveyors of urban values and lifestyles, but the public clamor for them was difficult to resist. As the theaters changed, becoming more elaborate and sophisticated, so did the films. Prior to 1915, movies were largely working-class entertainment, moralistic battles between good and evil in which virtue always prevailed. A 1913 film called *Traffic in Souls* broke with tradition, openly using sexuality to lure audiences. Its portrayal of "white slavery" was an instant success, and soon imitated. Only a few years later, viewers were introduced to the first movie "vamp" in the form of Theda Bara, whose pictures bore such sensational titles as *Eternal Sin, Purgatory, The Forbidden Path,* and *She-Devil.* Given the arrival of the middle-class audience, and America's increased involvement in world affairs, movie goers of the 1920s were offered increasingly worldly fare.

As we shall discover, the outcry against motion pictures well preceeded the introduction of sound. Moving images, alone, were deemed quite capable of evil influence; the addition of sound merely added insult to injury. The first major sound film success was *The Jazz Singer* (1927), starring Al Jolson, which utilized a synchronized phonograph record as sound track. The initial response to sound was to accept it as an amusing novelty. As the movie industry had entered a slump after its early boom years, novelty was welcome. The overabundance of theaters and the competition provided by a new media upstart—radio—had slowed the growth of cinema. Movie houses were resorting to a variety of gimmicks to lure back the crowds. Orchestras, vaudeville acts, talent contests, lotteries, and giveaways became the order of the day. A talking movie offered merely another gimmick. Few suspected that the silent movie was about to die. The "talkies," however, proved to be immensely popular, and a new era in motion pictures was soon under way.

Emergence of the Movie Menace

Even before the appearance of the nickelodeon the movies were under attack. As early as 1894, Senator James A. Bradley objected to the lewd display of ankles by Spanish dancer Carmencita in one of Edison's Kinetoscope "peep shows." Similarly, *Dolorita's Passion Dance* was removed from an Atlantic City arcade in 1895. A few years later there was considerable flap over the public taste for "fight films" when a movie of the Corbett-Fitzsimmons fight of 1897 proved to be a hit. The *New York Times* (1897) commented upon public attraction to prizefight films, finding it a regrettable aspect of human nature.

Shortly after the opening of the first nickelodeons, an article on "The Nickel Madness" appeared in *Harper's Weekly* (1907). Although generally favorable to the new medium, it indicated the harsh reception being given the movies in certain quarters:

> Crusades have been organized against these low-priced moving-picture theaters, and many conservators of the public morals have denounced them as vicious and demoralizing. Yet have they flourished amazingly, and carpen-

ters are busy hammering them up in every big and little community in the country.[1]

An editorial in the *Chicago Tribune* (1907) found that city's new movie houses to be "hopelessly bad" and "without a redeeming feature to warrant their existence." A New York Police Commissioner, in 1907, denounced the nickelodeons as "pernicious, demoralizing, and a direct menace to the young." He recommended to Mayor George B. McClellan cancellation of the licenses of all nickelodeons and penny arcades. The issue grew hotter over the next 18 months, as the movie houses became increasingly popular and numerous. Finally, on December 24, 1908, following a public meeting on the issue, McClellan issued an order to close all of the movie houses in New York City. A December 25 headline in the *New York Times* read: "Picture shows all put out of business." The mayor cited both complaints received from religious authorities on film content and concerns about "safety hazards" in the theaters. Theaters were invited to apply for new licenses, but these were only issued when owners agreed to close their theaters on Sundays (so as not to compete with Sunday Schools). Moreover, owners were notified that the licenses would be revoked should they exhibit films "which tend to degrade or injure the morals of the community."

The ministers were not alone in their complaints to the Mayor. Saloon keepers complained of injury to their trade, as patrons were lured to new forms of escape. Managers of legitimate theaters voiced similar complaints. Educators perceived the movies as offering mass audiences exposure to new values and behaviors, and thereby stealing their prerogatives. Local, state, and national moves in the direction of censorship were inevitable, and efforts in this regard quickly centered on motion picture portrayal of crime and sex. Such evils had to be controlled or eliminated.

A National Board of Censorship of Motion Pictures was organized in 1909, and for a number of years it inspected some 95 percent of the films produced for public exhibition in the United States. Once screened, films might be condemned entirely, ordered modified, or approved. A weekly bulletin described the films reviewed and the recommendations made, and this was mailed to mayors, police chiefs, and local censorship groups throughout the country for enforcement. The Board itself had no legal authority, exercising its power through "moral coercion." Any producer refusing to abide by the action of the Board could expect opposition to all his works throughout the country, leading to financial ruin. The Board insisted that it review *all* of a manufacturer's films, or *none,* and that failure to act upon its wishes on any film would lead to a termination of all relations with the manufacturer. The actual censoring work was done by voluntary committees of five to ten persons drawn from various religious, educational, and civic organizations.

Between 1909 and 1914 the Board reviewed some 20,000 films. Its standards prohibited not only "obscenity" but "vulgarity when it offends." Any detailed representation of crime, or "morbid scenes of crime," were prohibited. "Unnecessary elaboration" of scenes of suffering or violence was forbidden, as was "unnecessary offense against religious susceptibilities." Finally, the Board took the liberty of adding a still broader censorship mandate:

> In addition to the above specifications, the Board feels in general that it is right in forbidding scenes or films which, because of elements frequently very subtle which they contain, have a deteriorating tendency on the basic moralities or necessary social standards.[2]

In the first year of operation, about one-fifth of the films reviewed were deemed so bad as to preclude improvement. Films involving crimes of arson or realistic suicide were taboo on the grounds that this might cause viewers to attempt the same behaviors. Works involving marital infidelity were "discouraged"; kidnapping themes were usually rejected. Any cruelty to animals, including hunting or bull-fighting, was excluded. Censorship of the movies, arriving only a few years after the first nickelodeon, soon was firmly established.

Such was the power of the moving image, that the oversight and censorship of the National Board was insufficient to still the voice of alarm. An article in *Good Housekeeping* (1910), by Professor William McKeever, attacked the motion picture as "A Primary School for Criminals." He attributed the motion picture craze to the "realistic nature" of the medium. Such realism, however, was dangerous. Movies depicted the activities of robbers and murderers, corrupt policemen and politicians, adulterers, and so on. In the writer's opinion, no better means of teaching immorality, obscenity, and crime had ever been devised. Children viewing such movies would soon unlearn all the moral lessons of home, school, and church. The motion picture was an enemy akin to the dime novel, yet "ten times more poisonous and hurtful to the character." It was deemed even more harmful than the saloon. As to the mechanism of its evil effects:

> These moving pictures are more degrading than the dime novel, because they represent real flesh-and-blood forms, and impart their lessons directly

through the senses. The dime novel cannot lead the boy farther than his limited imagination will allow him to go, but the moving picture forces upon his view scenes that are new. That is, they give him first-hand experience.[3]

McKeever went on to offer readers a program for forcing reform upon the moving picture industry. Among the recommendations was one that would by used in most anti-media campaigns and that was later adapted by Wertham in his campaign against the comics. That is, readers were asked to be on the lookout for boys brought into juvenile court accused of committing crimes that might have been seen in the movies.

Those who decried the "evil moving picture" as undermining public morals soon found support from those who viewed the nickelodeon as a public health menace. An article in the *Independent* (1910) noted that the moving picture, while undoubtedly a fad destined to die out in a few years, nevertheless was a "menace to health." The theaters were described as poorly ventilated and often unclean, a setting in which patrons were "breathing in contamination from the breath of others." Members of the audience were prone to cough and to expectorate upon the floor, thereby spreading contagion. Moreover, the close seating was said to encourage the spread of "various kinds of vermin." Eye specialists soon identified a new illness, "moving picture eye," caused by exposure to the shifting and flickering images on the screen. According to an article in *Outlook* (1913), " . . . the movie fan lays himself open to overtaxed eye nerves, with the consequent headaches, indigestion, and general nervous complaints." Thus, if the movie *content* did not do you in, the theater and its machinery might do so.

The attack upon picture content, begun in earnest during the first decade of this century, rapidly picked up steam. Newspaper and magazine articles on this topic began to appear with increasing frequency. An article in *Current Opinion* (1914), for example, featuring the opinions of the head of a New York mission for unfortunate women, emphasized the profound psychological dangers involved in viewing movies. The author's argument was based upon the mechanisms of imitation and suggestion. That is, films about the Wild West caused boys to run away from home to seek their fortunes, and films about purported Indian tortures caused children to tie their playmates to stakes and light bonfires. As a more original contribution to the debate, she indicated that women of subnormal intellect, or with neurasthenic tendencies, were particularly at risk for ruin by the movies:

Consequently, what the psychologists call suggestion plays a much larger part in the lives of the border-line class than it is easy for ordinary people to comprehend. As to the effect on the neurasthenic, it is perhaps not best to go into it here. Suffice it to say that any physician with experience among such cases will testify to the immediate and serious mental results of this auto-suggestion.[4]

A contributor to the *Dial* (1914) editorial on "The Cinematographic Craze" wrote with concern of the psychological impact of all those film images on normal minds:

It is in a sense, the culmination of the process of substituting pictures for words—of actual images for the images which the stimulated mind creates—which was inaugurated when the photographic illustration began to invade our magazines and to disfigure our newspapers. It shows in a very striking way the demoralizing modern tendency to seek lines of least resistance in every form of activity, to convert education into amusement, and work into play, without giving the least thought to the way in which the process softens the mental fibre and saps the character . . . For the picture can never really be a substitute for the word, which is the equivalent to calling it a substitute for thought, and the intuitional elements which it supplies to the mental process are a poor exchange for the analytical elements of logical interpretation which reading and listening demand.[5]

The *Literary Digest,* in 1915, reported on "Movie Crimes Against Good Taste," citing the critique of Mr. Marion Reedy, a lover of the legitimate theater. Reedy was particularly upset with the cinematic treatment of great plays. Ibsen's "Ghosts," for example, was said to be "debased to the most sensational kind of yellow drama." Movie drama, in general, he characterized as "an insult to any intelligence above the dime-novel stage." Unless something was done about the movies, "the public taste must be hopelessly debauched, the public's sense of true values incalculably depraved." Because they were "based solely on sensation," films were ruining millions of viewers.

The "Scientific" Critique

Initially considered mere diversion, the motion picture soon was recognized as a cultural force to be reckoned with in American society. This brought it to the attention of the "progressive" element, those individuals dedicated to improving the lot of humanity in the new urban environment. Their most valued tool in this process was the application of rational, scientific thought to human problems, and they looked to government to institute the appropriate reforms. In the realms of psychology, sociology, and, particularly, education, scientific social reform became the order of the day. John Dewey's educational theories made it clear that the school system must help to reshape society through its impact upon children. Hence the educator came to have a social mission, a responsibility to safeguard the character and morality of the next generation, to protect them from evil influences. The emergence of social work, in this era, created yet another group dedicated to the eradication of urban social evils. Ordinary people began looking to this growing body of "experts" for advice in many areas of living, and these experts felt particularly compelled to speak out on the media issue.

Among the first to sound the alarm regarding motion pictures was Jane Addams, director of Hull House. Her book *The Spirit of Youth and City Streets* (1909) included an entire chapter on "The House of Dreams." She was alarmed at the growing popularity of the film and noted that it exposed many underprivileged children to a world that they would never attain. This unreal world was, at the very least, a cruel illusion for these impressionable viewers, a temporary escape from "sterner realities." Her concern went much further, however, as she pointed out that the moral code the movies transmitted often was at odds with religious values. Stories of violent crime and revenge dominated the screen, while the Church offered sermons of love and good will. She wrote of children stealing money to gain admission, and suggested that delinquency, neurosis, and other forms of unhealthy and antisocial behavior might be the ultimate fruit of the new medium.

Those attending a 1909 conference on child welfare heard Edward H. Chandler present a paper on the effects of theater attendance upon children. He described the motion picture as "a new and curious disease . . . selecting for its special victims only boys and girls from ten to fourteen years of age . . . " and he indicated its potential to "sap the mental and moral strength" of young people. The following year, John Collier warned child welfare conferees that the motion picture presented social workers with one of their most important and practical challenges, and he urged further scientific study.

William Healy, M.D., Director of the Psychopathic Institute in Chicago's Juvenile Court, launched a "scientific" attack on movies in his book *The Individual Delinquent* (1915). He argued that visual memory and visual imagery were the most dynamic elements of mental life and often among the wellsprings of criminal behaviors. "It is the mental representation of some sort of pictures of himself or others in the criminal act that leads the delinquent onward in his path." The motion picture was cited as a primary source of such "Criminalistic Mental Imagery." Healy also attacked the nickelodeons, noting that "Under cover of dimness evil communications readily pass and bad habits are taught.''

A forerunner of Wertham, Healy supplemented his opinions with a number of case histories. An eleven-year-old boy, described as very bright and from a nice family, repeatedly stole and stayed out all night. Healy reported that the boy had a "craze" for moving pictures, going to them as often as possible and paying for them with stolen money. Finally, the boy "had to be put in an institution." Movies, it was implied, ruined the child. A similar case was made for a twelve-year-old girl who reportedly learned about burglary from the picture shows, although it was noted in passing that her father was both an alcoholic and a criminal. And so on.

Hugo Munsterberg, a prominent psychologist, in 1916, published *The Photoplay: A Psychological Study*, attempting further scholarly analysis of the new medium. Although generally optimistic about the potential uses of film in education, he also wrote of its dangers: "The intensity with which the plays take hold of the audience cannot remain without strong social effects." Concerned that viewers' minds were completely surrendered to the moving picture, he offered the following warning:

> But it is evident that such a penetrating influence must be fraught with dangers. The more vividly the impressions force themselves on the mind, the more easily must they become starting points for imitation and other motor responses. The sight of crime and of vice may force itself on the consciousness with disastrous results. The normal resistance breaks down and the moral balance, which would have been kept under the habitual stimuli of the narrow routine life, may be lost under the pressure of the realistic suggestions . . . The possibilities of psychical infection and destruction cannot be overlooked.[6]

Many of these expert opinions eventually found their way into the political and legislative arenas, and the social movement to censor the movies proceeded to grow on many levels. The National Board of Censorship, already described, was not deemed sufficient response to a threat of this magnitude. Beginning with Chicago, cities instituted their own forms of censorship. Often this involved investing police with powers of inspection and licensing, leaving it to them to decide if a film was obscene, immoral, or otherwise objectionable. Other cities created their own boards of censorship. Meanwhile, censorship was also pursued at the state level. Pennsylvania was the first state to create its own board of censors (1911), which had to approve all films exhibited in the state. Ohio, Kansas, Maryland, and other states soon followed suit. When Ohio's censorship law was challenged in the U.S. Supreme Court (1915), the Court dismissed the complaint. Movies, it decided, were merely entertainments, spectacles, and not a part of the free press. Further, the Court noted that movies were " . . . capable of evil, having power for it, the greater because of their attractiveness and manner of exhibition." Communities were entitled to protect themselves from such evil influences.

The threat of federal censorship was rampant. In 1915, Congressman D. M. Hughes of Georgia introduced a bill to create a federal motion picture commission to examine, censor, and license movies. It was to be charged with preventing the exhibition of films that " . . . would tend to impair the health or corrupt the morals of children or adults, or incite to crime." After extensive hearings the bill was defeated, but many similar bills were introduced between 1915 and 1921.

Dissatisfied with censorship efforts, an article in the *North American Review* (1921) lamented the destructive impact of the movies upon intelligence and literacy:

> No wonder that the man with eyes to see is now watching with dismay the human race as it advances briskly along the highway back to illiteracy, fast drawing near the day when the movies will deliver it even from the alphabet, and when the ultimate glory of the twentieth century culture will be the return to the picture writing in vogue before letters were invented.[7]

Some groups of parents and educators attempted their own forms of censorship. Mrs. C. E. Mirriam, chairperson of the Better Films Committee of the National Congress of Mothers and Parent-Teacher Associations published an article on "Solving the Moving Picture Problem" (1924). She indicated her fears that all the good work done by parents and teachers, at home and in school, was being undone by the movies. Consequently, she urged parents "not to send the children to the movies before the age of ten years," and argued that an even higher age limit should be established. Films were said to be "too exciting and emotionally stimulating for the younger child." She suggested that mothers and teachers foster the habits of relaxation rather than permit or encourage overstimulation, because "the movies are making the children emotionally unstable and very nervous."

In an effort to avoid governmental regulation of the movies, the industry created its own self-regulatory machinery and hired lawyer/politician Will H. Hays as its president. Hays fought and won some battles against censorship laws, but failed to convince critics that the movies could be self-regulated. In a *Christian Century* article on "The

Menace of the Movies'' (1930), Fred Eastman reviewed the first eight years of attempted self-regulation:

> The testimony, therefore, seems overwhelming to the effect that the movies have not been cleaned up. Their character is shady. Their morals are a mess. Their pull is downward. They are sickening the better elements of the public. . . . But, worst of all, they are educating millions of young people daily in false standards of taste and conduct, false conceptions of human relationships.[8]

Eastman, a Professor of Religious Literature and Drama at Chicago Theological Seminary, led an extended *Christian Century* campaign against the movies and called for federal supervision of film production and distribution. Later in 1930 he escalated his attack, writing: '' . . . the cesspools of Hollywood are being piped unchecked to the minds of children everywhere.'' He characterized the business of the movies as showing '' . . . stupid and mean people doing stupid and mean things to one another.'' As for the effects of ''horror'' movies, Eastman (1933) noted that they ''sow the seeds of future nervous disorders.'' Twenty-eight articles eventually appeared as part of this anti-movie campaign.

The *Christian Century* campaign was encouraged by additional ''expert'' opinions in several books. In 1929, Alice M. Mitchell published *Children and Movies,* a study of the ''movie experience of the city child.'' This involved questionnaire research on over 10,000 Chicago children including groups of ''average'' public school students, juvenile delinquents, and children involved in Boy/Girl Scouts. Mitchell reported that over 90 percent of the children attended movies at regular intervals, but that the highest frequency of movie attendance was associated with the delinquent group and the lowest with the Scouts group. Scouts and average students also indicated a preference for playing football over going to the movies, while delinquents preferred the movies. Delinquent children also expressed a preference for movies over reading. Such findings were considered quite damning by critics who were quick to accept their validity and to infer that movie-going ''caused'' illiteracy and delinquency.

A series of studies of the effects of motion pictures upon youth, known as the Payne Fund Studies, were published in the early 1930s and promptly added fuel to critics' fires. *Movies, Delinquency, and Crime* (1933), by sociologists H. Blumer and P. Hauser, reported on questionnaires, autobiographical accounts, and interviews with criminals of various ages. They reported that some 10 percent of the male delinquents and criminals studied felt that motion pictures had contributed to their misdeeds. Moreover, 25 percent of the delinquent girls studied stated that they had had sexual relations with men after being aroused by a picture with passionate love scenes. The authors also published a large group of case reports in which criminals blamed the movies for one or another aspect of their behavior.

W. W. Charters, who chaired the Payne Fund Studies, summarized their findings in *Motion Pictures and Youth* (1933). He interpreted the findings as indicating that a kind of "emotional possession" strikes young children when they sit before a movie screen:

> He forgets his surroundings. He loses ordinary control of his feelings, his actions, and his thoughts. He identifies himself with the plot and loses himself in the picture . . . He is possessed by the drama.[9]

Among the important factors contributing to emotional possession, Charters includes the parade of visual images before the child's eyes. Whereas previously children had to provide their own images when reading books, they were now bombarded by "real" images complete with dramatic effects, stimulating actions, and colors. Charters was also willing to conclude that crime pictures had a "pronounced effect upon delinquents." As to the larger issue, the causation of crime or delinquency, he described the situation as "very complicated." That is, the power of films to influence behavior had not been assessed in comparison to the other influences: parents, school, companions, community customs. This point was not taken up by those in pursuit of evil influence, who found "emotional possession" the far more pleasing concept.

The campaign against movies conducted by the *Christian Century* and such religious groups as the Legion of Decency in the first half of the 1930s capped the era of anti-movie sentiment. There were, of course, subsequent outcries regarding gangster, horror, youth gang, and certain sexy movies, but by this time cinema was already too deeply embedded in American culture to be seriously threatened by censure.

Movies, Morals, and Mind

Well before movies were dreamt of, live stage performance was an established form of popular entertainment. The institution of theater, however, had its detractors from the time of Plato, with its fortunes rising and falling according to local politics and religious beliefs. The Puritans of colonial America, for example, condemned theater as a form of ungodly idleness, a workshop for the Devil. English neo-puritans in the early eighteenth century, such as Daniel Defoe and Jeremy

Collier, characterized theaters as "Houses of Sin and Nurseries of Vice" and waged campaigns to have them abolished. The arrival of burlesque and musical satire in the mid-nineteenth century rekindled American opposition to stage performances in many quarters. In some measure, then, early reactions against the movies may be viewed as following in this tradition. However, the movies offered society a radically new technology and the ability to reach millions of people in a relatively short time. They were inexpensive, hence available to the working class and to children, and they provided a dimension of realism previously unheard of in performance. Like novels, they had the ability to generate powerful fantasies and feelings, but they additionally provided both children and adults with vivid, ready-made, lifelike, visual images. Consequently, movies were perceived as a threat of far greater magnitude than existing forms of entertainment.

The rise of the social sciences during the 1920s brought new support to established anti-media forces. Social workers, psychologists, and progressive educators became increasingly concerned with the shaping of character and the promotion of mental health. Both psychoanalysis and "pop" psychology dictated that the experiences of childhood were critical in this regard. Using case studies and surveys, researchers set out to measure and thereby "prove" the evil influence of the motion picture upon youth. What began as a moral/religious/social issue became increasingly redefined as a scientific one. The complexity of the subject, however, ensured that such studies fell short of their goal. A scientific consensus to the effect that the movies were evil could not be achieved. Of course, consensus was not necessary to the purposes of the anti-media forces. The case studies and the statistics were sufficiently frightening to convince vast numbers of parents and legislators that their children were in immediate danger.

The arguments offered against the movies were quite similar to those marshalled against the newspaper and the novel. Although "unrealistic," these media forms were also too realistic. Their preoccupation with crime and sexuality undermined decency and promoted delinquency. The imagery they offered was too potent for much of the audience and would damage the mental health and morals of viewers; literacy and intelligence also were at risk. The power of their attraction was equated with a surrender of the will, which transformed human beings into passive repositories for all manner of suggestion. Censorship was invoked as the only possible way of protecting society from this new and potent form of evil influence.

The attack upon the movies certainly was escalated by the social transition occurring in America during the 1920s. The post-War gen-

eration was arousing anxiey and consternation with its independence
and provocativeness. Young people seemed deliberately to defy long-
standing social conventions, dismissing them as mere hypocrisies and
establishing their own codes of manners and morals. To the horror of
their elders, young women were wearing very short skirts and makeup,
and were commonly seen smoking and drinking in public. Young men
and women were openly speaking and joking about sexual matters and
partaking of new and vulgar jazz dances. Traditionalists soon were
overwhelmed by this youthful rebellion, understood as social disorder
and cultural disintegration. Progressives set out to save the younger
generation from various evil influences.

Both traditionalists and progressives found the movies objectionable,
although the latter dreamed of turning them eventually into a positive
force for education. The temptation was great to blame the cinema for
all unwelcome post-War cultural and behavioral transformations. Intellectuals of all persuasions, moreover, found that movies represented
a distinctly unwelcome break from the primacy of the written word.
Even a "bad" novel maintained some baseline of literacy in readers,
providing an avenue of eventual improvement through "better" read-
ings. Movies, on the other hand, offered sensation, emotion, and entertainment through mere images, without requiring or sustaining literacy. This seemed a return to a more primitive pre-alphabet form of
communication. Some feared the death knell of culture and the written
word had sounded in America.

Who could have imagined that this situation would soon get worse?

Notes

1. Barton W. Currie, "The Nickel Madness," *Harper's Weekly,* August 24,
   1907, p. 1246.
2. Frederic C. Howe, "What To Do With The Motion Picture Show: Shall It
   Be Censored?", *Outlook,* June 20, 1914, p. 415.
3. William A. McKeever, "A Primary School for Criminals," *Good Housekeeping,* August, 1910, p. 181.
4. Beverly Hazard, article in *Outlook,* cited in *Current Opinion,* April, 1914,
   p. 290.
5. Editorial, "The Cinematographic Craze," *Dial,* February 16, 1914, p. 130.
6. Hugo Munsterberg, *The Film: A Psychological Study* (1916) (New York:
   Dover, 1970), p. 95.
7. Article in *North American Review* (1921), cited in Robert Edward Davis
   Response To Innovation (New York: Arno Press, 1976), p. 180.
8. Fred Eastman, "The Menace of the Movies," *Christian Century,* January
   15, 1930, p. 77.
9. W. W. Charters, *Motion Pictures and Youth* (New York: Macmillan, 1933),
   pp. 38–39.

7

Radio Activity and Its Fallout: Radio

Into an America already beset by newspapers, cheap novels, comic strips, pulp magazines, and sensational cinema, yet another medium arrived. Unlike these mentioned forms, it was not at all tied to visual stimulation. "Radio," as it was called, was an art for the ear rather than the eye; it offered its audience a universe of entertainment possibilities totally removed from both print and picture. In some respects it seemed a throwback to the oral tradition, the stories and songs of the ancients, just as the comics had seemed a throwback to pictographic script. At the same time, however, it was thoroughly modern, the cutting edge of Western technology. In reach and speed it soon dwarfed all the other forms of entertainment media. Human consciousness was now to be bombarded with the inevitable diet of sensuality and violence through yet another sensory channel, undoubtedly with evil consequences. Perhaps this time we had gone too far; literacy, learning, morality, and mental health could hardly survive the additional burden.

Where had this "radio" come from, and where would it take us?

Waves and Voices

Broadcasting history began with a group of dedicated young physicists, sometimes characterized as "crackpot" inventors and lone tinkerers, who followed their esoteric technical interests despite public ridicule or indifference. Some labored in home workshops, supported by their families; others found support from educational institutions. Applying trial and error methods, these determined do-it-yourselfers instigated an enormous leap in communications technology and mass media.

Young Heinrich Hertz, working in a one-room laboratory in his parental home in Germany, investigated the new sciences of electricity and magnetism. In experiments between 1886 and 1888, he succeeded in discovering and measuring electromagnetic "waves" and continued to explore them until his untimely death at age thirty-seven. An Italian youth, Guglielmo Marconi, read about these "Hertzian waves" while vacationing in the Alps and decided to continue the work in his own home. His parents had considerable misgivings about the many hours the teenager spent closeted in his workshop amid coils and batteries. He soon succeeded, however, in an important experiment: ringing a bell by means of radio waves, without any intervening wires. Carrying his equipment out into the fields for remote tests, and adding a telegraph key, Marconi shortly thereafter became the father of "wireless telegraphy," the first form of radio.

With the support of his family, Marconi announced his findings and offered his invention to the Italian Minister of Post and Telegraph. The answer was that the government had no interest in Marconi's work. Marconi's mother, born Irish, suggested that the new invention might be better received in London. In 1896, she left for England with her son, accompanied by a black box bearing the young man's new device. Upon arrival, however, the Marconis were detained by customs officials on the lookout for anarchists and assassins. Deeming the mysterious black box suspicious, they smashed the wireless telegraph into a heap of coils and wires, ignoring the explanations and protestations of the young inventor and his mother. Radio had received its first reviews.

Marconi was able to purchase new parts in England and had soon reconstructed his invention. He brought it to the attention of the government, which tested the device and confirmed that it could send wireless signals for several miles. He became, in short order, the holder of a British patent, a businessman, and a celebrity. Along with a group of savvy financial advisors, he organized the Marconi Wireless Telegraph Company. He was 23 years old. The wireless soon proved its practical worth in communicating with ships at sea, thereby saving lives in nautical emergencies. It also permitted immediate news reporting of important yachting events.

Marconi was warmly welcomed in the United States and, in 1899, founded the Marconi Company of America in New Jersey. As holder of 600,000 shares of the company, Marconi, age 25, became a millionaire. In 1901, he further confirmed his place in history by orchestrating the first transatlantic radio transmissions. While Marconi was not actually the first person to send and receive radio signals, he is nevertheless credited with the invention of radio because he took it from raw invention to successful commercial application. He was awarded the Nobel Prize for physics in 1909.

Once it was established that messages could be transmitted through the air to remote locations, other visionaries considered the possibilities of transmitting the human voice. Reginald A. Fessenden, who had earlier worked in the Edison laboratories, considered the potential use of radio in providing vital weather information to farmers. He proposed that the transmission of dots and dashes be replaced by transmission of a continuous wave upon which voice would be superimposed by modulations. With the backing of General Electric he founded a transmitting station in Massachusetts and, in 1906, broadcast the first wireless voice transmissions. On Christmas Eve, Fessenden played his violin over the airwaves and read excerpts from the Bible to an amazed audience of radio amateurs and professional radio operators at sea. Commercial applications of this technology soon followed, with radio voices informing ships at sea as to which port offered the best prices for their goods.

Lee DeForest, another radio pioneer, wrote his doctoral thesis on "Hertzian Waves." He began his commercial radio enterprises in 1901 by contracting with the press to provide radio information on a yacht race. Borrowing enough cash to build the equipment, he worked frantically to prepare in time for the event, with little regard for his health. He succeeded in collapsing and being hospitalized and would have missed the race entirely had not the assassination of President McKinley required that it be postponed. Ultimately, he was able to attend the race but found that he had acquired two radio competitors working for different press groups. During the race, the three competing radio transmitters created an unintelligible chaos of mutual interference on the airwaves. DeForest was "saved," however, when his newspapers decided that direct radio reports would appeal to readers, and they published as "Radio Flashes" information received through normal channels. They also published feature stories on DeForest and his radio service. Thriving on this publicity, DeForest soon found additional financial backing and staged a variety of public demonstrations of wireless telegraphy.

In 1907, DeForest patented a new device for detecting weak radio signals. It was a vacuum tube with three electrodes, the "Audion," which could amplify radio signals to permit reception over greater distances. Several of these tubes could be used in a cascade arrangement to produce still greater amplification. The same type of tube, moreover, became the basis for a vastly improved type of radio transmitter. Ironically, DeForest was forced in 1912 to defend himself against impatient stockholders' charges of using the mails to defraud. Both he and the Audion eventually were exonerated. Thanks to DeForest, a radio revolution was getting under way; he had discovered "an invisible Empire of the Air."

In 1910, attempting to popularize the new medium, DeForest broadcast a live performance by Enrico Caruso from the Metropolitan Opera. Reception was poor, but the potential of radio for the transmission of entertainment and culture nevertheless was established. By 1916 he was broadcasting in New York with some regularity, with program content including phonograph records, a speech by his mother-in-law demanding the vote for women, and presidential election returns read from the newspapers. A better physicist than businessman, DeForest eventually was forced to sell most of his patents to AT&T in order to avoid bankruptcy.

Meanwhile, American Marconi continued to make strides toward widespread public acceptance of radio. In 1912 it won the attention of the world when David Sarnoff, one of its young radio-telegraph operators, picked up a transmission from the SS *Titanic* as it was sinking in the Atlantic. Sarnoff used the wireless to contact other ships in the area, thereby making possible the rescue of hundreds. Over a three-day period he relayed news of the rescue operations to the press and anxious relatives, while all other American transmitters were silenced by order of President Taft to avoid interference. Sarnoff, suddenly a national hero, went on to become a key figure in the development of broadcasting in the United States.

There was little public complaint regarding radio technology when it was primarily a device for communication with ships at sea. With the outbreak of World War I, moreover, it became clear that radio communications were vital to the coordination of battle plans. By the end of the war, in fact, the United States Navy was convinced that radio was too important to leave in the hands of the British-run American Marconi Company. Although it failed in its attempt to gain a radio monopoly of its own, the Navy succeeded in convincing Congress to take control of the airwaves. In 1919, the Radio Corporation of America was formed to wrest the new medium, including its patents, transmitters, and employees, away from "foreigners." Radio was becoming American.

Inventing an Audience

Prior to 1920, the only people listening to radio were the professional radio operators, both commercial and military, and the growing number of amateur radio operators. Nobody else had the interest, equipment, or know-how to tune in to the airwaves. One of the men responsible for changing this situation was Frank Conrad, a Westinghouse researcher and dedicated radio hobbyist. Conrad was broadcasting from a workshop over his garage, just outside Pittsburgh, and began transmitting evening phonograph concerts for his fellow radio enthusiasts. Of course, others had broadcast music before Conrad. The new element was the appearance of the following ad, placed by a department store in the Pittsburgh *Sun* (September 29, 1920):

> Victrola music, played into the air over a wireless telephone, was "picked up" by listeners on the wireless receiving station which was recently installed here for patrons interested in wireless experiments. The concert was heard Thursday night about 10 o'clock, and continued 20 minutes . . . Mr. Conrad is a wireless enthusiast and "puts on" the wireless concerts periodically for the entertainment of the many people in this district who have wireless sets. Amateur Wireless Sets, made by the maker of the set which is in operation in our store, are on sale here $10.00 up.[1]

If wireless sets could be sold in department stores, for use by ordinary people (rather than technically minded hobbyists), then the potential audience would be enormous; radio would become less a hobby and more a business. Westinghouse vice-president Harry P. Davis, Conrad's superior, immediately asked Conrad to construct a large transmitter for Westinghouse with the aim of broadcasting the election returns. Meanwhile, Westinghouse sold parts for radio sets and promised soon to offer complete, easy to use, receivers. After successfully transmitting election results to eager groups of listeners, Westinghouse began a daily schedule of broadcasts on their new station, KDKA. Band music, political speeches, weather reports, and a prizefight were among the groundbreaking broadcasts. Within a year, Westinghouse had established stations in Newark, New Jersey, Springfield, Massachusetts, and Chicago, Illinois. Soon it was invited to join in the new Radio Corporation of America.

When David Sarnoff, in 1916, had urged American Marconi to manufacture "Radio Music Boxes," the idea had been soundly rejected. Once the company became RCA, Sarnoff raised the idea again, with similar results. The success of KDKA, however, changed everything. In 1921, Sarnoff was made general manager of RCA and moved quickly to gear up for the manufacture and sale of radio sets. He also arranged to have the world championship boxing match between Jack Dempsey and Georges Carpentier broadcast to patrons of clubs and theaters (as well as to those owning their own wireless sets). The public needed to learn that radio was exciting, and it did. Only one year later, the sale of radio sets earned RCA some 11 million dollars. A substantial radio audience had been created, and it was to grow by leaps and bounds. In 1923 alone, more than half a million radio receivers were sold. By 1926 there were radios in some five million homes. Media historian John Tebbel noted:

> A door to the world had opened for millions of people in small towns and on lonely farms. With a twist of the dial they were transported to Carnegie Hall, to distant football fields, to nightclubs and ballrooms . . . It was a transformation in national life perhaps even more remarkable than the one produced later by television.[2]

Few early model radios had loudspeakers or other amenities, but listeners seemed willing to struggle with earphones, milk bottle-sized dry cells, and the considerable difficulties of tuning. Radio enthusiasts, with headphones in place, would endure terrible static in attempts to pick up distant stations, staying up half the night if necessary. Only through radio, after all, could one hear news, sports, and entertainment events as they were happening. Radio's sense of immediacy, of simultaneity, brought a new and exciting dimension to the media.

Exactly how was the new broadcasting industry to satisfy and maintain its new audience? Initially, the airwaves were filled with strains of phonograph records. The novelty of radio was such, however, that live performers were quite happy to go "on the air" without any pay; soon they were lining up for the privilege. This situation was short-lived, of course, and live talent eventually required payment. Broadcasters also were confronted by outraged composers, authors, and publishers who informed them that one could not play music or read articles and stories on the air without paying appropriate fees. How, then, was broadcasting to be programmed and financed? The answer, for better or worse, came in the form of broadcast advertising, or "commercials." The first, on WEAF, was a 10-minute pitch for apartments in Jackson Heights, New York. As the concept caught on, companies began sponsoring concerts, vaudeville acts, comics, and so on, in order to promote their goods. Thus the "Happiness Boys" pushed Happiness Candy, and listeners found dramatized classics on the "Eveready Hour" and concerts on the "Atwater Kent Hour." Soon the airwaves were filled with singers, actors, and comics, including such early notables as Fred Allen, Eddie Cantor, and Kate Smith; they were also filled with sponsors and commercials. Still, music predominated, and the entire country reverberated to the strains of "Yes, We Have No Bananas," "Barney Google," and so on.

In the late 1920s, radio broadcasting introduced a number of serial shows featuring earthy, ethnic characters. Among the most prominent were *Amos 'n' Andy* and *The Goldbergs*. Additional serials followed over the next few years, with melodrama coming into prominence. Titles included *Trouble House, Lonely Women, Other Wife, Road of Life,* and *Against the Storm.* Family-type serials included *One Man's Family, Today's Children, The Stepmother,* and *Those We Love.* Beginning as evening programs, the serials soon took over the daytime airwaves and, with the aid of nationwide network hookups, held millions of Americans spellbound. By the mid-1930s, the daytime serial drama, or "soap opera" (because of the many soap company sponsors), reigned supreme; a determined fan could listen to them all through the day. James Thurber once described the radio serial as a kind of sandwich:

> Between thick slices of advertising, spread twelve minutes of dialogue, add predicament, villainy, and female suffering in equal measure, throw in a dash of nobility, sprinkle with tears, season with organ music, cover with a rich announcer sauce, and serve five times a week.[3]

Gilbert Seldes (*The Great Audience,* 1950) described the soap opera as the great invention of radio, a new form of fiction in which virtually nothing happened in each installment. It often took weeks of the fifteen-minute dramas for the simplest action to be completed, and reactions of the various characters might consume another few weeks. The object, of course, was to sustain suspense while using a minimum of new material. At its best, Seldes noted, an installment consisted of "two desultory conversations of about four minutes each, the rest of the quarter-hour being taken by résumés, musical bridges of the most revolting quality, and commercials."

The 1930s also brought to radio such celebrities as Jack Benny, Bing Crosby, Fanny Brice, Burns and Allen, and Bob Hope. Even many news reporters and commentators became celebrities, such as H. V. Kaltenborn, Gabriel Heatter, and Lowell Thomas. Evening programming, however, became dominated increasingly by adventure, detective, crime, and suspense dramas featuring such notables as Sam Spade, Boston Blackie, The Thin Man, Captain Midnight, Buck Rogers, The Lone Ranger, the Green Hornet, and The Shadow. Many of these characters were taken from the popular novels, pulp magazines, and comic strips of the day. It was not long before horror shows arrived, such as *The Inner Sanctum, The Hermit's Cave,* and *Witch's Tales.*

Children's programming became a fact of life during the 1930s, although it was not always clear which programs were for children and which for adults. A survey of over 3,000 children, conducted in the mid-1930s, found that Eddie Cantor's variety show, with its songs and humor, topped their list of favorites. However, most other favorites were dramatic adventure shows: *Buck Rogers, Bobby Benson, Eno Crime Clues, Myrt and Marge, Little Orphan Annie,* and *Jack Armstrong,* to name a few. Children discussed the shows with their friends, included radio characters in their make-believe games, entered radio contests, joined radio clubs offering secret rings and/or handshakes, sent in cereal box-tops, and wrote letters to their favorite performers. Eisenberg (*Children and Radio Programs,* 1936) noted that ". . . radio, in all its ramifications, has become one of the principal leisure-time activities of children."

In the 1930s, then, it was clear that radio no longer served primarily as a means of "communication," but had become the nation's dominant vehicle for mass entertainment. Millions of American men, women, and children were thrilling to the squeaking door that opened *The Inner Sanctum,* the organ music that signaled the serial melodrama, the strains of the "William Tell Overture" that introduced *The Lone Ranger,* and so on. "Who knows what evil lurks in the hearts of men?" asked the introduction to *The Shadow.* Inevitably, a group of educators, social scientists, clergy, and parents began asking themselves what evil might lurk in this new medium of radio.

Evil in the Air

As early as 1927, with radio barely out of its infancy, an editorial in the *New Republic* complained that the great promise of the new medium had not materialized. It had not replaced print journalism, as many had predicted, nor had it proven to be a revolutionary vehicle for education. Rather, ". . . broadcasting in America is an advertising device." How long, the author asked, would Americans be willing to put up with inane commercial messages arriving in the midst of symphonies or serious news? Moreover, the radio industry had shown little inclination to enter the realm of important intellectual and social concerns, focusing instead on the delivery of jazz and other music. This form of radio could not, should not, last.

Two years later, an article in *The Forum* took the issue one step further by pointing out the "harm" being done by radio:

> And now we know definitely what we have got in radio—just another disintegrating toy, just another medium—like the newspapers, the magazines, the billboards, and the mailbox—for advertisers to use in pestering us . . .

we still had some leisure time. But radio, God's great gift to man, eliminated that last dangerous chance for Satan to find mischief for idle hands. There is now very little danger that Americans will resort to the use of thinking.[4]

The same article predicted that people would no longer socialize in the usual ways. Rather, they would spend evenings sitting around the radio listening to "so-called music interspersed with long lists of the bargains to be had at Whosit's Department Store." From time to time family members or guests might exchange nods, but little else. "Thus dies the art of conversation." Worse still, the latter would be replaced by ". . . the rattle and bang of incredibly frightful 'jazz' music . . . ." The brightest hope for the future, according to the author, was that advertising exploitation would succeed in killing off radio within a few years.

It was not merely the dominance of radio by advertising and jazz music that disturbed intellectuals, but their inability to gain any foothold in the medium. Radio in the 1920s was decidedly conservative, attempting to protect its listeners and its livelihood from the issues of socialism, liberalism, pacifism, sexuality, and so on. Broadcasting a lively debate on the important issues of the day, including unpopular points of view, might alienate a part of the audience. This was an unacceptable risk, hence forbidden. An article in *The Forum* (1931) noted: "Socialists, Pacifists, Communists, laborites, and such are almost always denied the use of the air on one pretext or another." Similarly, advocates of atheism and of birth control stood little chance of achieving radio exposure.

Lyman Bryson, writing of "The Revolt of the Radio Listeners" for the *Journal of Adult Education* warned educators of the dangers of radio:

> All great human inventions, even printing, even language itself, have proved to be two-edged swords. They can do as much evil as good . . . Radio is as great- and as dangerous- as any . . . and it can broadcast injury and discord and ugliness into the farthest reaches of inhabited space. To be light-minded about the radio is to jig along a precipice.[5]

Bryson took the usual swipe at advertising, indicating that broadcasting practices supported "the swindler, the slanderer, and the quack." However, he also brought a new element to the critique by pointing out that "our ears are less civilized than our eyes." That is, human beings had become ever more dependent upon their eyes since the development of writing and printing, so that our critical and discriminative abilities now lay predominantly in this realm. Consequently, radio and its advertising were reaching us on a level where we were more *vulnerable,* where our defensive measures failed to protect us. Unless radio advertising reformed, he warned, a revolt of the radio listeners might be required to force it off the air completely. He added: "Lies are lies, even if you are paying five thousand dollars an hour to tell them to the world."

In sum, intellectuals quickly found that radio was not a vehicle for their use, but merely another carrier of popular entertainment and advertising. They soundly rejected it in favor of print, and began alerting others as to its shortcomings and its alarming properties. Soon the message was carried to parents and elementary school teachers, and the conflict intensified.

In 1933, the Parent-Teacher Association of Scarsdale, New York, disturbed by the radio issue, distributed questionnaires to 286 pupils, ages 8–13. These were designed to determine the listening habits and preferences of the students. At the same time, another set of questionnaires was used with mothers and teachers who were asked to rate the quality of the various shows. The latter group gave "Excellent" ratings to such programs as *Current Events, Great Moments in History,* and *Dramatized News Events.* They rated as "Very Poor" (the lowest possible rating) such shows as *Little Orphan Annie, Myrt and Marge, The Shadow, Detectives Black and Blue, Skippy,* and *Howard Thurston—Magician.* Needless to say, parents and teachers were in considerable disagreement with their children, and the furor thus created was reported in an editorial entitled "The Children's Hour," which appeared in *The Nation* (1933). Its author noted: "What the parents rated poor and very poor the little savages almost invariably set down as their favorite entertainment."

Only one month later, an article by Arthur Mann entitled "The Children's Hour of Crime" appeared in *Scribner's* (1933). Mann introduced his thesis by noting that he removed the power tube from his radio daily between 4 p.m. and 8 p.m., thereby protecting his children from "four hours of lessons on the art of crime and higher skulduggery." He pointed out that "every form of crime known to man" appeared in the popular juvenile radio programs. Orphan Annie periodically was kidnapped, chloroformed, clubbed unconscious, held prisoner, and otherwise sadistically abused. Buck Rogers regularly encountered international and interplanetary thievery, espionage, counterfeiting, extortion, and assault. Young Bobby Benson of the H-Bar-O Ranch was always involved with cattle rustlers, shoot-outs, bandits, and other Wild West varieties of mayhem. Black and Blue, two bungling sleuths, regularly dealt with robbery, kidnapping, murder, arson, bribery, and so on. In fact, of the twenty-five shows he reviewed, Mann found only two worthy of recommendation. As for the vast majority of shows:

I should like to postpone my children's knowledge of how to rob a bank, scuttle a ship, shoot a sheriff, the emotional effects of romantic infidelity, jungle hazards, and the horrors of the drug habit for a few more years at least.[6]

The very next month, *New Outlook* (1933) launched a series of articles on the growth of radio, asking: "Was there ever an industry which in a few brief years made so many enemies?" The newspapers were cited as hostile competitors; the movie industry was said to be alarmed by low-cost entertainment in the home; legitimate theater was threatened; liberals feared a media form so dominated by "big business"; the church feared shrinking congregations due to competition from radio religious services; publishers complained that the radio lured people away from novels; intellectuals condemned program content and advertising practices. Organizing as the National Committee on Education by Radio, educators had become a particularly powerful enemy of commercial broadcasting. This group was demanding that 15 percent of available frequencies be set aside for educational broadcasting. The organization and its goals were backed by the National Catholic Educational Association, the National Congress of Parents and Teachers, the National Education Association, the Association of Land Grant Colleges and Universities, the National Association of State Universities, and so on.

Editor, essayist, and social critic H. L. Mencken offered a highly unfavorable comparison of American broadcasting with the British version:

We have an almost unbroken series of propaganda harangues by quacks with something to sell, and of idiotic comments on public events by persons devoid of both information and ideas. The British Broadcasting Company is a government agency, and is supported by a small annual tax on radio receiving sets. It sends nothing shabby, cheap or vulgar onto the air. There is no bad music by bad performers, there is no sordid touting of toothpastes, automobile oils, soaps, breakfast foods, soft drinks and patent medicines. In America, of course, the radio program costs nothing. But it is worth precisely the same.[7]

Opposition to the radio continued to spread among parents and teachers. The Central Council of the Parent-Teacher Association of Rochester, New York, passed a resolution condemning juvenile radio shows. It suggested that disapproving parents consider a boycott of sponsors' products whenever programs appeared to menace the welfare of children. A New York City Police Commissioner publicly criticized radio shows for providing dangerous ideas to young minds. His remarks were prompted by the suggestion that a kidnapping case might have been stimulated by a story on *Eno Crime Clues*. The following year found *Newsweek* (1934) reporting the condemnation of radio sales pitches to children by members of the Child Study Association of America. The association also criticized the many "gun-barking melodramas that scare children," while admitting that these shows are also the children's favorites. The association's chairwoman commented: "Radio seems to find parents more helpless than did the funnies . . . It cannot be locked out or the children locked in to escape it."

Some parents, however, did endeavor to limit access to the radio by banning certain shows. A survey reported by Eisenberg (1936) stated the following to be most often banned by parents: *Witch's Tales, Eno Crime Clues, Murder and Mystery, Crime Stories,* and *Buck Rogers.* The reasons for parental disapproval were predictable, focusing on exciting and frightening contents as well as criminal themes. These programs were, of course, among the favorites of many children.

After a few years of relative quiescence, the radio issue erupted again in 1937. Federal Communications Commissioner George Henry Payne pronounced a need to clean up children's programming. He was soon swamped with supportive mail from concerned parents. A *Newsweek* (1937) account of the situation described the effects of existing programs upon young listeners:

> They shudder delightedly while guns belch yellow flame and heads are split and hearts are broken. They gasp as airplanes roar down through imaginary skies to drop bombs . . . And their eyes widen appreciatively when men die suddenly on city pavements or wield blunt instruments with deplorable results.[8]

The author of an article for *American Mercury* (1938) on "Radio Horror," Worthington Gibson, charged that radio was breeding "a race of neurotic impressionables," with the message of terror firmly imprinted upon their minds. He also raised the issue of damaged morality:

> Come five o'clock every weekday afternoon, millions of American children drop whatever they are doing and rush to the nearest radio set. Here, with feverish eyes and cocked ears, they listen for that first earsplitting sound which indicates that the Children's Hour is at hand. This introductory signal may be the wail of a police siren, the rattle of a machine gun, the explosion of a hand grenade, the shriek of a dying woman, the bark of a gangster's pistol, or the groan of a soul in purgatory. Whatever it is, the implication

is the same: Radio has resumed its daily task of cultivating our children's morals—with blood-and-thunder effects.[9]

Gibson explicitly considered and rejected the notion that radio shockers might, in the long run, prove as harmless as the once-feared dime-novel. The evil influence of radio was deemed far more powerful by virtue of its impact upon the ear rather than the eye. This time, the mental and moral health of young Americans was indeed at risk. This theme was echoed by other critics, who emphasized the overstimulating effects of radio as a cause of nightmares, fingernail biting, and nervousness.

Preoccupation with events in Europe soon overshadowed worries about radio, and World War II brought this phase of the dialogue to a close. The condemnation of radio had peaked, although a post-war flare-up of the debate again found critics charging that radio left children with perverted moral values and an appetite for violence. Voices were raised, as well, about the effects of all those soap operas on adults. Were they getting over-involved, confusing the fantasy of the soaps with reality? Was the constant tension created by such programs contributing to physical illness and/or emotional instability?

One of the parents of radio, physicist Lee DeForest, in 1947, proclaimed his distress with its development:

> What have you gentlemen done with my child? He was conceived as a potent instrumentality for culture, fine music, the uplifting of America's mass intelligence. You have debased this child, you have sent him out on the street in rags of ragtime, tatters of jive and boogie-woogie, to collect money from all and sundry for hubba hubba and audio jitterbug. You have made him a laughing stock to the intelligence, surely a stench in the nostrils of the gods of the ionosphere . . . Soap opera without end or sense floods each household daily . . . Murder mysteries rule the waves by night and children are rendered psychopathic by your bedtime stories.[10]

DeForest's powerful indictment of radio broadcasting attracted a good deal of attention, but not for very long. The arrival of a new media threat called "television" soon eclipsed public concerns about radio.

The Radio Revolution

The reaction against radio, although intense, was more than matched by the passion of its large, admiring audience. The excitement generated by the broadcast of dramas, news reports, sports coverage, and music is difficult to imagine today, since the radio has become a very minor and relatively undistinguished household appliance. In its day, radio dominated the living rooms of America, becoming the first electronic hearth. It kept housewives company during the day, attracted the children in the evenings, and provided the entire family with its primary link to the greater world. By 1948, there were some seventy-five million radios in the United States. Given the size of its audience and its power to attract young and old, male and female, the reaction against radio was both predictable and inevitable. Mass entertainment, as we have seen, invites massive criticism.

To many intellectuals, the American romance with radio seemed a social reversion to a primitive, preliterate level of culture. McLuhan noted: "The subliminal depths of radio are charged with the resonating echoes of tribal horns and antique drums . . . radio is a profound archaic force, a time bond with the most ancient past and long-forgotten experience." Such connection to the early world of story and song was not welcomed by those committed to the world of print. The way of the voice and the ear was unfamiliar and threatening. It appealed to emotions rather than reason; it lacked logic, permanence, and elegance. A speech, for example, which rallied an entire nation when delivered over the air might, upon analysis of its written content, reveal little that was new or exciting. The human voice added a new and powerful dimension to communication, to be sure, but it was a dimension that had little to do with intellect.

There is a certain amount of irony in the fact that radio, which totally lacked the explicit visual imagery that had gotten the movies into trouble, was no less criticized. It, too, was deemed a moral and mental health hazard, able to touch the subconscious mind by means of unguarded pathways. Like the dime novel, it was said to stimulate unwholesome images in the minds of its audience, although the offending images were more often violent than sexual. Woman and children, once again, needed protection—the former from the stress and fantasy of the soaps, the latter from the over-stimulation and immorality of the serials.

While parents and teachers railed against the evils of radio drama, additional aspects of the radio problem came quietly to the fore. Observers of the political scene, for example, could not help but notice the growing significance of radio in national and world affairs. President Roosevelt used radio broadcasts to good effect as a means of calming the nation's financial panic. Orson Welles used it, on a memorable Halloween in 1938, to simulate an invasion from Mars, generating panic in many parts of the country. In Europe, Adolph Hitler used it to deliver powerful speeches that rallied his Fascist supporters and fueled his war machine. Clearly, one could influence many people rapidly, and in a variety of significant ways, using the radio.

Program content aside, many were uneasy with the power of the new medium, its ability to touch so many people at once. Radio brought to millions of listeners not only the news of distant events, but commentary and interpretations that indicated who our enemies were and where they were to be found. In the hands of a demagogue, radio broadcasting was an invitation to chaos, an ideal tool for propaganda, persecution, and hatred. Equally frightening to some was the specter of creeping collectivism, whether of a Communist or Fascist variety, imported into American living rooms via radio. Could our citizens adequately protect their individuality from the voices daily filling their ears, telling them what to eat, drink, and wear, what household products to buy, how to treat their ills, how to deal with family problems, how to understand the news, and so on?:

> We have erected safeguards against panic, but not against persuasion . . . the slow daily and weekly creation of a climate favorable to certain ideas, the unnoticed gentle nudges and pressures that turn people in one direction rather than another, the constant supply of images to populate our subconscious minds—these are not watched, and cannot be, so long as we think we are safe—because we can turn it off, can't we?[11]

If radio threatened to undermine individuality, it simultaneously instituted a wave of democratization hitherto unknown. The radio and its messages spoke to one and all, young and old, rich and poor, men and women, urban and rural communities, to people of all classes, races, and religions. Radio waves jumped the barriers of social stratification as readily as they did regional and national boundaries. This development, too, was not entirely welcome. To some, it threatened to usher in an age of homogeneity and mediocrity, in which specialized individual tastes were sacrificed in order to reach the "average" radio listener. Similar arguments had been advanced regarding the early movies. By the 1940s, consumers already had considerable choice in selecting movies and reading materials; one could find something for most any taste. Radio, however, seemed to offer little to the elite. Only in the New York City area, in the mid-1940s, could one find a few stations devoted exclusively to classical music and cultural/educational programming, and these attracted only a small audience.

Did radio offer something of value to anyone? Some argued otherwise, pointing out that the medium required enormous quantities of material to feed its daily audiences, and consequently could serve up only mush. Seldes pointed out that radio producers had no expectation or concern about producing lasting or memorable programming, but merely attempted to fill the airwaves with whatever the public and the sponsors would accept. Radio was immediate, but it was also immediately forgotten:

> . . . this pumping out of never-ending waters of oblivion may be the most serious count against radio as a public service. It reduces the created entertainment to the level of a commodity . . . to be quickly used and thrown away.[12]

Fortune (1947) magazine, exploring "The Revolt against Radio," noted the results of a national opinion poll in which 82 percent of radio listeners reported that the radio industry was doing a good-to-excellent job. Moreover, 62 percent of those polled thought radio advertising ought to be continued. The "voice of the people" had spoken; most listeners were satisfied. The most outspoken critics of radio, then, simply deplored the national taste. That is, people in the United States were by-and-large getting the entertainment they wanted, except for that small but vocal minority that found popular music, soap opera, slapstick humor, quiz shows, and commercials to be obnoxious or harmful. This highbrow minority group, broadcasters complained, was attempting to force all radio listeners to "enjoy" classical music and uplifting educational productions. Critics, on the other hand, accused broadcasters and sponsors of exploiting and perpetuating ignorance and bad taste while endangering moral decency and mental health. Psychologists studying the impact of radio upon individuals and society (*The Psychology of Radio,* 1935) quickly noted the class distinctions involved:

> The poor man escapes the confines of his poverty; the country dweller finds refuge from local gossip; the villager acquires cosmopolitan interests; the invalid forgets his loneliness and his pain; the city dweller enlarges his personal world through contact with strange lands and peoples. It is the middle classes and the underprivileged whose desires to share in the world's events have been most persistently thwarted, and it is these classes, therefore, that are the most loyal supporters of radio.[13]

The radio controversy, in its day, encompassed the evil content of radio programs, the horrors of advertising and commercialism, and the dangerous characteristics of the medium itself. In the newspapers and magazines, virtually all aspects of radio eventually were challenged as potentially or actually harmful to individuals and to society. These articles regularly fanned the smouldering fears of parents and teachers regarding evil influences. The critique was not based upon research findings but upon the opinions and convictions of social critics. The various evils attributed radio broadcasting, of course, did not pass away at mid-century, when radio lost much of its prominence. Rather, they were transformed, soon to reappear as the evils of television.

Radio remains very much with us; millions of Americans wake up to its music and news and listen to it while driving to and from work. Today, however, it is rarely controversial. Even its constant outpouring of rock-and-roll, once a favorite target of parents and teachers, now draws little attention; other targets are more compelling. The few remaining social scientists to study radio generally find it to be a benign or positive influence, a "portable friend" to youngsters, a diverting companion to the elderly and the shut-in. As for the adventure dramas of the 1930s and 1940s, a few stations have brought some back as nostalgia items, and several of the original programs remain available to the public on audio cassette tapes, marketed as radio "classics." Nevertheless, as noted by Jim Harmon in his retrospective on *The Great Radio Heroes* (1967): "The true art of radio was its drama, which has faded back into the darkness whence it came."

Notes

1. Ad in the Pittsburgh *Sun,* cited in Erik Barnouw, *Tube of Plenty* (New York: Oxford University Press, 1979), p. 30.
2. John Tebbel, *The Media in America* (New York: Crowell, 1974), p. 361.
3. James Thurber, cited in Russel Nye, *The Unembarrassed Muse: The Popular Arts in America* (New York: Dial, 1970), p. 396.
4. Jack Woodford, "Radio—A Blessing or a Curse?", *Forum,* March, 1929, p. 169.
5. Lyman Bryson, "The Revolt of the Radio Listeners," *Journal of Adult Education,* 1932, 4, p. 234.
6. Arthur Mann, "The Children's Hour of Crime," *Scribners,* May, 1933, p. 315.
7. H. L. Mencken, cited by Allen Raymond, "Static Ahead!", *New Outlook,* July, 1933, p. 18–19.
8. "Radio Gore Criticized," *Newsweek,* November 8, 1937, p. 26.
9. Worthington Gibson, "Radio Horror: For Children Only," *American Mercury,* July 6, 1938, p. 294.
10. Lee DeForest (1947), cited in "The Revolt against Radio," *Fortune,* Vol. 35(3), 1947, p. 101.
11. Gilbert Seldes, *The Great Audience* (New York: Viking, 1951), p. 139.
12. Ibid., p. 110.
13. Hadley Cantril and Gordon W. Allport, *The Psychology of Radio* (New York: Harper Brothers, 1935), p. 259.

8

The Vast Wasteland: Television

The death of radio was widely predicted but never occurred. With the arrival of television at mid-century, however, radio was forced to alter its programming drastically and to focus its efforts on broadcasting music. In this manner, the "menace" of its dramatic presentations was quietly and effectively vanquished. A mass exodus of performers ensued, with television clearly becoming the "in" form of entertainment. Radio was virtually abandoned to its disc jockeys, who were able to provide the lowest priced form of broadcast entertainment. News, weather, traffic reports, and "talk" shows also survived, although clearly ancillary to the "Top Twenty" hit tunes. Television, meanwhile, rapidly acquired the power to attract a mass audience. It could literally clear the streets on Tuesday nights, when "Mr. Television," Milton Berle, offered his comic routines, or on Saturday nights, when Sid Caesar and Imogene Coca performed. Although young and inexperienced, the new medium was already a force to be reckoned with—for good or ill.

Our excursion into television must be prefaced with a caveat. Popular and scientific literature on television has reached the point where it cannot be thoroughly reviewed in a single chapter. The technical aspects of television research methodology alone require book-length elaboration. Consequently, we will be dealing only with a limited selection of documents deemed (by me) either important or particularly illustrative of the enduring crusades against evil influence.

Creating Television

The basic principles upon which television would operate were suggested as early as 1880. The transmission technique involved a rapid "scanning" of each element in a picture, line by line, frame by frame. Reception relied upon the tendency of images to persist in human vision, which would let the mind organize and assemble rapidly presented elements into a whole picture. In 1884, Paul Nipkow, in Germany, took an important first step in realizing the dream of television. He patented a mechanical, rotating disk which featured a series of square holes arranged in a spiral pattern. Each hole, as it rotated, scanned one line of a target image; a full rotation scanned the entire image. Each line could then be represented as a series of brightness values indicating patterns of light and shade. Using a photoelectric cell, one could then translate the brightness values into electrical values for transmission by wire or radio. The process simply was reversed at the other end, using the electrical values to light a lamp in the proper sequence behind an identical disk rotating in synchrony with the first. Although slow and primitive, and quite limited in resolution, the Nipkow disk was used in all early television systems.

Technical improvements were not long in coming. In 1897, K. F. Braun, of Germany, introduced a cathode-ray tube with a florescent screen that produced light when struck by a beam of electrons. Russian scientist Boris Rosing, in 1907, suggested its use in a television receiver and succeeded in transmitting and receiving geometrical patterns. The first demonstration of "true" television pictures, by J. L. Baird in England, awaited 1926, and these were crude, flickering images only a few inches high. Only a few years later, Baird offered the first practical demonstration of color television transmission.

Mechanical systems of image transmission were slow and lacked the sensitivity needed for greater image resolution. An electronic method of scanning was needed, and a Russian immigrant to the United States, V. K. Zworykin, soon patented such a device (the Iconoscope) for R.C.A. By 1932, R.C.A. had demonstrated and filed patent for an all electronic color television system. To the consternation of R.C.A., it found that it was not alone in the field of electronic television. A young inventor named Philo T. Farnsworth, working alone in an apartment, had quietly applied for a patent on electronic television before R.C.A. Their attorneys contested the application, but without success. Farnsworth, age 24, was awarded the patent in 1930. As he proved unwilling to sell his patent outright, corporate giant R.C.A. was forced to purchase a license from the youth and pay him royalties. Another independent researcher, Edwin H. Armstrong, was far less fortunate. The inventor of F.M. radio transmission, which was adapted for the audio portion of television transmission, Armstrong remained locked in ongoing legal struggles with R.C.A. until his death by apparent suicide. His widow, shortly thereafter, accepted a cash settlement.

Among the earliest noteworthy television programming events was the 1927 appearance of Secretary of Commerce Herbert Hoover, in

Washington, D.C., for viewing by a select audience in Manhattan. The following year saw the first dramatic production for television, *The Queen's Messenger*. Such experimentation with television soon ground to a halt, however, with the onset of the Great Depression. Only radio flourished, as audiences sought an inexpensive means of relieving the misery of the era.

It was not until 1939 that R.C.A and NBC formally introduced the new medium to the public. The vehicle selected for the debut was the New York City World's Fair, and this was where many Americans thrilled to their first look at television. Daily programming was initiated, with one program originating in a studio, another from a mobile unit, and additional programming time devoted to movies. In the same year, CBS began its own broadcasts, beginning with a speech by New York City Mayor Jimmy Walker, songs by Kate Smith, and a piano solo by George Gershwin. The performers worked under the blazing lights required by primitive television cameras, sometimes resorting to salt pills to keep from passing out. Viewers were few in number and most watched sets equipped with 5-inch picture tubes, which cost somewhere between $600 and $1000. By 1940, there were twenty-three television broadcasting stations in the United States and the future looked bright for television. The year 1941 saw the first commercial programming on television. It was a report on the time, temperature, and weather, sponsored by the Bulova Watch Company. At about this time, however, the nation began preparing for war; set manufacturing and programming began to diminish. Once the United States entered World War II, television development was abandoned and many stations left the air.

Although the war years saw little television programming, they brought considerable advances in electronic technology, including radar and radio transmission. Engineers and technicians who had studied the application of electronics to warfare found their skills welcome in the commercial broadcasting industry at war's end. Although only nine stations remained in operation in 1945, the industry soon began its recovery. When ABC televised the Joe Louis—Billy Conn heavyweight championship match, in 1946, cabinet members, congressmen, generals, and other dignitaries gathered to watch the proceedings on television sets installed at the Washington, D.C. Statler Hilton Hotel. Shortly thereafter, tavern owners began ordering TV sets so that their customers might linger over similar sporting events while devouring spirits and snacks. Some 5,000 new sets were manufactured in the initial year of recovery; one year later, over 150,000 sets were produced.

Programming began in earnest in 1947. The *Kraft Television Theater* made its debut, offering both classical drama and new plays. Children's television appeared in the form of *Howdy Doody* and *Kukla, Fran and Ollie*. Long-time radio hit *Meet The Press* moved onto the screen, and such news events as the opening session of Congress were televised. The following year brought comedy, in the form of Milton Berle's *Texaco Star Theater*, and variety, with Ed Sullivan's *Toast of the Town*. About 100 broadcasting stations had been licensed, and both New York City and Los Angeles boasted seven stations each. Most cities, however, had only one station or none at all. Still, momentum was growing, and nearly a million receiving sets were produced in the United States.

By 1949, the nation began to feel the impact of the new medium. The restaurant business was suffering, for example, as people rushed home to spend evenings with the TV set. The public library reported an alarming drop in book circulation. Publishers and bookstores complained of a reduction in sales. Even the radio industry, riding high through both depression and war, found it was losing its audience. New programs, such as *Your Show of Shows,* with Sid Caesar and Imogene Coca, and *Men Against Crime,* added to the lure of television. President Truman's inauguration was covered by thirty-four stations in sixteen states. Moreover, sponsors had begun to discover the power of the medium for advertising. Hazel Bishop, a tiny cosmetic business, began television advertising in 1950 and rapidly grew into a multimillion dollar operation.

The early 1950s have come to represent, to some, an era of "classic" television programming, when serious, "live" drama was offered viewers by the *Philco Television Playhouse, Goodyear Television Playhouse, Kraft Television Theater, Studio One,* and so on. Paddy Chayefsky's *Marty,* for example, appeared on the *Goodyear Television Playhouse* in 1953, with Rod Steiger in the title role. Serious drama did not survive for long, however, and by 1955 these programs were on the decline. Sponsors had not been comfortable with the dramatic exploration of emotional and social issues as a vehicle for selling their products. They began to demand more control over scripts and productions, attempting to minimize controversial material. One major manufacturer/sponsor, for example, dictated a set of script requirements that eliminated any material that might give offense, directly or indirectly, to organized minority groups, organizations, institutions, residents of any state or section, political organizations, labor groups, business organizations, and so on. There was to be no material for or against national or regional controversial issues. Furthermore, scripts could not suggest in any manner that business persons were often cold, ruthless, or otherwise lacking in personal or spiritual values. Other sponsors quickly followed suit, setting their own standards as to appropriate program content. The commercial side of television had begun to exert its muscle, and a different sort of programming was demanded. The new shows had to appeal to almost everyone and offend no one. Mass appeal, after all, was the key to mass sales.

During the 1950s, the character of American television gradually became established as certain programming genres emerged. The soaps, for example, successfully moved from radio to television. Serials such as *Search for Tomorrow, Love of Life,* and *Guiding Light* had their television debuts in the first two years of the decade. The number and length of the soaps regularly increased until they became a major force in daytime television. The mid-1950s, also saw the rise of television quiz and game shows: *$64,000 Question, The Big Surprise, High Finance, Treasure Hunt, Twenty-One,* and so on. In July of 1957, ratings of the American Research Bureau found five of the top ten TV shows to be quizzes, with the *$64,000 Question* in the lead. The discovery, in 1959, that some of the leading shows were "fixed," in the name of generating greater excitement, soon soured the public on big-money quizzes. In the Nielsen ratings of August, 1959, they were nowhere to be found. Still, a taste had been established, and the quizzes and games were destined to return.

The mid-1950s also saw the emergence of Western drama, above and beyond the usual Western movies. *Cheyenne, Maverick, Wyatt Earp, Gunsmoke,* and a host of others quickly established a place for themselves. By 1958, twenty-two Western series were represented in prime-time television, dominating every network. Top-rated television shows in August, 1959, were *Gunsmoke, Have Gun—Will Travel,* and *Rifleman.* Crime and mystery shows were also on the upswing in this period, following the example of *Dragnet.* Shows included *Big Town, Highway Patrol, Racket Squad, Perry Mason,* and so on. Suspense/adventure shows soon followed: *Captain Midnight, Dangerous Assignment, I Led Three Lives, Superman, Passport to Danger,* and others.

In many respects, then, the new medium simply followed the path taken by radio, bringing its audience soaps, quizzes, comedies, Westerns, crime stories, and adventures that already had proven popular. Shows, characters, and plots were taken directly from radio, comics, movies, and novels; variety and comedy shows were cast in the vaudeville tradition. By 1957, television entertainment reached into forty million American homes on ever-larger screens, and color television was catching on. Some 500 stations were broadcasting, and it was estimated that sets were turned on about five hours daily. Thousands of sponsors already were providing the industry with an operating capital of about a billion dollars a year.

With the character of television essentially established, Newton Minow, a lawyer appointed by President Kennedy as chairman of the Federal Communications Commission, offered a memorable speech on the subject. Addressing a 1961 meeting of the National Association of Broadcasters, he first noted that the industry was in the best of financial health, and that it had made some considerable achievements. As for programming, however, he went on as follows:

> I invite you to sit down in front of your television set when your station goes on the air and stay there without a book, magazine, newspaper, profit and loss sheet or rating book to distract you—and keep your eyes glued to that set until the station signs off. I can assure you that you will observe a vast wasteland. You will see a procession of game shows, violence, audience participation shows, formula comedies about totally unbelievable families, blood and thunder, mayhem, violence, sadism, murder, western badmen, western goodmen, private eyes, gangsters, more violence, and cartoons. And endlessly, commercials—many screaming, cajoling, and offending . . .[1]

He went on to note that the power of instantaneous transmission of sight and sound was both new and awesome. "It has limitless capabilities for good—and for evil." Minow's remarks, while forceful and dramatic, were scarcely original. By the time of his 1961 address, television had already been widely criticized for more than a decade.

Early Reactions

The December 1, 1947 issue of *Life* presented readers a profusely illustrated article on a new medium: "Television: It is a commercial reality but not yet an art." While complimenting both news and sports coverage, the author offered highly critical comments on early programming efforts. Television was accused of reviving the "hoariest acts in vaudeville," and filling the screen with "the worst aspects of radio." Other programming featured "implausible dramatics" and "witless chitchat." Indeed, early television had little identity of its own and drew heavily upon radio, movies, and vaudeville for its program ideas. A writer for the *New Republic* (1948) accused the medium of being so focused upon technical improvements as to forget the necessity of good programming.

Business Week, in 1948, acknowledged that television was rapidly becoming a "big-volume business," and that big profits were soon to be made. Other observers were less enthusiastic. A contributor to

Harper's, for example, indicated that television was poised for an "all-out invasion of the living rooms of America" and called for government regulation of the medium "before it is too late." *Time* magazine noted that the "young monster," television, was producing cracks in the foundations of such well-established industries as radio, movies, sports, and book publishing.

A 1948 article in *The Commonweal* was concerned with "How Illiterate Can Television Make Us?" Its author noted that one could turn on the radio "and let it drool by the hour," while simultaneously washing dishes, painting a wall, or even reading a book. Television, on the other hand, was more demanding, monopolizing all attention. In order to partake, one had to stay wherever the television set was located and both look at and listen to programming. "And there you see why I'm afraid" stated the author, concerned that passive television consumption would overwhelm the habits of literacy in all but the most intelligent and strong willed.

With the industry still in its infancy, the *New York Times Magazine,* in 1949, already was asking "What is Television Doing to Us?" Writer Jack Gould, on the basis of a survey of television households, noted that these families were now spending more time physically together, but members were not necessarily talking to one another. Conversation, at least in the early period of set ownership, was suffering; predictions of the "death of conversation," previously offered in relation to radio, were once again forthcoming. The survey found that reading activities initially declined in favor of watching the new set, but tended to return within several months to pre-TV levels. As for its effects upon children, estimated to be viewing some 2–4 hours daily, few conclusions were drawn. Instead, a dire warning was issued: "When it offers a daily diet of Western pictures and vaudeville by the hour, television often seems destined to entertain the child into a state of mental paralysis." Predictions of evil influence, then, greeted the new medium almost from its inception.

The critics of television, Gould noted, already were predicting "the death of culture," despite the fact that its social effects would be largely unknown for a generation. Clearly, they had been primed by recent encounters with radio. He also reported a growing concern that:

> . . . television will cause the American public to withdraw from active participation in events in favor of the indolent pleasure of just looking at them. If children at an early age become addicted to such 'spectator-itis,' it has been suggested, they may be less prepared to cope with the give-and-take of adult life.[2]

The following year, another *New York Times Magazine* article identified television with the dreaded comic book. Youngsters, it was reported, viewed television as "comics that move." Moreover, librarians were complaining that children's reading rooms were deserted by 5 p.m., the hour when popular children's TV shows began. The author noted that parents' groups had not yet organized resistance to television, as they had to comics, but that the dissatisfactions and concerns were quite similar. A supervisor at the New York Public Library indicated that fault lay not with the youngsters, but with all Americans who submit to "passive recreation without exerting any judgment in choice or sufficient discrimination."

One of the early leaders of the attack on television was Norman Cousins. In an editorial for *The Saturday Review of Literature* (1949), he indicated that television shows were taking over from the comics as "prime movers in juvenile misconduct and delinquency." He went on to accuse the medium of "an assault against the human mind," "a mobilized attack on the imagination," and "an invasion against good taste." Its unimaginative, stereotyped programming and its "terror and torture specials," indicated that the new medium was being "murdered in the cradle."

Readers of a *Better Homes and Gardens* (1950) article "Should you tear 'em away from TV?" learned that the effects of television on children had become the leading topic at parent-teacher meetings. The authors of this article offered their suspicions that a certain amount of hysteria and scapegoating might be going on, but these observations received little attention. Surveys of parental reactions to television, aimed at proving the medium harmful to youngsters, were already appearing regularly in newsletters and journals. Specific charges included overstimulation, creation of aggressive and destructive tendencies, passivity, illiteracy, eye damage, anxiety, and nightmares. Some middle-class parents already had declared a "boycott" of television, refusing to allow it in their homes. A *Readers Digest* article characterized television as "Hypnosis in Your Living Room," and commented: "With a television set there isn't much more conversation than in entombment."

At mid-century, after only a few years of programming, crime and violence on television were already hot issues. A series of TV monitoring studies supported by the Ford Foundation tabulated the occasions of actual or threatened violence on the screen. In New York City, for example, it was said that one could witness nearly 3,000 such incidents a week. The *Nation* (1950) commented on the rapidly multiplying television crime stories which dealt regularly with murder.

"People are killed with ice picks, axes, and poison in these all too graphic shows, and the effect on the youthful mind can hardly be salutary." Other writers warned that TV was encouraging "a craving for violence and fantasy" among children.

An article in *Survey* (1950) suggested that the real difficulty with television lay with parental misuse of the new medium as a pacifier for children:

> There is no doubt that television can keep the kids "occupied" and "quiet"—
> but by a method that may be as drastic as the one adopted by the nineteenth
> century European peasant women who accomplished the same results by
> lacing the little one's milk with a jigger of distilled potato juice.[3]

Several reports had also appeared by 1950 on the dangers of "television eyes," an eye malady presumably caused by watching the TV screen. *Parents Magazine* (1949), warned readers to carefully supervise their children's television-viewing habits and offered "rules" for healthy viewing. Children were to sit between 6 and 12 feet away from the set, with a light on in the room. Sitting on the floor was prohibited, as the angle of vision was said to produce eyestrain. Inappropriate focusing of the set was deemed another a danger to the eyes. Even in the mid-1950s, the warnings of eye specialists regarding television viewing were being reported. Decades earlier, of course, similar articles and cautions had appeared regarding "motion picture eyes."

In the very first years of its existence, then, television programming was already condemned by many educators and intellectuals as a public health menace, damaging to mental, moral, and physical health. Its fruits were said to include illiteracy, passivity, craving for violence, mental paralysis, juvenile delinquency, anxiety, eye damage, overstimulation, and so on.

Food for Fear

The debate over television programming continued in a steady stream of newspaper, journal, and magazine articles, as well as in a spate of books devoted to the topic. Social scientists, educators, mental health workers, and journalists found the topic quite irresistible, and concerned parents, teachers, and legislators constituted a sizable and receptive audience. The really popular works, of course, were those declaring a crisis and sounding the alarm. Individuals already concerned with the evil influence of television soon found much to fuel their fears.

'The theme of television-as-soporific, for example, was taken up by Ernest Van den Haag (1957) and deemed even more injurious than television violence:

> Before television the cradle was rocked, or poppy juice given, to inhibit the initiative and motility of small children. Television, unlike these physical sedatives, tranquilizes by means of substitute gratifications. Manufactured activities and plots are offered to still the child's hunger for experiencing life. They effectively neutralize initiative and channel imagination.[4]

Journalist Harold Mehling extended the argument to include adults. In *The Great Time Killer* (1962) he charged that the interference of sponsors with program content had turned television into a national pacifier:

> . . . television today is a national soma-dispenser, delivering a population into blissful vacuousness . . . while the world experiences radical upheaval that demands perception and understanding, the gurgle-gurgle box insulates us from that world and substitutes a narcoticland in which we sit, stare, and kill time, while everything always turns out all right in the end.[5]

Along similar lines, TV news journalist Daniel Schorr (1977) wrote that television had created a national, electronic "seance," and was gradually separating viewers from reality:

> Millions sit figuratively holding hands as they are exposed to a stream of images and suggestions, mixed up facts and fancies, playing more on their senses than their intellects. Television may be on its way to . . . dulling the sense of the objective and tangible and making the perceived more important than the fact.[6]

Sociologist Rose Goldsen warned in *The Show and Tell Machine* (1977) that television was having a profound effect upon American hearts and minds. Programming designed to stir emotions in viewers, she noted, was regularly interrupted by commercial breaks. Just as one experienced a peak of excitement, laughter, anger, or sadness, the emotion was interrupted and rendered meaningless. Constant repetition of this pattern, she warned, constituted a "desensitization" procedure in which strong feelings of all kinds were gradually eliminated. Eventually one would be able to view situations that once had been of great concern or distress with little or no emotional arousal. In short, viewers were being conditioned out of their emotions, turned into passive zombies.

Author Marie Winn expanded upon this theme in a highly influential work *The Plug-In Drug* (1977). Winn indicated that lobbying groups focusing their efforts on mere reform of programming *content* were misunderstanding the problem. It was the television *experience*, per se, which was pathogenic, not the nature of the program. Television viewing represented a return to a "passive mode of functioning" at a time when children needed real-life experience with parents and peers. Lacking such opportunities, children would learn to deal with others as if they were mere television characters rather than real human beings. The narcotizing, addictive power of television particularly was emphasized. Like drugs or alcohol, television was said to allow viewers to blot out the real world in favor of a pleasurable and passive mental state, an addictive mental "trip."

Jerry Mander, an advertising executive turned author, in 1978 published his *Four Arguments for the Elimination of Television*. He claimed that the evils of television were far too pervasive and resistent for reform; elimination was the only alternative if Americans were to preserve a sane and democratic society. For one thing, television removed people from "real" experiences, substituting arbitrary, artificial ones. The result was described as "utter confusion as to what is real and what is not." Control of the new, artificial reality was in the hands of a group of powerful corporations. A tool of big business, television shaped minds, feelings, and culture through advertising technology and the manipulation of program content. As for its effects upon the mental health of viewers, Mander noted the creation of a "passive mental attitude," and suggested that television was received largely in the unconscious regions of the mind. "We may have entered an era when information is fed directly into the mass subconscious." Viewers were reduced to mere containers, vessels into which television images were poured. These took up residence in the unconscious, replacing the ordinary images of human imagination, and thereafter influenced our dreams, daydreams, and behaviors. Mander summarized matters as follows:

> If the arguments of the preceding pages are even partially correct, then television produces such a diverse collection of dangerous effects—mental, physiological, ecological, economic, political; effects that are dangerous to the person and also to society and the planet—then it seems to me only logical to propose that it never should have been introduced, or once introduced, be permitted to continue.[7]

The Science and Politics of Evil Influence

In 1951, a Roman Catholic Archbishop in Chicago informed the faithful in his archdiocese of the serious moral responsibility involved in purchasing a television set. He noted that children who are allowed too much or inappropriate television viewing gave evidence of "great nervousness and inability to concentrate in the classroom." Parents were urged to supervise and limit programming and to follow the recommendations of the Legion of Decency, so as to guard the health and morals of their children. The following year, *The Christian Century* reported that more and more parents were growing concerned about the nature of television programming. Before long, an Arkansas Congressman had introduced a resolution for an investigation of the matter. The content of television programming was becoming a political issue, with many angry voters calling for action.

Observing the growing tumult over television, Mary Seagoe attempted to provide some historical perspective via an article in the *Quarterly of Film, Radio and Television* (1952):

> Television is the newest addition to the illustrious family of our mass entertainment enthusiasms. We have had dime novels, movies, radio, comics—and now television. Every time we seem to go through the same stages. We remember the alarm raised soon after the advent of the talking picture . . . then when we had examined the matter and learned how to use movies, the alarm died away. The same thing happened with the widespread use of radio . . . The same thing went on in relation to the comics. Now we are starting that cycle with television.[8]

Historical perspective was quickly lost in the national groundswell of alarm regarding television violence. *Cosmopolitan* (1953) reported that parents, educators, and doctors were concerned with the "appalling crime wave regularly beamed at 70 million American viewers." Crime dramas on television were characterized as a "dangerously underestimated menace to child health." Crime and Western drama was said to constitute 30 percent of children's programming. In *Cosmopolitan's* survey of "medical and educational authorities," all indicated that television crime shows were potentially much more injurious than movies, radio, or comic books. Schoolteachers were found to be the most vehement in denouncing television programming.

The initial congressional inquiry into television programming eventually produced a report that concluded crime shows were not suitable for children. This was hardly the end of the matter. In 1954, a Special Senate Subcommittee on Juvenile Delinquency, chaired by Robert C. Hendrickson of New Jersey, held further hearings on the subject. Members watched excerpts from TV shows and took testimony from assorted experts. Psychiatrist Edward Podolsky, for example, provided the following testimony:

Seeing constant brutality, viciousness and unsocial acts results in hardness, intense selfishness, even in mercilessness, proportionate to the amount of exposure and its play on the native temperament of the child. Some cease to show resentment to insults, to indignities, and even cruelty toward helpless old people, to women and other children.[9]

In the same year, a report by the National Association for Better Radio and Television expressed dismay over the volume of crime and the degree of violence in children's television programming. It noted that four times as many television crime shows were being produced in 1954 as compared with 1951. ". . . Murder, torture, sadism, morbid suspense, and other fear-and-tension-inducing elements are saturating children's minds."

The pressure on television continued, and the Hendrickson subcommittee soon became the Kefauver subcommittee. Estes Kefauver, who earlier had headed the investigation of comic books, set out once again to tame the media monster. When all the expert testimony and other materials were collected and examined, the subcommittee conceded that it could not prove a direct causal relationship between criminal behaviors and television viewing. This did not prevent it from censuring the industry, however, and emphasizing its potential for harm. "Television, available at the flick of a knob and combining visual and audible aspects into a 'live' story, has a greater impact on its child audience." The report suggested both the establishment of citizen review boards and the use of fines and/or license revocation by the Federal Communications Committee where violations of standards occurred.

Television violence remained in the political arena for many years. After the Kefauver subcommittee came the Thomas Dodd hearings of 1961 and 1964. Later came Milton Eisenhower's National Commission on the Causes and Prevention of Violence, followed by Senator John O. Pastore's inquiry in the late 1960s. Parents kept up the pressure by forming lobbying groups such as Action for Children's Television (ACT). Researchers developed a Violence Index by which to measure TV shows, and lobbyists began circulating lists of the most violent shows and their sponsors.

A major investigation of television violence by the Surgeon General's Committee, formed in 1969, yielded a 5-volume report in 1972. Having evaluated several tons of research reports, the latter committee concluded there was a "preliminary and tentative indication of a causal relationship between viewing violence on television and aggressive behavior" but only for "some children . . . in some environmental contexts." This was hardly the condemnation of television sought by its critics. The fears of parents, teachers, mental health workers, and intellectuals demanded a simple and decisive answer, and politicians sought to oblige, but all were foiled by the real complexities of the issue. Meanwhile, programming was little influenced and audiences grew larger. If televised violence had the power to undo an entire generation of Americans, it also had ample opportunity to do so.

Over the next decade, virtually no area of programming escaped potentially devastating criticism. In addition to the action/adventure/crime shows, soaps, sit-coms, political debates, commercials, cartoons, news reporting, and so on, were all attacked as destructive to the mentality of children and/or adults, to culture, or to social order. The extent of the criticism was proportional only to the popularity of the medium, which was, and is, without parallel.

It was in 1982 that the National Institutes of Mental Health offered a more definite conclusion on the violence issue. *Television and Behavior: Ten Years of Scientific Progress and Implications for the Eighties* was a two-volume work intended as an update to the earlier surgeon general's report. This time, a distinguished panel of experts reviewed the studies in the area and concluded that a causal relationship existed between television violence and "aggressive behavior." This was widely considered the long-awaited indictment of television, even though the experts did not indicate that television violence was the only, or even the main, factor in creating aggression in children.

Media experts from the broadcasting industry were quick to point out that the research studies under consideration by the NIMH rarely attempted to measure violent or criminal behaviors. More typically, they studied "aggressiveness" toward toys or playmates during a period of observed play in the laboratory. A considerable leap of faith would be required to conclude that television instigated or supported criminal violence in natural settings. (Perhaps the aggressive TV watchers went on to become great entrepreneurs or salespersons.) They also noted the tendency of scientific journals to exclude studies reporting only a lack of association between variables, a bias which would necessarily distort the scientific literature on this issue. Although the government and its experts had finally taken a position on the television question, then, the debate was hardly over. Only two years later, for example, Canadian psychologist Jonathan Freedman reviewed those studies, more limited in number, which dealt with the effects of television on behavior in natural settings outside the laboratory. He characterized their results as "unimpressive," and concluded that they could not support any causal relationship between TV violence and real-life violence.

The Ultimate Evil

Once it had been thought that newspapers exposed people to unnecessary and irrelevant information while overstimulating them with violence, scandals, illustrations, photographs, and headlines. Their pages provided unnatural groupings of the serious with the ridiculous and required unusual eye movements to read. Novels and storypapers were said to have promoted escapism and sensuality and injured the morals of young readers. Comic strips and comic books had challenged literacy and had created more graphic representations of crime and violence with which to corrupt the young and vulnerable. Movies were more graphic still, and deemed far too realistic, offering detailed instruction in crime and sexuality while injuring eyesight. Radio, lacking visual representations, managed nevertheless to offer dramatic productions that created overly graphic images in the minds of listeners. It brought objectionable crime, horror, and action/adventure shows right into the livingroom, causing overstimulation and nightmares. It threatened an end to conversation and encouraged passive withdrawal from social involvement and healthy outdoor activities. Radio also brought advertising into the home every few minutes, often aiming its sales efforts at children. All of these evils already had befallen American families. Television, combining elements of all the above, inevitably was perceived as the ultimate evil influence.

Like the radio in prior decades, the television set came to occupy a dominant position in the household. Living rooms revolved around the new "electronic hearth," and sets were turned on much of the day. Family-time activities centered more and more on its offerings. Providing both audio and visual stimulation, television made great demands on the attention of viewers, limiting conversation and presumably threatening eyesight. Programming included the sensual and the violent, emphasizing the latter, thereby raising concerns about the stimulation of real violence and crime. Commercials constantly intruded upon the consciousness of viewers, interfering with the normal processes of thinking and feeling; many were aimed at children. Youngsters were sufficiently fascinated with television (even the commercials) to devote many hours to it, raising once again the specters of illiteracy, passivity, and addiction. Daily immersion in the fiction and fantasy of television was seen as threatening to reality orientation, hence mental health, and undermining of family values. All in all, it looked to critics as if television was the supreme media threat to civilization.

That earlier evils remained with us only made the situation worse. Newspapers had survived, if fewer in number. Comic strips and comic books remained very much in evidence, with early editions avidly sought as collectors items. Paperback novels were everywhere. Radio lacked its dramas but filled the airwaves with sensual and suggestive rock music. Movies remained popular and had entered the living room by way of the television set. Individuals who grew up in, or simply lived through the television era of the last four decades, then, were exposed to a truly vast array of presumably evil media influences. Believers in the doctrine of evil influence could only expect the cumulative effects to be staggering, perhaps crippling to the Television Generation(s). A Gallup survey of November, 1954, for example, reported that 70 percent of adults sampled placed at least part of the blame for juvenile delinquency on comics, radio, and television. Dr. Fredric Wertham warned that TV shows, radio programs, and comic books were "schools for violence" training the "potential rapists of tomorrow." Columnist Walter Lippmann wrote that the movies, television, and comic books were "purveying violence and lust to a vicious and intolerable degree" and predicted dire consequences. Condemnations, warnings, and investigations proliferated, and many parents feared for the future of their children.

In *Great Expectations* (1980), Landon Y. Jones noted the extent of the charges against television and its presumed impact upon the "Baby Boom" generation:

> Barely a year has gone by since 1954 without a report or study mounting a quixotic charge against the windmill of antennas. In fact, the evils these studies pointed out have almost told us more about particular problems afflicting society at any given time than they have about television's role in them. At various times we have faulted television for causing juvenile delinquency, crippling reading ability in schools, impoverishing family life, narcotizing the imagination, promoting mindless acquisitiveness, shortening attention spans, eroding respect for authority, and increasing everything from drug use to the divorce rate.[10]

What actually became of the children of television? Were they a different breed of humanity—passive spectators incapable of sustaining involvement with real events and real people, yet prone to violence? Those convinced of the pathological passivity of the television generations must have been surprised by the political activism and commitment shown by so many young people during the Vietnam War. Believers in the aggressiveness of television viewers probably understood the peace movement in terms of social irresponsibility, or a new form of violence. Still, Harvard's Class of 1969, whose students seized campus buildings in the course of demonstrations, a decade later had produced about as many doctors, lawyers, and bankers as previous classes.

Along similar lines, the relatively conservative, career-minded college students of the 1980s seem unlikely products of the television years, unless explained in terms of a triumph of the materialistic values inherent in the media. The same explanation might be applied to the arrival of Yuppies, who represent the 1980s version of the American success story. The upsurge of fundamentalist religious beliefs in the 1980s is also difficult to explain in a generation corrupted by television, unless interpreted as a passive acceptance of powerful church leadership. As for the energy and commitment of the Women's Liberation movement, one could always interpret this in terms of increased aggression, selfishness, and materialism in women of the television era. On the other hand, one might venture that mass media influences had not been as decisive in defining (and destroying) two generations of young people as critics feared.

Despite nearly total saturation of the country by television, the expected epidemic of videocy, the generation of zombies, never materialized. Even literacy, often deemed failing, remained in reasonable health. With so many millions of individuals involved, in various stages of development, adjustment, vulnerability, and pathology, it cannot be argued that the onslaught of mass media violence and/or sensuality was harmful to none. Nevertheless, the historical record indicates that the power of television to undermine health and welfare was exaggerated out of all proportion by frightened parents, teachers, health care practitioners, and assorted "experts."

Television was but another media target for longstanding but poorly defined fears. Consequently, it was condemned almost as soon as it appeared. It represented the most decisive break yet with the familiar world of linear, logical, abstract thought structures, the most massive media intrusion of the visual, sensual, emotional, and the fantastic into consciousness. Combining elements of the novel, newspaper, comic book, cinema, and radio, television reached the largest mass audiences yet assembled and daily held its attention. Inevitably, its power to attract millions of men, women, and children aroused terror among the guardians of society, culture, and the status quo. To intellectuals, as we shall see, the popular (or "mass") culture it promulgated so effectively was anathema.

Notes

1. Newton Minow (1961), cited in Barnouw, E., *Tube of Plenty* (Oxford: Oxford University Press, 1979), p. 300.

2. Jack Gould, "What is Television Doing to Us?", *New York Times Magazine,* June 12, 1949, p. 28.
3. Frank Riley and James A. Peterson, "The Social Impact of Television," *Survey,* 1950, 86, p. 484.
4. Ernest Van den Haag, "Of Happiness and of Despair We Have No Measure," in Rosenberg, B. and White, D. M., *Mass Culture* (New York: The Free Press, 1957), p. 530.
5. Harold Mehling, *The Great Time Killer* (Cleveland, OH: World, 1962), pp. 14–15.
6. David Schorr, "The National Seance," in Gumpert, G. and Cathcart, R., *Inter/Media* (New York: Oxford University Press, 1979), p. 341.
7. Jerry Mander, *Four Arguments for the Elimination of Television* (New York: Morrow, 1978), p. 348.
8. Mary Seagoe, cited in Wartella, E., and Reeves, B., "Historical Trends in Research on Children and the Media: 1900–1960," *Journal of Communication,* 1985, 35, p. 120.
9. Edward Podolsky, cited by Walter Goodman, "Bang-Bang! You're Dead!", *New Republic,* Nov. 1, 1954, p. 12.
10. Landon Y. Jones, *Great Expectations* (New York: Ballantine, 1981), p. 142.

9

Invaders of the Eighties: Recent Threats

Having examined alarmed and outraged responses to the novel, newspaper, comic book, cinema, and the broadcasting media, we have seen that public reaction to mass media and mass culture has been surprisingly consistent over the last few centuries. That is, once any new media form or application achieved a broad enough audience, it was perceived in certain quarters (e.g., intellectuals, clergy, educators) as a menace to the public health and welfare. Self-proclaimed experts quickly condemned it as preoccupied with violence and/or sensuality, overly graphic in form, and overpowering in its effects upon the young and the innocent. Its influence upon literacy, as well as physical, mental, moral, and spiritual health was deemed unwholesome, and society itself was proclaimed at risk. The fears first voiced by intellectuals, clergy, educators, physicians, and/or social scientists were taken up and amplified by a larger portion of the middle class. This led to legal and political actions aimed at restriction and restraint of the new medium, with only the most limited and temporary success. In each case, however, the widely predicted fall of literacy, sanity, and civilization somehow failed to materialize. In fact, as each media threat was replaced by a new one, the older forms became ever more accepted and respected. Many early movies, comics, and radio shows, for example, came to be considered classics, avidly sought by collectors and nostalgia buffs; newspapers and magazines are today a part of American daily life at virtually all levels of society; the photograph and the novel have been accepted as legitimate art forms.

Has all of this historical precedent left us wiser with regard to the mass media, less vulnerable to panic? The evidence of the 1980s, I submit, suggests otherwise. In fact, the escalating pace of technological and social change has merely made it possible for several threats to be perceived in the time span previously allocated to one. While the literature regarding these new forms is less than complete, a survey in this regard will document the dogged continuation of the standard crusade against mass media.

Revenge of the Tube

Criticism of television has remained a part of the American scene since the early 1950s, although specific complaints have varied. Programming for adults has been deemed hopeless by intellectual critics, who report that televised sex and violence, soaps, and quiz shows threaten to undermine the cognitive, moral, and motivational foundations of our society. With few exceptions, childrens' programming has met with similar criticism, particularly the Saturday morning cartoons. Even *Sesame Street,* beloved of millions of children and parents, acquired critics who found its fast-paced format inimical to childhood cognitive development. News programming has been condemned as superficial and sensational, more oriented toward slick presentation than rational and thorough analysis. Coverage of the political process by television has been attacked as ruinous to American politics and government, encouraging voters to focus on "image" rather than substance. America's love affair with the tube, then, has coexisted for decades with a steady stream of harsh criticism from intellectual leaders and their worried followers.

By the 1980s, the television industry had evolved in several ways, and its new characteristics occasioned yet another set of fearful and angry protests. Among the emerging sources of evil influence: cable television, music video, and the video cassette recorder (VCR). Related developments in consumer electronics included the personal computer and the video game. All of these innovations quickly found eager audiences. At the same time, however, they met with the ambivalent reception generally accorded commercially successful media innovation in our society. That is, many greeted them with extreme mistrust and/or outright condemnation. Alarmed by the warnings of experts, a number of parents and teachers set out to defend their homes and classrooms against these electronic invaders of their domains.

Cable—Cable television originated simply as a method of improving television reception for viewers in remote areas. In the late 1940s, when commercial television was just getting under way, there were many areas out of reach of existing television stations. People living in hilly or mountainous areas had very poor reception, if any. A cable system was created in 1948, in Pennsylvania, to bring TV reception to a coal-mining town in the Appalachians. It was merely a central TV antenna atop a mountain, with lines running to subscribers' homes. This approach was soon widely imitated, and the community-antenna television system, or CATV, was born. By 1955 there were about 400 such systems in operation, with 150,000 subscribers. Still, these systems were merely passive conduits for broadcast television signals.

By the latter part of the 1950s, cable systems began to do more than pick up and carry local TV signals. They started to import distant programming using microwave relay systems, and they became increasingly selective about what sort of programming they provided their subscribers. Several companies made early ventures into pay television schemes involving scrambled TV images and unscrambling devices. These experiments were not at first successful. Broadcasters were firmly opposed to any system of pay television, finding it an unwelcome competitor to existing operations. It was opposed, as well, by theater and restaurant owners, who wanted people going out of their homes for movies, sports, and special events.

During the 1970's, both cable television and pay television became firmly established. Home Box Office (HBO) was organized in 1971 and began transmitting programs via communications satellites in 1975; Showtime appeared in 1978. In 1979 the floodgates opened, and among the new channels were the Movie Channel, Nickelodeon, Cable News Network, Entertainment and Sports Programming Network, and so on. There followed a boom period in the growth of the industry, although profits were not forthcoming until the mid-1980's. By the end of 1984, some 40 percent of American TV households subscribed to a cable television service.

Unlike traditional broadcast television, cable systems did not make use of the public airwaves. Consequently, they were free of the censorship otherwise imposed by the Federal Communications Commission. For the first time, via cable, movies and shows involving adult themes and nudity could be received in viewers' homes. In fact, channels dedicated to such programming soon appeared, e.g., Playboy and Escapade. Public reaction against this development was inevitable.

An article in *Ladies Home Journal* (1984) on the problem of "cable porn" reported that an increasing number of communities across the country were involved in fights to ban cable channels featuring nudity and strong language. Groups such as Morality in Media were arguing that cable television ought to be subject to the same regulations as commercial television. Several communities had already acted to ban cable channels considered obscene or indecent, but these laws had been ruled unconstitutional. Like other publishers, cable operators were deemed by the federal courts to be protected by the first amendment to the constitution. Nevertheless, the pressure continued. In Yakima, Washington, a group of parents, educators and ministers formed a Steering Committee for Television Awareness and lobbied for removal of a station offering R-rated fare; in Memphis, Tennessee more than 6,000 people demonstrated in an effort to force a cable operator to drop the Playboy channel. A bill was introduced into the United States Senate to extend federal obscenity laws for broadcast television to include cable TV. An Attorney General's Commission on Pornography was appointed by President Reagan, and the Attorney General singled out cable TV and video cassettes as large-scale distributors of pornography. (A previous commission of this sort, in 1970, concluded that the pornography had no significant effect upon social behavior.) Cable television was under the gun.

Music Video—The evils of cable television were compounded by the arrival of a new form of entertainment: the rock music video. In 1981, Warner Amex Satellite Entertainment Company launched MTV, a cable channel devoted exclusively to video productions of rock music and related aspects of rock culture. Any day of the week, at any hour of the day or night, cable subscribers could tune in to MTV for music video fare. Programming consisted of brief (3–5 minute) movies, or videos, produced by record companies to illustrate and/or interpret popular recordings. Productions were often fast-paced and slick, involving fancy editing techniques, computer-generated graphics, and/or animation; surrealistic fantasy themes were not uncommon. Viewers were encouraged to vote for their favorite videos, to enter various contests, and to purchase recordings and related products.

The MTV experiment proved highly successful; the station had entered the homes of twenty-two million subscribers by 1984. The music video concept had also spread to a number of other channels, generating such programming as Friday Night Video, Night Tracks, Night Flight, Album Flash, Take Five, Hot Rocks, and Video Jukebox. One 1983 survey found that 43 percent of cable subscribers had watched MTV in the past week; another found that viewers had a median age of 23. The channel attracted a large teenage audience, and these young viewers tended to watch in peer groups rather than individually, often participating in the form of dancing and singing. The content of music video hits, consistent with the long-standing tradition of rock-and-roll music, frequently concerned adolescent sexual longings and fantasies as well as anti-authority themes. Such expressions could not long escape censure.

Many of those in the nascent music video business considered themselves pioneers in the area of video expression, a form of post-modern art. Indeed, music video was bursting with energy and experimentation at a time when commercial television had, by and large, settled into a pattern of "safe," imitative, formula programming. It was sufficiently dynamic to cause a boom in the record industry and to exert a profound influence on all forms of advertising. Critics complained, however, that most videos lacked coherence and failed to tell any sort of story. This was true, but irrelevant; videos were not intended to tell stories. Instead, they offered viewers a series of emotions, or mood states, through the combination of musical rhythms, lyrics, and powerful, transient images. They appealed directly to feelings, bypassing logic and reason; they were less "films" than "experiences." Marsha Kinder, writing in *Film Quarterly* (1984), noted strong parallels between the structures of music videos and dreams. Both involve streams of visual imagery characterized by abruptly changing, loosely connected scenes, lack of coherent logic, violations of natural laws, and so on. To those expecting or demanding traditional narrative structures, the video appears to be a hopeless jumble. Of course, the same may be said of representational versus abstract expressionist paintings.

A 1984 article in *New Leader* characterized programming on the new music video television as "MTV Torture." Videos were denigrated as mere commercials (for records), separated from one another by commercials for other products. Although visually striking, music video productions were said to be "like seeing somebody's innermost fantasies on TV." That is, they ranged from incomprehensible to very embarrassing. The pace was so fast, the author noted, that one might never be bored, but neither could one get interested or involved. All in all, the experience of an evening with MTV was likened to Chinese water torture, or to watching the same commercials over and over again. Along similar lines, an article in *Christianity Today* (1984) characterized MTV as a "24-hour-a-day pacifier" for youth of the television generation. Author Lloyd Billingsley summed it up as follows:

> . . . MTV is television incarnate: noisy, indifferent to pain, containing all the joy of a tax audit, plotless, and all too often, meaningless. Behind the gloss lies little more than hype, shiny images, and, of course, wads of money. What was long feared has come to pass: 'We interrupt this commercial to bring you a commercial.'"[1]

The following year, *Newsweek* described music video as incorporating all the worst aspects of television into one package. Health-care professionals were quoted as to the presumed evil influence of music videos. Dr. Eli Newberger at Children's Hospital, Boston, reported: "Children are being bombarded with messages of violence and sexuality that are very confusing and suggest easy ways out of complex problems." A Member of the American Academy of Pediatrics' Task Force on TV and Children, Dr. Victor Strasburger, noted: ". . . seeing a video can teach you that if you're not sexually active there's something wrong with you. Once you've depicted the song, you've magnified the effect a hundredfold." He conceded that there was little data to support this point of view.

A National Coalition on Television Violence, highly critical of the content of music videos, attempted to document violence in such programming over a 7-month period. Using a very broad definition of violence, they reported a considerable rate of violent acts or threats in music videos. Subsequent studies by the School of Journalism and Mass Communications at the University of Georgia, however, reported that while 56 percent of concept videos did portray violence, this compared favorably to 75 percent of prime-time TV shows. The sexual content of videos, moreover, was found to be "more implied than overt," and was again reported to be less than that of traditional TV programs. Such findings, of course, did little or nothing to quell the stream of fear and criticism.

VCR—The VCR revolution followed close upon the heels of cable television, with VCR ownership growing at an astounding rate in the early 1980s. In 1982 only about five million units were owned in the United States; this number grew to nearly twenty-four million by the end of 1985. That is, about one in three television homes contained VCRs. The recorders were used in three ways: to record television programs for later replay, to build home libraries of recorded programs and films, and to play rented or purchased cassettes. The vast majority of prerecorded cassettes contained movies, but self-help titles, particularly exercise routines, were also available.

In some respects, the VCR was the answer to many early criticisms of television. Using its technology, viewers could exercise greater selection of programming; they were free of the constraints of network schedules. When viewing their recorded shows they were also free to fast-forward the commercials. With a bit of extra effort they could even record shows without commercials. Moreover, they could now choose among thousands of prerecorded cassettes if dissatisfied with television programming; some 40,000 titles were available in 1984. Determined parents could tape their own programming for young children, selecting both the content and the schedule. In some respects, the arrival of the

VCR signaled the decline of the passive viewer, the "couch potato." Viewers had gained a new degree of power and control over the television set.

The merits of the VCR, however, could not long stay the inevitable attack. The children of the 1980s, after all, would be the first VCR generation, and critics questioned whether its effects would be beneficial. Concerns were raised, for example, about "information inequities" and "knowledge gaps" created as a result of exclusion of the poor from VCR ownership and tape rentals. Researchers soon began studying youths and families in relation to their ownership of VCRs. Early studies found that those with VCRs watched more TV, recorded or otherwise, but also read more books, newspapers, and magazines; they were more likely to have access to cable TV, pay cable stations, and home computers. These were media-oriented people. Their households had higher income and educational levels; parents were more likely to be away at work during the day. Some of these data, of course, became obsolete once the cost of VCRs plummeted.

While the long-term effects of VCR ownership on youths were unknown, it was already clear that they might now be exposed to R-rated movies at home. Critics noted with despair that sex and violence had found yet another passage to the minds of the young and innocent. Adult society was also deemed at risk, as X-rated materials became commonly available through local rental outlets.

Video Games and Computers—What else could television/video technology have to offer in the way of objectionable entertainment? It just so happened that the cathode ray (picture) tube could also be utilized in a manner quite independent of the broadcasting industry, the cable system, and the VCR. That is, it could function as a screen for viewing and interacting with dedicated video game machines as well as personal computers. The latter innovations, of course, created a whole new realm of possibilities for evil influence.

In 1972, Magnavox Company pioneered the home video game business with its Odyssey system. By 1975, Atari, Inc., a company that had already taken the lead in coin-operated electronic amusements, was turning out some 3,000 units per day of a home version of Pong. The game involved player manipulation of video paddles in attempting to hit a video ball; it was an electronic version of Ping Pong. Sears Roebuck, the initial retailer of the Pong game, was selling out as fast as the units were delivered. Other games began to appear, and it was soon clear that something new and exciting had been born. In December of 1975, *Business Week* wrote about "TV's Hot New Star," and one year later *Time* referred to electronic games as "TV's New Superhit." By the end of 1976, some 40 manufacturers were producing electronic games, and sales were about 10 times those in the preceding year. *Time* reported more than 50 different varieties of video games to be already available, ranging from tic-tac-toe to tank warfare.

Video games offered yet another escape from the passivity and commercialism so harshly criticized in television viewing. Participation certainly was not passive, and the games involved no commercials. An article in *Saturday Review* (November, 1977) welcomed Pong as a use of the television screen that permitted viewers not only to be active but to interact with one another. Over the next few years, however, as video games (both home and arcade versions) grew in numbers and sophistication, the attitudes of establishment observers gradually were transformed. In 1981 alone, the market for video games tripled, and magazines such as *Forbes* and *Macleans* began using the word "addiction" in describing the popularity of such games as Space Invaders, Asteroids, and Pac-Man. These games had generated sufficient excitement and attracted sufficiently high audiences to arouse the usual concerns about emerging media forms. By 1982, people were spending more money on video games than on movies and records combined. In February of that year, *U.S. News and World Report* was asking whether arcade games posed a serious threat to American children and teenagers. Concerns about electronic addiction soon extended beyond video games, as parents were alerted in numerous articles that excessive exposure to computer programming might transform their children into socially withdrawn, bleary-eyed, frenzied, and compulsive computer "hackers." Thus, while the personal computer was hailed by *Time* magazine (1983) as its Man or Woman of the Year, it was also damned by many people who viewed it primarily as a source of addictive video games, compulsive programming, dehumanization, and computer crime.

The video game issue had, by 1982, become a political one, and local governments were taking action to protect their communities. According to *U.S. News and World Report:* "In town after town, local officials are struggling to cope with a craze that has swept the country: Arcade video games, that gobble up the time and money of America's teenagers." In Bradley, Illinois children under 16 were barred from playing video games. Its mayor complained that the children were losing their lunch money to the machines, along with any other money they could get their hands on. Marlborough, Massachusetts prohibited those under 18 years of age from using the arcades during school hours or late at night. Its mayor noted that some Massachusetts youths had been breaking into parking meters to acquire quarters for video games. A Mesquite, Texas law limited the use of coin-operated games to persons age 17 or older unless accompanied by a parent. All in all, the public reaction was quite similar to that which greeted the nickelodeons many years earlier and the pinball machine a generation before.

The worst fears of parents were reinforced when Harvard psychiatrist Alvin Poussaint warned that video games were teaching children that violence was acceptable behavior and that the games might well contribute to the problem of violence in society. Based upon interviews with a sample of parents, the *New York Times,* in 1983, reported that "... no other toy in recent memory has caused them so much perplexity, ambivalence and soul-searching." The article cited Dr. Michael Lewis, professor of psychiatry at Rutgers University Medical School, as warning that the special intensity of the video game experience might promote an erosion of reality orientation. As for violence, Lewis warned that the active participation in violence that was possible in video games was far worse than the passive viewing of violence on television or in movies.

Psychologist Patricia M. Greenfield (*Mind and Media,* 1984), in a volume examining the effects of media upon the young, acknowledged the rising anxiety about video games and microcomputers:

> In the past few years a new medium has come along to fascinate young people and worry their elders: video games. Some adults fear that, even more than television, the games are at best frivolous and at worst mindless, numbing, and violent. While many see the popularity of microcomputers among the young as a promising trend, others fear that they reinforce asocial or even antisocial tendencies.[2]

Author Craig Brod, writing on *Technostress* (1984), charged that video games were luring children away from healthful physical activities. Moreover, they were reinforcing disengagement from reality, impulsive thinking, and a false sense of omnipotence, while impeding the development of imagination. The pace and intensity of the video game experience were such that all else, even television, seemed slow and boring to children by comparison.

Public anxieties over video games reached new heights when Linda Wolfe, writing in *New York* (1984), published her article "Death in the video arcade." This described an incident in which two youths armed with a baseball bat entered an arcade in search of some particular "enemy" they intended to punish. In the course of pushing around several young patrons, presumably for information, they attacked and killed a young man trying to leave the arcade. Although the incident had nothing to do with video games "per se," and could as well have occurred in a park or playground, readers were left feeling otherwise. The author warned that ". . . similar video parlors still remain open, drawing young people from all corners of the city."

The mobilization against video games, however, suddenly lost steam with the collapse of Atari and the withdrawal of other manufacturers from the business. *Forbes* (1984) magazine, in fact, announced that video games were "dead." What could have happened? The *Forbes* analysis indicated that children had simply "moved on" to other things, particularly to MTV. So much for the "addictive" powers of the video game. Of course, video games were not really dead, and they eventually staged a comeback, but their rapid decline in popularity caught the business world by surprise and temporarily relieved the anxieties of many opponents.

The escalating crusade, in the 1980s, against invasion by video technology reflected the growing realization that commercial television, once the ultimate evil influence, had merely been one aspect of a new video age. The arrival of cable, pay channels, music video, VCRs, personal computers, and video games made it quite clear that the world, long dominated by the written word, would never be the same. The enduring order, logic, rationality, and abstraction that characterized the society of the alphabet and the printing press were challenged as never before by the emotionality, sensuality, immediacy, and intensity of the visual video image. Where the young embraced and celebrated the new developments as "progress," the intellectual establishment and other conservative elements in society found them immensely threatening and potentially pathogenic. Opposition was soon organized, and it focused upon the classic issues: graphic violence and sensuality as public health hazards, presumed addictive properties, and the threat to literacy. The old arguments against novels, newspapers, comics, radio, and television were dusted off and polished up in an effort to make them appear thoroughly new and insightful. Yet another cycle had begun in the crusades against evil media influences.

Another Dragon

Not all of the invaders of the 1980s were electronic in nature. Critics in search of another media dragon to slay found one in the fantasy role-playing game Dungeons and Dragons (D&D). Manufactured by TSR Hobbies in Lake Geneva, and first marketed in 1973, the game soon drew fire from a number of experts and lobbying groups. By 1985, some eight million copies had been sold, along with innumerable accessory

items, and a weekly cartoon show had been generated. TSR estimated that about four million people, mostly teenagers and young adults, were playing the game.

The basic components of a D&D game are a set of specially fashioned dice and hundreds of pages of instruction manuals. No board is involved, but maps and figurines may be used as accessories. A group of players take an imaginary journey into a realm filled with sorcerers, dragons, demons, treasures, and sundry dangers. They must overcome all obstacles, by means of combat, magic, or strategy, while attempting to collect treasure, effect a rescue, or perform some other mission. An advanced player takes the role of Dungeon Master (DM), keeper of the rules and arbiter of all conflicts. The DM describes the various situations and obstacles, and the players must decide how to deal with them. Dice are rolled to determine the outcome of various activities, particularly battles.

In 1981, an article in *Christianity Today* inquired whether D&D was merely a "fantasy fad," an expensive waste of time, an obsessive escape from reality, or even a form of "dabbling in the demonic." It reported on "a barrage of criticism from evangelicals," including one minister who wanted to collect enough money to buy and burn every copy. The violence inherent to the game was only part of the issue. Ministers were particularly concerned that the cast of characters in the game might include not only villains and dragons, but also demons, witches, zombies, and other occult figures. Worse still, a variety of deities and demigods, drawn from multiple religions, might also join in the action. These included Ra, Osiris, Isis, Vishnu, Odin, Loki, and many others. The practice of making playmates of deities and demons did not sit well with the clergy, who feared this might promote occultism and undermine Christian values.

Criticism of Dungeons and Dragons peaked in 1985, when the National Coalition on Television Violence (NCTV) attempted to link the game to teenage suicides and murders. The group petitioned the Federal Trade Commission and the Consumer Protection Agency to require warnings on all game books indicating that the game had been linked to violent deaths. The Federal Trade Commission was asked to require that similar warnings be transmitted during the cartoon show. All three agencies rejected the requests, but the organization continued to lobby Congress on these issues.

Dr. Thomas Radecki, psychiatrist at the University of Illinois School of Medicine and chairman of the National Coalition on Television Violence, in an interview with *Newsweek* claimed "The game causes young men to kill themselves and others . . . The kids start living in the fantasy." Another group opposing the game was called Bothered About D&D, or BADD. It was founded by the mother of a boy who committed suicide. She attributed his death, and those of other teenagers, to playing Dungeons and Dragons. The evidence of its evil influence was anecdotal, but she noted that the written materials of the game originated in demonology, witchcraft, and the occult.

It was the intensity of the interest in D&D that frightened critics and parents. The game had generated great excitement on college campuses and had later filtered down to the high school set and even younger players. Devotees would spend hours pouring over the complex rule books, creating new fantasy characters, collecting or creating accessories, in addition to actual game playing. Inevitably, such excitement was soon labeled as an addiction. Moreover, the immersion in fantasy, which the game supported, was attacked as detrimental to mental health. Instead of learning to live in the real world, critics charged, teens were escaping into their D&D fantasy worlds and gradually losing the ability to separate the two. Over-identification with such fantasy was said to be specifically responsible for some teen suicides.

The attack on Dungeons and Dragons occurred within the context of a rising teenage suicide rate; such statistics were frightening to many. *Newsweek* (1985) noted: ". . . it is not surprising that parents are looking for something to blame." A form of mass entertainment involving fantasy and violence was therefore an easy target, following in the tradition of attacks on novels, comics, movies, cartoons, music videos, and so on. Another complex social problem was thereby transformed into an easier one with an obvious solution.

As far as can be ascertained, children have always immersed themselves in fantasy role-playing activities as a part of their natural play. They have inevitably summoned up evil and magical characters with which to do combat, drawing upon materials from mythology, fairy tales, dreams, and imagination. The addition of a complex set of rules, some dice, and a compendium of suggested characters has done little to alter the basic psychology of play. Of course, there have long been those sharply critical of fantasy play in any form, finding it either a waste of valuable time or a threat to normal adjustment. This has always been one aspect of the enduring moralistic attack on mass media. Nevertheless, the evidence linking fantasy play with psychopathology has never been forthcoming. Indeed, research findings have tended to support just the opposite conclusion, that the ability to indulge in a rich, far-ranging fantasy life is a sign of psychological strength and creative potential.

What will become of Dungeons and Dragons and the other "invaders'' of the 1980s? It is likely that opposition to cable television, music videos, video tapes, video games, personal computers, and role-playing games will remain with us for some time. Cable television is young and continuing to develop, offering new channels, new services, and becoming increasingly interactive with consumers. Similarly, new and more sophisticated video games are appearing regularly, some involving interaction with television shows, others interfacing with optical disk technology. Personal computers are evolving in power and ability at an astounding rate, making dazzling graphics, music, and voice creations increasingly available in the home. Role-playing games have multiplied rapidly, so that youths may now choose to adventure in a variety of possible worlds or universes, including those created by J. R. R. Tolkein, Ian Flemming, Michael Moorcock, and others. (Popular titles include *Middle Earth, Star Frontiers, Gamma World, Top Secret, Rune Quest, Ghostbusters,* and so on.) The history of media innovation suggests that the pressure to contain and/or censor these media developments will continue until something new, and presumably more threatening, comes along.

It seems safe to predict that a generation from now, parents will be longing for the ''good old days'' of such simple diversions as Pac-Man, D&D, and MTV, while trying to save their children from some contemporary evil media influence.

Notes

1. Lloyd Billingsley, ''Rock Video: 24-hour-a-day Pacifier for TV Babies.'' *Christianity Today,* July 13, 1984, p. 70.
2. Patricia M. Greenfield, *Mind and Media: The Effects of Television, Video Games and Computers.* (Cambridge, MA: Harvard University Press, 1984), p. 2.

Part III
Social and Psychological Perspectives

10

Masscult Menace: Popular Culture

The arrival of media forms capable of achieving vast mass audiences gave the issue of "evil influence" new prominence and urgency in the twentieth century. In magazine articles, newspapers, and books, the experts, namely social scientists, clerics, health professionals, educators, journalists, and intellectuals, regularly warned their worried audiences regarding the latest media threats. As a result, frightened parents and teachers willingly enlisted in furious legal and political battles against the offending mass media. Specific targets changed, but the cycle of hostile encounters continued.

While frightened consumers fought each of the new media in the courts and through the congress, a less visible but no less significant battle was being waged in intellectual circles regarding the status of *mass culture*. The collective mass media undeniably were responsible for spewing and spreading a national mass ("popular") culture. As to the worth of such mass cultural artifacts, professor of philosophy William Gass charged: "the products of popular culture, by and large, have no more esthetic quality than a brick in the street." Gass also condemned mass culture as "the product of an industrial machine which makes baubles to amuse the savages while missionaries steal their souls and merchants steal their money."

The term "mass culture," according to sociologist Herbert J. Gans, combines two German ideas: Masse and Kulture. Masse referred to the bulk of European society: the nonaristocratic, the uneducated, the unprivileged. These are the people we today designate as lower-middle class, working class, and poor. Kulture referred to the arts, music, literature, and lifestyle of the aristocracy. "Mass culture" became a pejorative term referring to the lifestyle and amusements of the mob. Essayist Dwight Macdonald later renamed it Masscult. Eventually, the more neutral term "popular culture" was adopted by those aspiring to greater objectivity.

Debate about popular culture was concerned with the impact of multiple mass media forms on contemporary life and values. It did not often address presumed media threats to health and sanity, but explored more philosophical issues regarding the role of the arts in a democratic society. Nevertheless, the intellectual critique of popular culture provided the framework for derivative arguments and charges regarding public health, criminal behavior, and immorality.

The Birth of Masscult

The intellectual debate about mass media and popular culture began to take its modern form in eighteenth-century England. In prior centuries, writers and other artists had required patronage by upper-class benefactors, and economic survival had depended entirely upon pleasing them. At this point in history, however, an increasingly literate urban middle class made its appearance, an unforseen byproduct of rampant industrialization. As individuals, middle-class citizens lacked the wealth to support hungry artists, but as a group they comprised an audience of considerable size and means. Writers soon discovered that they could achieve financial independence from their patrons by appealing directly to the middle-class audience. Among the vehicles for reaching the new audience were newspapers, magazines, novels, and storypapers.

It had been hoped by some in the aristocracy and clergy that the rapid spread of the print medium would help to educate, improve, and "uplift" the populace. As it turned out, the populace did not wish to be uplifted so much as diverted and entertained, and they supported those who pleased them. Consequently, a new set of artistic standards began to appear based upon the wishes of this "mass" audience. An aspiring poet or author could choose to write for the elite upper-class audience, but also had the option of writing for the broader, "popular" audience. During the course of this century, the latter group came to include even some ordinary, working-class citizens. The appearance of two distinct audiences, with differing standards, set the stage for an enduring controversy as to the legitimacy and relative goodness of the products endorsed by each. Thereafter, the defenders of the traditional "high" culture perceived themselves, their children, and their society as threatened by evil influences originating in the new mass culture.

Similar issues had been raised prior to the arrival of mass media, of course, but in a considerably more theoretical manner. It had once been debated, for example, whether the voice of the masses ("vox populi") had a special place in the affairs of humanity or whether governance by an enlightened few was more sensible. Most of the landed and learned gentry of Europe viewed democratic notions as naive and destructive, tending to preclude the attainment of "excellence" by a country or culture. European aristocracies, after all, were built on the assumption of superior blood lines and supported by impenetrable class boundaries. Democracy, in this context, was interpreted as anarchy or "mob rule." Laws, standards of conduct, and standards of taste were clearly matters to be determined by the priviliged. The relative merits of "entertainment" for the masses had also been argued, with most civil and religious authorities suspicious of any lower-class activity unrelated to work or spiritual attainment.

With the creation of a sizable, literate, urban middle-class, with access to mass media, the clarity of the social order was forever diminished. These volume consumers of the media were creating their own standards of conduct and culture. Indeed, a new age was beginning in which the middle class was to gain control over most aspects of society. The emergence of mass culture was a part of this revolution, hence it was quickly recognized as an enemy of the establishment. "High" culture then became the bastion of the privileged minority, the elite, the truly civilized, in the face of encroaching barbarism. From its lofty ramparts its champions could, and did, constantly fire barbs at the minions of masscult.

Along with other writers of the era, Oliver Goldsmith initially expressed reservations regarding popular forms and the new audience. He feared that men of genius would be ruined by attempting to pander to popular tastes and that young artists would be "seduced" into "idle endeavours after literary fame." Moreover, the notion of linking artistic productivity to the marketplace, like any other business activity, was repugnant: "A long habit of writing for bread thus turns the ambition of every author at last into avarice."

Only a few years later, however, when Goldsmith had earned some much needed coin through his own efforts at writing for the marketplace, he wrote in glowing terms of the patronage of the public. Moreover, he described the meaning of the new audience to the self-respect and independence of the artist:

> He may now refuse an invitation to dinner without fearing to incur his patron's displeasure, or to starve by remaining at home. He may now venture to appear in company with just such clothes as other men generally wear, and talk even to princes . . . he can bravely assert the dignity of independence.[1]

While a number of writers forged ahead in the new marketplace, a more conservative group remained loyal to the established norms and openly criticized the rapidly multiplying popular works. Within a relatively short period of time, both drama and literature had been drastically altered as a result of the popular audience. "Realism" made its appearance on stage and in novels, and the affairs of the aristocracy began to take second place in literature to the problems of middle-class or working-class individuals. This was the era of Pamela and her many imitators (Chapter 4). For the first time, literature and drama became dominated by realistic characters and activities with which mass audiences could readily identify. Villainy, vice, and virtue were offered up as entertainment to the new audience, and presented in such a manner as to maximize the interest of potential consumers. Sentimentality, and detailed depictions of violence and horror, were soon found to be the most reliable means of attracting the attention of the mass audience. The outpouring of such works, their acceptance by large numbers of avid fans, and their dissemination through circulating libraries and book clubs, constituted the birth of English mass culture.

Long before the advent of electronic technology, then, English society of the eighteenth century was confronted with the problem of media-promulgated popular culture and its potential effects upon individuals and the social order. Initially concerned with matters of aesthetics and good taste, conservative critics of the popular forms soon were expressing fears that the impact of excessive realism and emotional content on the unsophisticated might well be *dangerous*. Among the dangers lay the possibility that one might closely identify with a fictional character and thereby be *influenced* to act in similar, possibly reprehensible, ways. The "evil influence" view of the mass media had been born, and marketplace-oriented mass culture had become a matter of great concern to the intellectual/artistic establishment.

By the nineteenth century, artists had largely freed themselves from dependence upon the elite, but some found their growing dependence upon the marketplace equally distasteful. Artistic integrity, after all, demanded uncompromising self-expression and a search for truth and beauty. Several artists attempted to educate the public in the appreciation of the great works of art, all the while condemning the popularizers as corrupting the public. Nevertheless, improvements in printing technology assured that citizens in England and America were flooded with inexpensive newspapers, magazines, and novels. It was the abundance of such materials that escalated the debate regarding the threat to high culture. Libraries were now large and well established, and the bookstalls at English railway stations were overflowing with "Yellow Backs" and other railway literature. How could "real" art hope to compete? How could artistic standards be maintained?

William Wordsworth, at the very beginning of the nineteenth century, wrote that the beauty and dignity of literature were threatened by "frantic novels, sickly and stupid German tragedies, and the deluge of idle and extravagant stories in verse." He went on to condemn the use of "gross and violent stimulants" in popular literature that would blunt the discriminating powers of the mind and engender passivity. His own work, of course, was intended to counteract these influences. Later in the century, William Hazlitt described the public taste as "a millstone round the neck of all original genius." The consequence of pandering to common taste, he noted, was the inevitable decay of high culture. As for his estimation of the general public: "It reads, it admires, it extols only because it is the fashion, not from any love of the subject or the man."

Alexis De Tocqueville, writing about *Democracy in America* (1835), indicated that the wealthy aristocracy of European society naturally had the time and resources required to appreciate the finer things. Under the American democratic system, on the other hand, where wealth and social standing were fluid and often elusive, attention was diverted to the process of economic survival. This meant, among other things, that little time or effort could be devoted to producing work of the highest quality. Instead, artists and craftsman alike had to be concerned with the *quantity* of their productions and the requirements of the marketplace. "In aristocracies a few great pictures are produced; in democratic countries a vast number of insignificant ones."

Literary style under democracy, according to De Tocqueville, was "fantastic, incorrect, overburdened, and loose, almost always vehement and bold." Its object was "to astonish rather than to please, and to stir passions more than to charm the taste." As for the audiences:

> . . . they must have what is unexpected and new. Accustomed to the struggle, the crosses, and the monotony of practical life, they require strong and rapid emotions, startling passages, truths or errors brilliant enough to rouse them up and to plunge them at once, as if by violence, into the midst of the subject.[2]

The autobiography of Sir Egerton Brydges (1834) revealed similar feelings about the effects of democratization upon European literature. The spread of literacy well beyond the aristocracy, and the revolution in printing technology, had created a significant threat to the ascendancy of the elite:

It is a vile evil that literature has become so much a trade all over Europe. Nothing has gone so far to nurture a corrupt taste, and to give the unintellectual power over the intellectual. Merit is now universally estimated by the multitude of readers that an author can attract . . . the mob do not love truth—they relish only what feeds their appetites and passions.[3]

Later in the century Sir Edmund Gosse (1889) reported signs of "a revolt of the mob against our literary masters," particularly in America. Again, the cause was attributed to democratic sentiment, such that matters of taste appeared to be decided by popular vote. The common folk, it was said, were sitting in judgment on matters that could not possibly comprehend. Gosse warned: "The revolution against taste, once begun, will land us in irreparable chaos."

Clearly, the split into two audiences, which had occurred in the eighteenth century, deepened, during the nineteenth, into a chasm. The attack upon popular culture became more bitter, as the elite felt themselves continuing to lose ground to the mass audience. The triumph of democratic forms of government and thought, combined with advances in mass media technology, had created a new world in which traditional class distinctions and priviliges were severely curtailed. "High" culture, one of the few remaining preserves of the elite, was defended more fiercely against encroachment by the "mob." In America, of course, where nothing was sacred, many feared for the future of High Culture. As the twentieth century approached, then, a kind of "class warfare" had been under way for some time, with an elite minority struggling for the salvation of its own culture in an increasingly democratic world. Gans described the situation as follows:

. . . the mass culture critique is an attack by one element in society against another: by the cultured against the uncultured, the educated against the uneducated, the sophisticated against the unsophisticated, the more affluent against the less affluent, and the cultural experts against the laity. In each case, the former criticize the latter for not living up to their own standard of the good life.[4]

The New Elite

Mass culture in the twentieth century has had the distinction of being attacked by both ends of the political spectrum, conservatives and socialists. Conservatives were threatened by the increasing political power of the masses, reflected in their power to influence culture. Socialists and liberals were unhappy that the increasing liberation of the masses had not resulted in their embracing high culture. Paul F. Lazarfeld (1948) remarked:

The liberals of today feel terribly gypped. For decades they and their intellectual ancestors fought to attain certain basic goals—more leisure time, more education, higher wages. They were motivated by the idealistic hope that when these goals were reached, the "masses" would develop into fine human beings. But what happened? After the liberals won their victories, the people spent their newly acquired time and money on movies, radio, magazines.[5]

Conservative and liberal intellectuals alike rejected the notion of cultural democracy in favor of defending high culture from all perceived threats. Taking a "neo-elitist" perspective, they insisted that groups of the highly educated and cultured must retain control over the arts lest they be debased and destroyed. Many neo-elitists were New York City based writers and professional critics who claimed the right to set exclusive standards for what was "good" in American culture. Comic books, most movies, radio, and nearly all television were soundly condemned as destructive to taste and high culture. To such critics, television represented evil influence on a cultural, as well as a personal, level.

Dwight Macdonald, influential spokesman of the new elite, described mass culture, or Masscult (1960), as a "parody of High Culture," including almost all radio, television, and cinema productions in this definition. He viewed movies as relatively uniform products of a production line, intended only to generate effortless "distraction." They demanded nothing of the audience and gave as much in return. "Those who consume Masscult might as well be eating ice-cream sodas."

Macdonald's attack was focused on the impersonality of Masscult and its lack of standards. High culture was said to involve an expression of feelings, ideas, and tastes by an individual, with audiences responding to the vision of the artist. Both artist and audience accepted and respected certain standards based upon past achievements. Masscult, on the other hand, dealt with products deliberately fashioned by "technicians" to conform to the presumed wishes of the largest possible audience. It lacked all values but the central goal of pleasing the greatest number of consumers. Once a pleasing product was found, the Masscult mills produced it in vast quantities and set to work on generating equally pleasing imitations. Although the process was democratic, in the sense of breaking down traditional barriers of class and tradition, and pleasing the largest number of people, Macdonald vehemently objected to the tasteless, homogenized culture it yielded.

Although Masscult was a "cultural nightmare," Macdonald found another, greater threat to High Culture. Americans, confronted with the choice between Masscult and true culture, had turned to a "middlebrow compromise" termed "Midcult." The large, educated middle class, possessed of money, leisure, and knowledge, had created a middle culture that possessed the essential qualities of Masscult but aspired toward High Culture. Midcult "pretends to respect the standards of High Culture while in fact it waters them down and vulgarizes them." Such an enemy was deemed more dangerous than blatant Masscult; it quietly corrupted High Culture and attempted to replace it. Among the examples cited by Macdonald were the Revised Standard Version of the Bible, intended to replace "our greatest monument of English prose" the King James Version; the Book-of-the-Month Club; Hemingway's *The Old Man and the Sea* and Wilder's *Our Town;* the popularized sociology of Vance Packard's *The Hidden Persuaders* and *The Status Seekers;* and such magazines as *Harper's* and the *Atlantic.*

Macdonald longed for the days when class distinctions protected the arts from the masses and the troublesome mass media did not exist. "The great cultures of the past have all been elite affairs, centering in small upper-class communities . . ." He admired England for having maintained a functional class system and found something "damnably American" about Midcult. Aware that the prospects for restoring an aristocracy in America were nil, his proposed solution to the threats of Masscult and Midcult was the deliberate creation of a cultural elite to counteract their effects. Artists were enjoined to ignore the tastes of the majority and deal instead with the standards of appreciative subgroups, thereby avoiding both "Masscult depths" and "the agreeable ooze of the Midcult swamp."

Ernest Van den Haag was another prominent critic of popular culture and spokesman for the new elite. He noted that art was systematically excluded from the mass media lest it fail to attract enough consumers or be found offensive by someone. The standards created to "protect" audiences from the media, he noted, had also created a formula approach to their utilization that ruled out both risk and art. Instead, the media offered pseudoproblems, action-packed plots, and cliche solutions while shielding people from real problems and their complexities. Should art be attempted, it was invariably corrupted: Shakespeare was transformed into musical comedy, Freud offered up in newspaper advice columns, novels condensed, the Bible rewritten, and so on.

Popular culture, for Van den Haag, was a form of diversion for the bored and lonely, but it tended to produce a habitual withdrawal from "meaningful experience." Where art deepened the appreciation of reality, the addiction to popular culture permitted evasion from reality and diminished the capacity for experiencing life. The yearning for diversion, which popular culture engendered, could not, after all, be sated;

diversion merely numbs temporarily. No amount of mass-produced diversion could relieve "the burden which oozes from nonfulfillment." Even the Second Coming, he suggested, would be reduced to "just another barren thrill to be watched on television."

The vulgarization of high culture was also a concern of Bernard Rosenberg, who blamed the problem on industrialization and technology rather than political democracy. While technology had freed much of humanity from manual labor, it had not left them free to improve their sensibilities and heighten their understanding. Rather, technology had created the mass media, complete with a horde of "popularizers," to prevent cultural progress:

> No art form, no body of knowledge, no system of ethics is strong enough to withstand vulgarization. A kind of cultural alchemy transforms them all into the same soft currency. Never before have the sacred and the profane, the genuine and the specious, the exalted and the debased, been so thoroughly mixed that they are all but indistinguishable. Who can sort one from the other when they are built into a single slushy compost?[6]

The production of popular culture artifacts sometimes involved appropriation of elements from high culture, leading to elitist pronouncements against "kitsch." The term probably is derived from the German "verkitschen," to make cheap. An object was described as kitsch when it attempted to appear artistic, cultured, or profound when, in fact, it was manufactured for mass tastes and the mass market. Items condemned as kitsch by critics included: a packaged collection of the World's Greatest Music; a coffee-table book of French Impressionist paintings; a living room full of imitation "Colonial," "Early American," or "French Provincial" furniture; plaster-cast lawn statues in the form of classic sculpture; and so on. These were decried by intellectuals as phoney art, packaged culture, and vulgarization. Kitsch was said to undermine true quality in the arts and crafts, substituting the illusion of quality and mass marketing techniques.

The elitists shared a distain for ordinary people and their lives. This perspective was forcefully expressed by Gass in his description of the "average man":

> The average man does not want to know how he looks when he eats; he defecates in darkness, reading the *Readers Digest* . . . his work is futile, his thought is shallow, his joys ephemeral, his howls helpless and agony incompetent; his hopes are purchased, his play is mechanical . . . futilely he feeds, he voids, he screws, he smokes, he motorboats, he squats before the tube, he spends at least a week each year in touring . . . and dies like merchandise gone out of season.[7]

Another prominent elitist, Q. D. Leavis, wrote of ordinary people as collectively constituting a "herd," and noted that the average individual could not be expected to stand against it. She attributed the widespread acceptance of Ernest Hemingway's work to herd attitudes and pressures:

> It is more than difficult, it is next to impossible, for the ordinary uncritical man to resist when, whichever way he looks in the street, from poster and hoarding, and advertisement in bus and tramcar, whichever paper or novel he picks up, whatever play or film he attends for amusement, the pressure of the herd is brought to bear upon him . . . it is pleasanter to be one of the herd, i.e., less wear and tear is involved in conforming than in standing out against mass sentiment.[8]

In an earlier era, an aristocratic elite could readily and safely ignore the tastes and desires of the common folk; workers and peasants lived in one world, the elite in another. The masses could not hope to understand or appreciate the cultural products of the literate, and the elite had little concern with folk culture. In the twentieth century, however, the products of popular culture became impossible to escape or ignore. Mere possession of a radio or television ensured exposure to sit-coms, soaps, quiz shows, mysteries, westerns, superheroes, rock stars, and so on. Even the finest newspapers featured "best-seller" lists or comic strips. Forced in this manner to confront the cultural products of the mass audience, the intellectual elite became vociferous in expressing dissatisfaction with mass media and popular culture.

The broadcast media of the twentieth century simply brought to a head the festering class-conflict regarding popular culture. The intellectual elite remained heavily invested in the older print culture as the source of its knowledge and power. It had struggled, in the prior two centuries, against impurities in the print medium as newspapers, story-papers, and novels challenged the supremacy of the linear, logical, dispassionate, analytic format. The growing infusion of illustration, photography, realism, violence, and sensuality into print was perceived as an invasion of lower-class values and tastes. The bestial, brutal, sensual aspect of the lower-class nature had tainted the clarity and beauty of knowledge and culture. Once the film and the broadcast media arrived, the challenge to print culture was deemed monstrous, and fears for literacy were rampant. Masscult and/or Midcult were everywhere.

For the new elite, the stakes of the conflict between mass culture and high culture were considerable; civilization itself was deemed at risk. More immediately, however, the power and status of the intellectual establishment were on the line. As each new media development blossomed and became yet another vehicle for popular culture, the elite became more and more removed from social power and leadership. The machinery of mass culture, after all, daily influenced millions. Movie stars, television personalities, sports figures, and popularizers earned millions of dollars by pleasing the huge and eager mass audience. Meanwhile, many of the elite struggled along on meager university or editorial salaries, hard-won grants, or inherited funds. Gans aptly described high culture as a "low-wage industry."

The evils of popular culture and mass media were not simply abstract, impersonal phenomena to the new elite but immediate sources of frustration, deprivation, and humiliation. What sort of aristocracy is it, after all, that grows powerless and poor by comparison with the entertainers of the herd? The anger and frustration of the elite inevitably fueled the century's social/political controversies regarding the evil influence of the mass media. Social scientists, meanwhile, discovered that research into the dire predictions of intellectual critics was a highly profitable enterprise. Every danger to society, after all, warranted research grants and public attention, and findings were eagerly awaited by ambitious politicians and a book-buying public.

There were also some moderate voices raised in the mass media/culture debate, those willing to consider the possibility that society was not about to perish under a mound of trash. Sociologist Herbert Gans (*Popular Culture and High Culture,* 1974) was numbered among these. Tracing the history of the mass culture critique, he noted that it had appeared whenever intellectuals were losing power and status but became dormant when these were regained. The peak of criticism in the late 1940s and 1950s, for example, he attributed to the loss of affluence, power, and status by intellectuals during the Eisenhower administration and the McCarthy era.

Gans attempted to place popular and high cultures on a more equal footing by referring to both as "taste cultures." All taste cultures were said to have the functions of entertaining, informing, and beautifying life while expressing aesthetic (and sometimes political) values. Beyond "high" and "low," taste cultures might also be upper- or lower-middle class, youth, black, ethnic, and so on. Until all Americans had equal educational backgrounds, Gans argued, one could not expect them to choose taste cultures that required a college education. Moreover, he found little reason to criticize people for participating in taste cultures that reflected their own educational levels and life experiences.

As for evil influences, Gans noted that despite the daily exposure of the vast majority of Americans to mass media and mass culture, he could not describe them as "atomized, narcotized, brutalized, escapist, or unable to cope with reality.'' Mental instability and criminal behavior, when they occurred, seemed to him much more closely related to the stresses and strains of poverty than exposure to mass media. Although the media may have had negative effects on a minority of people who consumed them in other than accepted ways, the power of the mass media over individuals was highly exaggerated. The mass culture critique, after all, was partly:

> . . . an ideology of defense, constructed to protect the cultural and political privileges of high culture. Like all such ideologies, it exaggerates the power of its opposition and the harmful consequences that would follow from permitting this opposition to exist.[9]

The tolerant view of popular culture offered by Gans, while widely recognized for its scholarship and sophistication, could not long compete for attention in the marketplace of ideas against dramatic prophesies of doom. Ironically, the mass media/culture critique had itself become part of popular culture; warnings about the evil effects of the media had proven to be effective in selling books, magazines, and newspapers. Doom-sayers repeatedly discovered new reasons for horror and outrage and always found a receptive audience for their concerns. Where the elite railed against the dangers to high culture, the social scientists, physicians, clergy, and social workers warned of the threat to higher cognitive functions and higher morality. Ultimately, they urged the nation's teachers, parents, and politicians to take action lest the vulnerable succumb to mental illness, immorality, or criminal behavior.

Over the past two centuries, each manifestation of the mass media that appealed to a large audience has promptly upset the elite; it has thereafter been attacked by a broader coalition as inimical to health and morality. The realism and sentimentality of early novels and story-papers; the illustrations, photographs, headlines, comics, and sensational aspects of newspapers; the imagery, fantasy, and graphic violence of comic books; the vivid imaginal productions suggested by radio; the pictorial realism, sensuality, and violence of cinema and television; and so on, have all encountered this pattern of response. Ironically, the mass culture critique initiated by the elite has been adopted in a ''popularized'' version by middle-class citizens, who interpreted it according to their own set of concerns. Here the emphasis was not upon art, truth, and beauty, but upon the health and welfare of women, children, the family, and society.

Clearly, the arrival of mass culture was experienced differently by the lower and middle classes in comparison to the elite. New media forms, formats, and byproducts were tremendously exciting to the lower class and soon won considerable followings. Initially, these individuals had little to lose in the way of power or status, and much to gain from the wealth of information and entertainment that became available to them. As the mass audience broadened still further in the twentieth century, however, an increasing portion of the middle class experienced a threat from "lower-class" influences. To the "upwardly mobile" in aspiration, the enjoyment of high culture came to be considered a personally and socially desirable goal. Moreover, shame and guilt were easily provoked when such folk learned that certain of their media pleasures were considered contemptible by the elite. Sex and violence had become too graphic they were told, and entertainment too passive; the way to upward mobility lay elsewhere, along a more genteel path.

That society was being polluted or corrupted by mass media influences, placing their children in peril, was a very palpable and motivating fear for the middle class. Let one authority figure hoist a banner that identified and condemned such a threat, and many felt compelled to rally. The very act of opposing such presumably degrading influences made many feel culturally elevated. Defenders of literacy, they became self-righteous and proud, literate or not. By the simple act of protesting low standards, they laid claim to high standards. By thus emulating the elite, they felt themselves become a part of that elite.

In sum, while it cannot be said that social class issues fully explain the public response to mass media innovation, it is clear that they have been lurking behind and contributing to the lengthy crusade against evil media influences.

Notes

1. Oliver Goldsmith, cited by Leo Lowenthal and Marjorie Fiske, "Art and Popular Culture in Eighteenth Century England," in M. Komarovsky (Ed.) *Common Frontiers of the Social Sciences* (Illinois: The Free Press, 1957), p. 69.
2. Alexis De Tocqueville, "In What Spirit the Americans Cultivate the Arts," reprinted from *Democracy in America* (1835), in B. Rosenberg and D. M. White (Eds.) *Mass Culture* (New York: The Free Press, 1957), p. 33.
3. Sir Egerton Brydges, cited in Q. D. Leavis *Fiction and The Reading Public* (London: Chatto and Windus, 1932), p. 188.
4. Herbert J. Gans, *Popular Culture and High Culture* (New York: Basic Books, 1974), pp. 3–4.
5. Paul F. Lazarfeld, in Norman Jacobs (Ed.) *Culture For The Millions* (Boston: Beacon Press, 1964), p. xiv.

172   **Evil Influences**

6. Bernard Rosenberg, *Mass Culture,* op. cit., p. 5.
7. William H. Gass, "Even if, by all the Oxen in the World (a polemic)," in R. B. Browne, R. H. Crowder, V. L. Lokke, W. T. Stafford (Eds.) *Frontiers of American Culture* (West Lafayette, IN: Purdue University, 1968), p. 196.
8. Q. D. Leavis, op. cit., p. 194.
9. Herbert J. Gans, op. cit., p. 63.

11

Moral Crusades: The Psychology of Fear

In previous chapters we examined a sampling of negative public responses to otherwise successful mass media innovations. Although we have not dealt with each and every such innovation-response cycle, enough examples have been provided to highlight the striking similarities among them. Early critics of the newspaper, for example, complained that its format hurt readers' eyes and powers of concentration; its rapid shifts of content matter disoriented the mind. The liberal use of imagery (illustrations, photographs) detracted from important written content and undermined literacy and critical thinking. Journalistic obsession with crime and sensuality undermined moral strictures, desensitized to violence, and encouraged imitative behaviors in the vulnerable. Such concerns, in retrospect, are consistent not only with complaints about early television, but also contemporary with criticism of music videos. Yet another set of critics warned that children would be giving up their lunch money and/or stealing money in order to get into seedy nickelodeons, where they would be adversely influenced by screen violence. This litany was echoed many decades later by the opponents of arcade video games. Those who condemned the early subscription libraries because the circulation of novels undermined morality would very likely feel at home with modern opponents of video cassette rentals. And so on. In this chapter, we examine these parallels from a psychological perspective, looking at unifying themes that help us to understand these persistent cycles of reaction, rejection, and attempted suppression.

Challenges to Cognition

Cognition refers to that set of mental processes by which we perceive, interpret, remember, and understand the world. In the last few decades, psychologists have been greatly interested in investigating how people receive, process, store, and use information in order to navigate life situations, make decisions, and solve problems. The relevance of such matters to mass media is clear—the latter present us with huge quantities of information on a daily basis. How it is presented (form, structure), what is presented (content), and what we do with it (processing, behavioral outcomes) are issues relevant to the crusade against mass media. An entire book might be devoted to analyzing the cognitive parameters of a single media form, but that is not our purpose here. The more limited task at hand is to apply a cognitive framework to the various incarnations of the mass media critique already presented, so as to clarify certain commonalities.

Mass media innovations inevitably have challenged well-established cognitive patterns and practices. Novels, films, television, video games, and the like have required that people receive or process information in new ways and in new quantities. While some found this exciting, even exhilarating, others found it exhausting, alien, and threatening. One of the most important dimensions of this cognitive challenge has already been mentioned in several chapters, that is, the shift from almost total reliance upon linear, logical, impersonal, abstract information structures to a pervasive use of nonlinear structures involving emotion, imagery, and fantasy. The transition occurred in a number of relatively small increments: the column format of newspapers, the use of headlines, the introduction of illustration and photography, the use of sentiment in the novel, and so on. Each increment met with resistance. Every time consumers were asked to use their sense organs and their minds in new ways, a part of society responded with fear, strenuously objecting to the change.

The image, in the form of penned illustration, photograph, movie, television, or vivid mental representation has stirred up the most dire concerns. It was just too powerful, too realistic, too evocative and arousing for comfort. Those accustomed and/or committed to cool, rational, abstract analysis found the image a most unwelcome intrusion. Sophisticated, intellectual critics proclaimed themselves relatively safe from such distractions but declared virtually everybody else to be vulnerable. The dynamic images of the movies were said to be still worse than the static images of photography. Images generated directly in the imagination via novels or radio were equally objectionable. A cabinet full of realistic, dynamic images, sharing or dominating the living room, comprised the greatest threat of all. The rapidly shifting dreamlike imagery, animation, and computer graphics of the music video only confirmed, for some, the intolerable aspects of television. The march toward increased reliance upon imagery in both communications and entertainment has been both inexorable and revolutionary.

Critics of the mass media repeatedly have cited "overstimulation" as one of the evils involved. This refers not only to the evocation of powerful emotions via images but also to the amount of information that images carry. A single cinematic or television image, briefly glimpsed, takes considerable time and effort to describe verbally or in print. This is because an image presents us with an entire "packet" of information all at once. Printed communications use a slower, "sequential" arrangement of letters, words, and sentences to present their information. In the transition from the printed word to a stream of rapidly moving images accompanied by sound, the amount of information presented for processing by the mass media increased manyfold. Critics long have feared that this avalanche of input would overload the nervous systems of the vulnerable. Even the morning newspaper, at the turn of the century, looked dangerously overstimulating to a prominent neurological expert.

Imagery is also the stuff of fantasy, of dreams, daydreams, reveries, hallucinations, and such. For many, it seemed the antithesis of rational, reality-oriented thought, and therefore dangerous. Daydreaming, itself, was seen for many years as undesirable or pathological in children and certainly not to be encouraged. Until recently, daydreaming in adults was seen as the regressive, neurotic behavior of ineffectual, Walter Mitty-like, individuals who could not cope with reality. Many mental health professionals confused normal fantasy with delusional or hallucinatory behavior, often citing daydreaming in children as an early sign of psychosis. Consequently, mass media innovations that encouraged imagery and fantasy were seen as dangerously weakening the boundaries between realistic and pathological thinking. Excitement about mass media innovation was redefined as "over-involvement," a first step toward pathology. Although considerable research has revealed imagery, fantasy, and daydreaming to be normal, healthy, and inevitable parts of mental life, these misconceptions continue today. Video games, fantasy role-playing games, and music videos are all under indictment in this regard.

The kind of cognitive flexibility that can most readily adapt to new forms of information input is found, of course, among the young. Their minds are still growing and stretching; they have not yet settled into comfortable and well-defined ways of looking at and thinking about things. Consequently, children and young adults have been most receptive to media innovation, finding it an adventure rather than a threat. They have thrived on an intensity of stimulation to mind and sensorium that was overpowering to the previous generation. They have pursued novels, cinema, television, video games, music videos, and so on, with an intensity that astonished their more cautious and cognitively conservative parents, who were readily panicked by any "expert" who suggested that such excitement and involvement would inevitably harm their children.

Challenges to Control

Another important unifying theme in the attack on mass media has been the fear of diminished control over personal and family life. The feeling of having significant control over one's life, however illusory, is well known to be an important prerequisite to feelings of safety and security. Being at the mercy of forces beyond one's control, on the other hand, is totally unacceptable—a common nightmare. Consequently, anything that lessens the feeling of control is a potential threat. Many successful mass media innovations have fallen squarely into this category.

One quality of mass media that threatened feelings of control was *intrusiveness*. With the technology of the printing press perfected, for example, printed matter began appearing everywhere. Novels, newspapers, and magazines were soon in evidence in stores, railway stations, neighbors' homes, barber shops, and so on. Still, there was some small hope of keeping these out of the home, if so desired. With the arrival of radio, the air around us was suddenly filled with media messages. In theory, one was not forced to purchase a radio, or to turn it on, but most felt the need to be connected to the rest of the country and the world. Once radio took up residence in the living room, however, it rapidly became an integral part of family life. (Woody Allen documented this phenomenon in the film *Radio Days*.) Traditions of dining, conversation, and other family activities were suddenly and irrevocably modified by the presence of a radio. The "invasion" of the home by the mass media had begun.

Once television appeared, spreading rapidly into millions of homes, mass media were virtually inescapable. An occasional self-declared intellectual might ban television from the home for a time, but its influence was omnipresent throughout the culture and not to be denied. The broadcast media had come home to live with us, to sing their varied messages to our wives and husbands, sons and daughters, teens and toddlers. Many people welcomed the media as entertaining and undemanding guests, while others felt intruded upon and violated. Guests, after all, come and go away; the media had come to stay.

The intrusiveness of the mass media might have been a relatively minor problem had it not carried the germ of yet another loss of control.

That is, the ability of parents and educators to direct the flow of information to children had been suddenly compromised. In a simpler time, children knew only what their parents, teachers, and clergy told them, along with tidbits gleaned from friends and neighbors. Mass media changed this situation completely and irrevocably as information of all kinds began to flow into the home. Newspapers offered the children comics, games, and stories; radios plied them with music, comedy, and drama; novels offered them all sorts of possibilities. The same box of electronic circuitry that brought politics, concerts, and international affairs into the home also brought game shows, cartoons, cowboys, detectives, R-rated movies, and MTV. Eventually, most family entertainment was preselected by sponsors and networks, leaving parents only the options of switching channels or pulling the plug. Consequently, children were increasingly exposed to material that might not meet with the express approval of their parents. Harmless or otherwise, it was all outside of parent/teacher/clergy control, and therefore threatening. Protest against children's "addiction" to comics, novels, video games, MTV, role-playing games, or computers was one way of saying that these media forms were seducing the young away from rightful authority. Potentially enriching aspects of media exposure were readily eclipsed once it was suggested that some evil influence had taken control of childhood.

It was not only control over children's formative years that seemed threatened by the ubiquitous mass media; many feared that adults were about to surrender control of their own lives as well. The enemy, in this regard, was *passivity*. Movies, comics, novels, radio, and particularly television were criticized as promoting mind-numbing and physically disabling passivity in consumers of all ages. In a society oriented toward action and accomplishment, the prospect of millions of people engaged in any sit-and-stare form of entertainment appeared decadent and dangerous. A closely related concern was an insidious loss of individuality, as consumers passively merged with a growing mass society. This was no small matter in America, where individualism had long been the cornerstone of society. The free and responsible individual, rather than the collective, has been the basic unit of American life. Capitalism demands that the individual, as entrepreneur, seek out creative ways to acquire wealth and become a "self-made" person. Passive acceptance of mass culture, it was feared, would thoroughly undermine the necessary innovative thought and initiative. Minds and bodies would grow flabby on a diet of mass media mush, becoming vulnerable to authoritarian domination. The society of Orwell's *1984* was cited, by critics, as a likely outcome of such mass-media domination. It must have surprised some of these critics to find health-conscious Americans of 1984 exercising to video tapes or cable TV shows and actively controlling home entertainment by means of VCR's, multichannel cable reception, personal computers, and remote-control "mute" switches.

Challenges to Defense

Psychological defenses, simply put, are mental maneuvers that permit us to deny, repress, suppress, or otherwise avoid the impact of information that is personally threatening, distasteful, or repulsive. Information about unpleasant aspects of *ourselves*—our wants and needs, impulses, guilts—are particularly choice targets for defensive operations. Many a sophisticated clinical treatise has been written on the nature of psychological defense, and a complete exposition of the concept is neither possible nor necessary here. The notion that defensive operations play a part in the crusade against mass media, on the other hand, has been little appreciated.

All mass media offer opportunities for "projection," that is, involvement of the "self." Novels, comics, movies, radio, and television have provided a means for audience members to put themselves temporarily into imaginary situations and experiences. Even the newspapers have offered this opportunity, albeit to a lesser degree; readers could see themselves as crime victims, criminals, politicians, and sports figures, with little effort or risk. The various media forms deliberately aimed to maximize this projective effect to facilitate personal involvement in order to create and hold as large an audience as possible. Reactions to the mass media, therefore, are not simply objective and intellectual judgments. They reflect, as well, emotional reactions to the kinds of imaginal experiences that have been encountered; personal responses to personal experiences. This helps to explain the tendency for reactions to become somewhat exaggerated. That is, we are seeing how people respond to the imaginal proximity of violence, death, and sexuality. Those most heavily defended against these aspects of their humanity are also most shocked and offended, most likely to do battle against the offending source of stimulation.

Defensive operations can readily be initiated by pleasurable activities, providing these evoke shame, guilt, anxiety, or merely conflict in individuals. American society, of course, began in a Puritan context, which held all pleasurable entertainments to be sinful. The early colonies adopted strict regulations "in detestation of idleness"; all were expected to devote themselves to work and worship. By law, no person was permitted to "spend his time idly or unprofitably." In New England, authorities attempted to suppress almost every form of amusement and recreation: dice, cards, bowling, shuffleboard, theater, song, and dance. Recreation and other frivolity was seen as inherently evil and sinful. Even the Sabbath was not intended for enjoyment, but for religious observation and pious reflection. Early laws specifically prohibited Sunday amusements, including unnecessary walking in the streets or fields. Only children under seven years of age were exempt from these austere, intolerant rules. Such were the origins of American culture, and some aspects of this heritage long adhered to the evolving Protestant ethic. Little wonder that the "entertainment" aspects of early mass media innovations were found to be threatening, content aside. To this day, the notion of an "addiction" to mass media forms expresses the fear that purely pleasurable activities inevitably undermine work responsibilities and thwart self-improvement.

As for mass media *content,* even the most casual perusal of the previous chapters indicates that the furor over evil influence has focused again and again upon imaginal representations of sexuality and/or aggression. Sex and aggression, of course, are the very issues that psychoanalytic thought placed at the heart of human conflict, and that were presumed to underlie defensive and neurotic behaviors. Just as individuals may defend themselves against blatant sexual or aggressive impulses from within, they may defend themselves against representations of these impulses in their environment. The novel, newspaper, comic book, radio, television, and related media innovations have all confronted society with vivid sexual and/or aggressive images. While the latter have been important factors in the success of these media forms, they have also been responsible for stimulating powerful defensive reactions in some portion of the audience. Human fascination with sexuality and aggression, both in the psyche and in mass media, is opposed by defensive forces that reject the very same themes. Personal ambivalence and conflict regarding these two extremely powerful motives is mirrored in cultural ambivalence about their representation in the media.

Examining charges against mass media content, Leslie Fiedler noted:

> It has been charged against vulgar art that it is sadistic, fetishistic, brutal, full of terror; that it pictures women with exaggeratedly full breasts and rumps, portrays death on the printed page, is often covertly homosexual, etc., etc. About these charges there are two obvious things to say. First, by and large, they are true. Second, they are also true about much of the most serious art of our time, especially that produced in America . . . Behind the opposition to vulgar literature there is at work the same fear of the

archetypal and the unconscious itself that motivated similar attacks on Elizabethan drama and on the eighteenth-century novel.[1]

From Challenge to Threat

Having examined the specifics of past anti-media crusades, we have now noted and grouped their regularities. This approach has yielded a number of social (ch. 10) and psychological factors, which contribute to the evocation of public outrage. Challenges/threats to the social status, cognitive abilities, sense of control, and defensive operations of the audience were preeminent in this regard. Viewed from this perspective, the cycles of outcry against novels, newspapers, radio, comic books, television, video games, and so on, appear relatively indistinguishable. The specifics of mass media innovation, it seems, were relatively unimportant in shaping the public response, except insofar as all provided an opportunity for *vivid imaginal experiences*. These experiences created the challenges, which, perceived as threats, initiated cycles of reaction and rejection. Threats to cognition, control, and defense were compounded by threats to social class. Attempts to suppress the sources for such experiences repeatedly met with failure, yet each media innovation occasioned another attempt and renewed prophecies of doom.

Writing on America's reaction to the juvenile delinquent in the 1950s, historian James Gilbert (*A Cycle of Outrage,* 1986) recently referred to the episodic nature of certain accusations:

> Thus, the debate over mass culture and its effects on children during the 1950's indicates the reappearance of an old worry. Its roots lie in a reoccurring criticism of American culture attributing misbehavior and delinquency to a hostile cultural environment. Since this is such a common accusation, with so many reappearances in American history, it should be considered an example of what I would call an *episodic* notion . . . the seduction of the innocent by culture is a primary example of an episodic notion.[2]

Gilbert also noted that episodic notions cannot be accepted at face value but must be studied for their social functions and underlying messages. The recurring accusation of mass culture and mass media, for example, was thought to reflect a "large measure of insecurity and resistance to cultural change." Such observations are highly consonant with those offered here, and some specifics have now been provided as to the nature of the public's "insecurity."

The anxiety generated by the psychosocial challenges of media innovation repeatedly has led significant numbers of people to turn upon it, to brand it as evil. Psychologist Milton Rokeach and his colleagues (*The Open and Closed Mind,* 1960) noted that anxiety from any cause predisposes us to perceive menace. As a diffuse, undirected type of fear it cries out for definition and structure. What a relief, after all, to know exactly what one fears, to clearly identify the "enemy." In the face of such motivation, an answer eventually occurs. At that point, belief systems begin to contract and become rigid, becoming closed to further considerations. Anxiety is reduced because uncertainty is (apparently) eliminated. This is the state of mind that leads to scapegoating, intolerance, and prejudice of all kinds. A clear-cut scapegoat, once identified, provides an ideal target for all frustration and hostility. The mass media have served admirably in this regard.

It is undeniable that aspects of the mass media have frequently demonstrated mediocrity and bad taste. It is also perfectly reasonable to believe that the media have been abused by some consumers. Perhaps mass media have some suggestive power in highly susceptible or deranged individuals. Recent research into television violence may even have demonstrated a link to increased aggressive behavior in children (this is not universally accepted). However, the charges against mass media over the past two centuries go far beyond these relatively mild statements. As we have seen, the rhetoric of the mass media debate generally has been shrill. The media have been branded as potent sources of physical, psychological, and moral deterioration, sufficiently powerful to overcome the beneficial effects of family life, education, and religion. The media "habit" has been condemned with the same sense of moral outrage and dread once reserved for masturbatory activity. Such charges bear little relation to the findings of serious academic researchers in their attempts to identify and study the multiple, complex, and subtle forms of interaction between media and audience.

Popular Crusades against the Media

The original "crusades" were military expeditions undertaken by the Christian nations in the eleventh to thirteenth centuries to win the Holy Land from Islam. The same term, however, may be applied to any remedial enterprise undertaken in the name of moral or religious outrage; its application to the cycles of attack upon the mass media therefore seems quite appropriate. Crusades, of course, always have political aspects. Moral issues serve as rallying points, and they are readily seized upon by those in search of a political following. There have always been politicians willing and able to lead a fight to censor or otherwise suppress the mass media. Once the media are condemned as spreading evil influence, those leading the charge are credited with attempting to rescue the land for the righteous. This is a time-tested procedure for building a devoted following. All this sounds melodramatic, but melodrama has been a consistent characteristic of such crusades.

The crusaders against the media have not merely exaggerated its influence upon health and welfare, but consistently have underestimated the adaptive capability of humanity. They have offered up their vision of consumers, particularly women and children, as passive, helpless victims requiring rescue after rescue. They have indicated that all the efforts of parents, teachers, and clergy have little impact upon children once captured by the media. The notion that healthy children cannot learn to place the media into proper perspective in their lives, however, seems shortsighted, particularly when so many of today's adults have survived their childhood encounters with television, radio, movies, comics, and more. Moreover, the implication that parents, teachers, and clergy are not responsible for helping with this process is an unfortunate avoidance of responsibility. Crusaders typically direct all their considerable energies toward suppression, thereby missing the opportunity to educate in any positive sense. Fortunately, researchers recently have begun to investigate such topics as the role of the media in stimulating healthy imagination and the role of parents in buffering the effects of television viewing upon young children.

The march of the media seems destined to continue, and today's crusades will be quickly recycled as the next innovations come along. The best preparation for all of this change, I believe, will be a history of confronting and dealing with earlier media challenges, not one of being protected from these by well-meaning crusaders.

Notes

1. Leslie Fiedler, "The Middle Against Both Ends," in Rosenberg, B. and White, D. M., *Mass Culture* (New York: The Free Press, 1957), p. 542.
2. James Gilbert, *A Cycle of Outrage* (New York: Oxford University Press, 1986), p. 4.

Bibliography

I. Books and Journal Articles

Addams, Jane. *The Spirit of Youth and the City Streets* (1909). Urbana: University of Illinois, 1972.

Aufderheide, Pat. "The Look of the Sound." In *Watching Television*, pp. 111–35. Edited by Todd Gitlin. New York: Pantheon, 1987.

Bakwin, Ruth M. "Psychologic Aspects of Pediatrics: The Comics." *Journal of Pediatrics,* 1953, 42, pp. 633–35.

Barnouw, Erik. *Tube of Plenty.* New York: Oxford University Press, 1979.

Beard, George M. *American Nervousness.* New York: G. P. Putnam's Sons, 1881.

Becker, Stephen. *Comic Art in America.* New York: Simon and Schuster, 1959.

Bender, Lauretta. "The Psychology of Children's Reading and the Comics." *Journal of Educational Sociology,* 1944, 18, pp. 223–31.

Bender, L. and Lourie, R. S. "The Effect of Comic Books on the Ideology of Children." *American Journal of Orthopsychiatry,* 1941, 11, pp. 540–50.

Berger, Arthur A. *The Comic-Stripped American.* Baltimore, MD: Penguin, 1974.

Blumer, Herbert. *Movies and Conduct.* New York: Macmillan, 1933.

Blumer, H. and Hauser, Philip M. *Movies, Delinquency, and Crime.* New York: Macmillan, 1933.

Bode, Carl. *The Anatomy of American Popular Culture.* Berkeley, CA: University of California Press, 1959.

Bogart, Leo. *The Age of Television.* New York: Frederick Unger, 1972.

Bogart, Leo. "Warning: The Surgeon General Has Determined That TV Violence is Moderately Dangerous To Your Child's Mental Health." *Public Opinion Quarterly,* 1972–73, 36, pp. 491–552.

Brown, Herbert Ross. *The Sentimental Novel in America 1789–1860.* Durham, N.C.: Duke University, 1940.

Brown, Lee. *The Reluctant Reformation*. New York: David McKay, 1974.

Browne, R. B., Crowder, R. H., Lokke, V. L., Stafford, W. T. (Eds.). *Frontiers of American Culture*. West Lafayette, IN: Purdue University, 1968.

Bryson, Lyman. "The Revolt of the Radio Listeners," *Journal of Adult Education*, 1932, 4, pp. 234–39.

Cantor, M. G. and Pingree, S. *The Soap Opera*. Beverly Hills, CA: Sage, 1983.

Cantril, Hadley and Allport, Gordon W. *The Psychology of Radio*. New York: Harper Brothers, 1935.

Carothers, J. C. "Culture, Psychiatry, and the Written Word," *Psychiatry*, 1959, 22, pp. 307–20.

Carroll, John (Ed.) *Samuel Richardson*. Englewood Cliffs, NJ: Prentice-Hall, 1969.

Chaffee, S. H., Gerbner, G., Hamberg, B. A., Pierce, C. M., Rubenstein, E. A., Siegel, A. E., and Singer, J. L. "Defending the Indefensible." *Society*, 1984, September, pp. 30–35.

Charters, W. W. *Motion Pictures and Youth*. New York: Macmillan, 1933.

Csikszentmihalyi, M. and Kubey, R. "Television and the Rest of Life: A Systematic Comparison of Subjective Experience." *Public Opinion Quarterly*, 1981, 45, pp. 317–28.

Dalziel, Margaret. *Popular Fiction 100 Years Ago*. London: Cohen and West, 1957.

Daniels, Les. *Comix: A History of Comic Books in America*. New York: Bonanza, 1971.

Davis, Robert Edward. *Response To Innovation*. New York: Arno Press, 1976.

DeFleur, M. L. and Ball-Rokeach, S. *Theories of Mass Communication*. New York: David McKay, 1966.

Diringer, David. *The Alphabet*. New York: Philosophic Library, 1948.

Diringer, David. *The Book Before Printing*. New York: Dover, 1982.

Dominick, Joseph R. "Videogames, Television Violence, and Aggression in Teenagers." *Journal of Communication*, 1984, 34, pp. 136–47.

Dorfles, Gillo. *Kitsch: The World of Bad Taste*. New York: Bell, 1968.

Dulles, Foster R. *A History of Recreation*. New York: Appleton-Century-Crofts, 1965.

Eisenberg, Azriel L. *Children and Radio Programs*. New York: Columbia University, 1936.

Emery, E., Ault, P. H., and Agee, W. K. *Introduction to Mass Communication*. New York: Dodd, Mead & Co., 1974.

Eron, Leonard D. "Parent-Child Interaction, Television Violence, and Aggression of Children." *American Psychologist*, 1982, 37, pp. 197–211.

Eysenck, H. J. and Nias, D. K. B. *Sex, Violence and the Media.* London: Maurice Temple Smith, 1978.

Fass, Paula S. *The Damned and the Beautiful: American Youth in the 1920's.* New York: Oxford University Press, 1977.

Fiedler, Leslie. *What was Literature?* New York: Simon and Schuster, 1982.

Foreman, Henry J. *Our Movie Made Children.* New York: Arno Press, 1970.

Fox, R. W. and Lears, T. J. J. *The Culture of Consumption.* New York: Pantheon, 1983.

Frank, Josette. "What's in the Comics?" *Journal of Educational Sociology,* 1944, 18, pp. 214–22.

Freedman, Jonathan L. "Effect of Television Violence on Aggressiveness." *Psychological Bulletin,* 1984, 96, pp. 227–46.

Gans, Herbert J. *Popular Culture and High Culture.* New York: Basic Books, 1974.

Gass, William H. "Even if, by all the Oxen in the World." In *Frontiers of American Culture,* pp. 194–99. Edited by Ray B. Browne, Richard H. Crowder, Virgil L. Lokke, William T. Stafford. West Lafayette, IN: Purdue University, 1968.

Geller, Evelyn. *Forbidden Books in American Public Libraries, 1876–1939.* Westport, CT: Greenwood Press, 1984.

Gifford, Denis. *The International Book of Comics.* New York: Crescent Books, 1984.

Gilbert, James. *A Cycle of Outrage.* New York: Oxford University Press, 1986.

Gitlin, Todd (Ed.) *Watching Television.* New York: Pantheon, 1987.

Glessing, R. J. and White, W. P. *Mass Media: The Invisible Environment.* Chicago: Science Research Associates, 1973.

Goldsen, Rose K. *The Show and Tell Machine.* New York: Dial, 1977.

Greenberg, B. S. and Heeter, C. "VCR's and Young People: The Picture at 39% Penetration." *American Behavioral Scientist,* 1987, 30, pp. 509–21.

Greenfield, Patricia M. *Mind and Media: The Effects of Television, Video Games and Computers.* Cambridge, MA: Harvard University Press, 1984.

Gumpart, Gary and Cathcart, Robert. (Ed.) *Inter/Media.* New York: Oxford University Press, 1979.

Gunter, B. and Levy, Mark R. "Social Contexts of Video Use." *American Behavioral Scientist,* 1987, 30, pp. 486–94.

Hart, James D. *The Popular Book.* Berkeley: University of California, 1961.

Healy, William. *The Individual Delinquent.* Montclair, NJ: Patterson Smith, 1969.

Hendrickson, Robert. *The Literary Life and Other Curiosities*. New York: Penguin, 1982.

Herd, Harold. *The March of Journalism*. London: George Allen and Unwin, 1952.

Holmgren, R. and Norton, W. *The Mass Media Book*. Englewood Cliffs, NJ: Prentice-Hall, 1972.

Hoult, Thomas F. "Comic Books and Juvenile Delinquency." *Sociology and Social Research,* 1949, 33, pp. 279–84.

Hughes, Michael. "The Fruits of Cultivation Analysis: A Reexamination of Some Effects of Television Watching." *Public Opinion Quarterly,* 1980, Fall, pp. 287–301.

Jacobs, Norman (Ed.). *Culture For The Millions*. Boston: Beacon Press, 1964.

Jones, Landon Y. *Great Expectations*. New York: Ballantine, 1981.

Jowett, Garth. *Film: The Democratic Art*. Boston: Focal, 1976.

Kreissman, Bernard. *Pamela-Shamela*. Lincoln, NE: University of Nebraska, 1960.

Landsdowne, James D. "The Viciousness of the Comic Book." *Journal of Education,* 1944, 127, pp. 14–15.

Larned, J. N. *Books, Character and Culture*. Boston: Houghton Mifflin, 1906.

Larsen, Otto N. (Ed.) *Violence and the Media*. New York: Harper and Row, 1968.

Leavis, Q. D. *Fiction and The Reading Public*. London: Chatto & Windus, 1932.

Legman, Gershom. *Love and Death*. New York: Hacker Art Books, 1963.

Lounsbury, Myron. "Flashes of Lightening: The Motion Picture in the Progressive Era." *Journal of Popular Culture,* 1970, 3, pp. 769–97.

Lowenthal, Leo and Fiske, Marjorie. "Art and Popular Culture in Eighteenth Century England." In *Common Frontiers of the Social Sciences,* pp. 33–112. Edited by Mirra Komarovsky. New York: The Free Press, 1957.

Macdonald, Dwight. *Against The American Grain*. New York: Random House, 1962.

McGlashan, Alan. "Daily Paper Pantheon." *Lancet,* 1953, 1, pp. 238–39.

McIlwraith, R. D. and Schallow, J. R. "Adult Fantasy Life and Patterns of Media Use." *Journal of Communication,* 1983, 33, pp. 78–91.

McLuhan, Marshall. *Understanding Media*. New York: New American Library, 1964.

McLuhan, Marshall. *The Gutenberg Galaxy*. Toronto: University of Toronto, 1962.

Mander, Jerry. *Four Arguments for the Elimination of Television*. New York: Morrow, 1978.

Mehling, Harold. *The Great Time Killer*. Cleveland, OH: World, 1962.

Mitchell, Alice M. *Children and Movies*. Chicago: University of Chicago, 1929.

Mitchell, Curtis. *Cavalcade of Broadcasting*. Chicago: Follett, 1970.

Moody, Kate. *Growing Up on Television*. New York: Times Books, 1980.

Mott, Frank Luther. *Golden Multitudes: The Story of Best Sellers in the United States*. New York: R. R. Bowker, 1947.

Mott, Frank Luther. *American Journalism*. New York: Macmillan, 1962.

Munsterberg, Hugo. *The Film: A Psychological Study* (1916). New York: Dover, 1970.

Newcomb, Horace (Ed.) *Television: The Critical View*. New York: Oxford University Press, 1979.

Noel, M. *Villains Galore: The Heyday of the Popular Story Weekly*. New York: Macmillan, 1954.

Nye, Russel. *The Unembarrassed Muse: The Popular Arts in America*. New York: Dial, 1970.

Orians, G. Harrison. "Censure of Fiction in American Romances and Magazines, 1789–1800," *Publications of the Modern Language Association of America,* 1937, 52, pp. 195–214.

Ornstein, Robert. *The Psychology of Consciousness*. New York: Harcourt Brace Jovanovich, 1977.

Peterson, T. *Magazines in the Twentieth Century*. Urbana: University of Illinois Press, 1964.

Pierce, Chester M. "Television and Violence: Social Psychiatric Perspectives." *American Journal of Social Psychiatry,* 1984, 4, pp. 41–44.

Plato, *The Dialogues of Plato*. New York: Random House, 1937, Vol. 1, "Phaedrus," translated by B. Jowett.

Postman, Neil. *Amusing Ourselves To Death*. New York: Viking, 1985.

Reitberger, Reinhold, and Fuchs, Wolfgang. *Comics: Anatomy of a Mass Medium*. Boston: Little, Brown, 1972.

Riley, Frank and Peterson, James A. "The Social Impact of Television," *Survey,* 1950, 86, pp. 482–64.

Rivers, William L. and Schramm, Wilbur. *Responsibility in Mass Communication*. New York: Harper and Row, 1969.

Robinson, Edward S. "Are Radio Fans Influenced?" *Survey,* 1932, 68, pp. 546–47, 567–70.

Rokeach, Milton. *The Open and Closed Mind*. New York: Basic Books, 1960.

Rosenberg, B. and White, D. M. *Mass Culture: The Popular Arts in America*. New York: The Free Press, 1957.

Schallow, J. R. and McIlwraith, R. D. "Is Television Viewing Really Bad for Your Imagination?" *Imagination, Cognition, and Personality,* 1986, 6, pp. 25–42.

Schramm, Wilbur and Roberts, Donald. *The Process and Effects of Mass Communication.* Urbana, IL: University of Illinois Press, 1974.
Schudson, Michael. *Discovering the News.* New York: Basic Books, 1978.
Schultz, Henry E. "Censorship or Self-Regulation?" *Journal of Educational Sociology,* 1949, 23, pp. 215–23.
Seabury, William M. *The Public and the Motion Picture Industry.* New York: Macmillan, 1926.
Seldes, Gilbert. *The Great Audience.* New York: Viking, 1951.
Sellers, L. L. and Rivers, W. L. (Eds.). *Mass Media Issues.* Englewood Cliffs, NJ: Prentice-Hall, 1977.
Sherif, M. and Sargent, S. S. "Ego Involvement and the Mass Media." *Journal of Social Issues,* 1947, 3, pp. 8–16.
Sherman, Barry L. and Dominick, Joseph R. "Violence and Sex in Music Videos: TV and Rock 'n' Roll." *Journal of Communication,* 1986, 36, pp. 79–93.
Singer, Dorothy G. "Television and Imaginative Play." *Journal of Mental Imagery,* 1978, 2, pp. 145–64.
Singer, Dorothy G. "Reading, Imagination, and Television." *School Library Journal,* 1979, 26, pp. 31–34.
Singer, Dorothy G. and Singer, Jerome L. "Television Viewing and Aggressive Behavior in Preschool Children A Field Study." *Annals New York Academy of Sciences,* 1980, 347, pp. 289–303.
Sobel, Robert. *The Manipulators.* Garden City, NY: Anchor/Doubleday, 1976.
Stevenson, Lionel. *The English Novel.* Boston: Houghton Mifflin, 1960.
Tebbel, John. *The Media in America.* New York: Thomas Cromwell, 1974.
Thompson, D. and Lupoff, D. *The Comic Book Book.* New Rochelle, NY: Arlington House, 1974.
Thrasher, Frederic M. "The Comics and Delinquency: Cause or Scapegoat," *Journal of Educational Sociology,* 1949, 23, pp. 195–205.
Turkle, Sherry. *The Second Self.* New York: Simon and Schuster, 1984.
Wagner, Geoffrey. *The Novel and the Cinema.* Cranbury, NJ: Associated University Presses, 1975.
Wartella, E. and Reeves, B. "Historical Trends in Research on Children and the Media: 1900–1960," *Journal of Communication,* 1985, 35, pp. 118–33.
Watt, Ian. *The Rise of the Novel.* Berkeley: University of California, 1967.
Waugh, Coulton. *The Comics.* New York: Macmillan, 1947.
Wells, Alan (Ed.) *Mass Media and Society.* Palo Alto, CA.: National Press, 1972.

Wertham, Fredric. *Seduction of the Innocent.* New York: Rinehart, 1954.

Wertham, Fredric. *A Sign for Cain.* New York: Macmillan, 1966.

Whitney, Frederick C. *Mass Media and Mass Communications in Society.* Dubuque, IA: Wm. C. Brown, 1975.

Winn, Marie. *The Plug-In Drug.* New York: Bantam, 1978.

Wood, Donald N. *Mass Media and the Individual.* St. Paul, Minnesota: West, 1983.

Woods, L. B. *A Decade of Censorship in America.* Metuchen, NJ: Scarecrow Press, 1979.

Wurtzel, A. and Lometti, G. "Researching Television Violence." *Society,* 1984, September, pp. 22–30.

Wurtzel, A. and Lometti, G. "Smoking Out the Critics." *Society,* 1984, September, pp. 36–40.

Zorbaugh, Harvey. "What Adults Think of Comics as Reading for Children." *Journal of Educational Sociology,* 1949, 23, pp. 225–35.

Zorbaugh, Harvey. "The Comics—There They Stand!" *Journal of Educational Sociology,* 1944, 18, pp. 196–203.

II. Magazine Articles

Radio

"Adults Condemn Air Hair-Raisers for Youngsters." *Newsweek,* December 1, 1934, pp. 27–28.

Benedict, Agnes E. "A United Front on Children's Radio Programs." *Parents Magazine,* June, 1935, pp. 22–23, 42, 58.

"Can Radio Be Rescued?" *New Republic,* October 26, 1927, pp. 251–52.

"The Children's Hour." *The Nation,* April 5, 1933, p. 362.

Dawson, Mitchell. "Censorship on the Air." *American Mercury,* March, 1934, pp. 257–68.

Denison, Merrill. "Why Isn't Radio Better?" *Harper's Monthly,* April, 1934, pp. 576–86.

Frank, Josette. "Chills and Thrills in Radio, Movies and Comics." *Child Study,* 1948, 25, pp. 42–48.

Gibson, Worthington. "Radio Horror: For Children Only," *American Mercury,* July 6, 1938, pp. 294–96.

Kaltenborn, Ralph. "Can Anything Be Done for American Radio?" *The Saturday Review,* January 31, 1948, pp. 6–7, 30–31.

Lauter, V. and Friend, J. H. "Radio and the Censors." *Forum,* December, 1931, pp. 359–65.

Mann, Arthur. "The Children's Hour of Crime." *Scribners,* May, 1933, pp. 313–15.

"Mothers Chasing the Ether Bogeyman." *Newsweek,* March 11, 1933, p. 30.

"Poison Over the Airwaves." *Newsweek,* April 16, 1945, p. 75.

"Radio for Children—Parents Listen In." *Child Study,* April, 1933, pp. 193–98, 214.

"Radio Gore Criticized for Making Children's Hour a Pause That Depresses." *Newsweek,* November 8, 1937, p. 26.

Raymond, Allen. "Static Ahead!", *New Outlook,* July, 1933, pp. 17–21.

"Revolt Against Radio." *Fortune,* March, 1947, pp. 101–03, 172, 174–76.

Watson, Elmo S. "Does Radio Harm Our Children?" *The Rotarian,* November, 1938, pp. 13–14, 60–61.

Woodford, Jack. "Radio—A Blessing or a Curse?", *Forum,* March, 1929, pp. 169–71.

Cinema

"Are Movies the Opium of the People?" *Christian Century,* January 8, 1947, p. 36.

"The Cinematographic Craze." *Dial,* February 16, 1914, pp. 129–31.

Clements, Traverse. "Censoring the Talkies." *New Republic,* June 5, 1929, pp. 64–66.

Currie, Barton W. "The Nickel Madness," *Harper's Weekly,* August 24, 1907, pp. 1246–47.

"Do Motion Pictures Tire the Eyes?" *Scientific American,* May, 1927, p. 343.

Eastman, Fred. "The Menace of the Movies," *Christian Century,* January 15, 1930, pp. 75–78.

Eastman, Fred. "What Can We Do About the Movies?" *Parents Magazine,* November, 1931, pp. 19, 52–54.

Eaton, Walter P. "The Menace of the Movies." *American Magazine,* September, 1913, pp. 55–60.

"Gangster Movies and Children." *Christian Century,* August 12, 1931, pp. 1015–16.

Howe, Frederic C. "What To Do With The Motion Picture Show: Shall It Be Censored?", *Outlook,* June 20, 1914, pp. 412–16.

Levenson, Joseph. "Censorship of the Movies." *Forum,* April, 1923, pp. 1404–14.

McKeever, William A. "The Moving Picture: A Primary School for Criminals," *Good Housekeeping,* August, 1910, pp. 181–86.

"The Moral Havoc Wrought by Moving Picture Shows." *Current Opinion,* April, 1914, p. 290.

"Morals and Movies." *The Nation,* September, 18, 1929, pp. 291–92.

"Movie Crimes Against Good Taste." *Literary Digest,* September 18, 1915, pp. 591–92.

"Moving Pictures and Child Welfare." *School and Society,* January 12, 1918, pp. 55–57.

Poffenberger, A. T. "Motion Pictures and Crime." *Scientific Monthly*, April, 1921, pp. 336–39.

"Should Children Go to the Movies?" *Parents Magazine*, February, 1930, pp. 14–16, 42–44.

Tevis, Charles V. "Censoring the Five-Cent Drama." *The World Today*, 19, October, 1910, pp. 1132–39.

"Threats of Federal Censorship Send a Shudder Through the Movie World." *Current Opinion*, March, 1917, pp. 185–86.

White, William A. "Are the Movies a Mess or a Menace?" *Colliers*, January 16, 1926, pp. 5–6, 45.

Woolf, Virginia. "The Movies and Reality." *New Republic*, 47, August 4, 1926, pp. 308–10.

Comics

"Are Comics Fascist?" *Time*, October 22, 1945, p. 67.

"Aspects of Comic Journalism." *The Nation*, February 22, 1906, pp. 153–54.

Berkman, Aaron. "Sociology of the Comic Strip." *American Spectator*, June, 1936, pp. 51–54.

Brennecke, Ernest. "The Real Mission of the Funny Paper." *Century*, March 24, 1924, pp. 665–75.

Brown, John Mason. "The Case Against the Comics." *Saturday Review of Literature*, March 20, 1948, pp. 31–32.

Christ, Judith. "Horror in the Nursery." *Colliers*, March 27, 1948, pp. 22–23, 95–97.

"Comic Books Regain Their Readership—and Outlets." *Publishers Weekly*, December 6, 1985, pp. 34–35.

"The Comic Nuisance." *Outlook*, March 6, 1909, pp. 527–29.

"Comics-Radio-Movies." *Better Homes and Gardens*, November, 1945, pp. 22–23, 73–75, 108.

"A Crime Against American Children." *The Ladies' Home Journal*, January, 1909, p. 5.

"Cultivating Dreamfulness." *The Independent*, June 27, 1907, pp. 1538–39.

Freedman, Alex M. "Gadzooks! Comics Attract Investor Interest." *The Wall Street Journal*, July 30, 1986, p. 21.

"Funnies: Colored Comic Strips In the Best of Health at 40" *Newsweek*, December 1, 1934, pp. 26–27.

Henry, Gordon M. "Bang! Pow! Zap! Heroes Are Back." *Time*, October 6, 1986, p. 62.

Johnston, William. "Curing the Comic Supplement." *Good Housekeeping*, July, 1910, pp. 81–83.

Lowrie, Sarah D. "The Comic Strips." *Forum*, April, 1928, pp. 527–36.

McCord, David F. "The Social Rise of the Comics," *American Mercury,* July, 1935, pp. 360–64.

Muhlen, Norbert. "Comic Books and Other Horrors." *Commentary,* January, 1949, pp. 80–87.

"Opposition to the Comics." *School Review,* March, 1949, pp. 133–34.

Pedrick, Mary G. "The Sunday Comic Supplement," *Good Housekeeping,* May, 1910, pp. 625–27.

Pennell, Elizabeth R. "Our Tragic Comics." *North American Review,* February 20, 1920, pp. 248–58.

Ryan, John K. "Are the Comics Moral?" *Forum,* May, 1936, pp. 301–4.

"Sounding the Doom of the Comics." *Current Literature,* 45, 1908, pp. 630–33.

Stuart, Lyle. "Don't Get Even, Get Mad." *Publishers Weekly,* January 10, p. 80.

"The Vulgar Supplement Again." *Outlook,* June 5, 1909, pp. 306–7.

Wertham, Frederic. "The Comics . . . Very Funny!", *The Saturday Review of Literature,* May 29, 1948, pp. 6–7, 27–29.

Wigransky, David P. "Cain Before Comics." *The Saturday Review of Literature,* July 24, 1948, pp. 19–20.

Television

Billingsley, Lloyd. "Rock Video: 24-hour-a-day Pacifier for TV Babies." *Christianity Today,* July 13, 1984, p. 70.

Boyle, Deirdre. "The Library, Television, and the Unconscious Mind." *Wilson Library Bulletin,* May, 1978, pp. 696–702.

Carson, Saul. "A Look at Television." *New Republic,* June 7, 1948, pp. 15–17.

"Catholic Archbishop Warns Televiewers." *Christian Century,* December 26, 1951, p. 1499.

Cousins, Norman. "The Time Trap." *Saturday Review of Literature,* December 24, 1949, p. 20.

Diamond, D. and Tenenbaum, F. "Should You Tear 'Em Away From TV?" *Better Homes and Gardens,* September, 1950, pp. 56–57, 239–40.

"Ending Mayhem." *Time,* June 7, 1976, p. 63.

Gelman, Eric. "MTV's Message." *Newsweek,* December 30, 1985, pp. 54–56.

Goodman, Walter. "Bang-Bang! You're Dead!", *New Republic,* Nov. 1, 1954, pp. 12–14.

Gould, Jack. "What is Television Doing to Us?", *New York Times Magazine,* June 12, 1949, pp. 7, 24–28.

"Hypnosis in Your Living Room." *Readers Digest,* April, 1949, pp. 70–72.

Kinder, Marsha, "Music Video and the Spectator: Television, Ideology and Dream." *Film Quarterly,* Fall, 1984, pp. 2–15.

Kitman, Marvin. "M-TV Torture." *New Leader,* January 9, 1984, pp. 20–21.

Lobsenz, Norman M. "The Fight Over Cable Porn." *Ladies' Home Journal,* February, 1984, pp. 56–60.

Mander, Jerry. "Television: The Evil Eye." *Medical Self-Care,* Spring, 1980, pp. 30–32.

Martin, Thomas M. "The Psychological Impact of Television on the Child Today." *New Catholic World,* September, 1984, pp. 228–32.

"Mass Media and Their Impact." *Senior Scholastic,* December 1, 1969, pp. 4–11.

McFaddon, Dorothy L. "Television Comes to Our Children." *Parents Magazine,* January, 1949, pp. 26–27, 73–74.

McNichol, T. "Smutbusters Take Aim at Video." *Channels of Communications,* September, 1985, pp. 58–59.

Meyerson, Michael I. "Cable's 'New Obnoxiousness' Tests the First Amendment." *Channels of Communications,* March, 1985, pp. 40–42.

Shayon, Robert L. "The Pied Piper of Video." *Saturday Review of Literature,* November 25, 1950, pp. 9–11, 49–51.

Sherman, Charles L. "Television: You Can Have It!" *Rotarian,* May, 1948, pp. 10–12.

Singer, D. G., Singer, J. L., and Zuckerman, D. M. "What Every Parent Should Know About Television." *American Film,* January, 1981, pp. 39–44.

Smith, Bernard B. "Television: There Ought to be a Law." *Harper's Magazine,* September, 1948, pp. 34–42.

Spring, Beth. "As TV Violence Grows, the Campaign Against It Alters Course." *Christianity Today,* November 25, 1983, pp. 48–49.

"Television: It is a Commercial Reality But Not Yet an Art." *Life,* December 1, 1947, pp. 117–28.

"Television Reaches Stage of Big Volume." *Business Week,* January 10, 1948, pp. 24–34.

Toffler, A. "Crime in Your Parlor." *The Nation,* October 15, 1955, pp. 323–24.

Utley, Clifton M. "How Illiterate Can Television Make Us?" *Commonweal,* November 19, 1948, pp. 137–39.

Vamos, Mark N. and Atchison, Sandra D. "Cable TV, Older and Wiser, Looks Like a Good Bet Again." *Business Week,* July 22, 1985, p. 126.

Wall, James M. "Out-of-Control Media Hear Harsh Criticism." *Christian Century,* October 9, 1985, pp. 883–84.

Wall, James L. "Cable TV: Dangerous to Health." *Christian Century,* November 23, 1983, p. 1067.

Wanner, Eric. "The Electronic Boogyman." *Psychology Today,* October, 1982, pp. 8–11.

"What TV Does to Kids." *Readers Digest,* June 1977, pp. 80–84.

Whiteside, Thomas. "Onward and Upward With the Arts: Cable." *The New Yorker,* May 20 (Part I), pp. 45–87, May 27 (Part II), pp. 43–56, June 3 (Part III), pp. 82–99, 1985.

Witty, P. and Bricker, H. "Your Child and TV." *Parents Magazine,* December, 1952, pp. 36–37, 74–78.

Wylie, Evan M. "Violence on TV—Entertainment or Menace?" *Cosmopolitan,* February, 1953, pp. 34–39.

Computers and Video Games

"Addictive Video Games." *Psychology Today,* May, 1983, p. 87.

"Are They Games or Electronic Caffene?" *People Weekly,* May 31, 1982, pp. 79–80.

Blotnick, Srully. "From Pac-Man to GI Joe." *Forbes,* August 13, 1984, pp. 138–39.

Brod, Craig. "Children and Video: Computing the Effects." *Consumers Research Magazine,* June, 1986, pp. 19–22.

Collins, Glenn. "Video Games: A Diversion or a Danger?" *New York Times,* February 17, 1983, section C, pp. 1, 6.

Cory, Christopher T. "Pac-Man as Playmate." *Psychology Today,* January, 1983, p. 58.

"Games Addicts Play" *Forbes,* April 13, 1981, p. 102.

Kidd, Joanna. "Game for a New Addiction." *Macleans,* March 30, 1981, p. 58.

Salk, Lee. "How Computers Can Affect Your Kids." *McCalls,* April, 1984, p. 70.

"TV's Hot New Star: The Electronic Game." *Business Week,* December 29, 1975, pp. 24–25.

"TV's New Superhit: Jocktronics." *Time,* December 13, 1976, p. 80.

Tucker, Carll. "Sociable Pong." *Saturday Review,* November 26, 1977, p. 56.

"Video Games Are Harmful to Kids, Psychiatrist Says." *Jet,* November 29, 1982, p. 12.

"Video Games Are Suddenly A $2 Billion Industry." *Business Week,* May 24, 1982, pp. 78–79.

"Videogames: Fun or Serious Threat?" *U. S. News and World Report,* February 22, 1982, p. 7.

Wolfe, Linda. "Death in the Video Arcade." *New York,* April 19, 1984, pp. 52–59.

Other

Adler, J. and Doherty, S. "Kids: The Deadliest Game?" *Newsweek,* September 9, 1985, p. 93.

Atherton, Gertrude. "Literary Merchandise." *New Republic,* July 3, 1915, pp. 223–25.

Elshop, Phyllis T. "D&D: A Fantasy Fad or Dabbling in the Demonic?" *Christianity Today,* September 4, 1981, p. 56.

Holmes, John E. "Confessions of a Dungeon Master." *Psychology Today,* November, 1980, pp. 84–94.

Kellman, Jerold L. "Games to Magazines to Children's Books is the Multimillion-Dollar Wisconsin Saga of TSR." *Publishers Weekly,* July 8, 1983, pp. 34–35.

Mills, Barbara K. "If Students' Tails Are Dragon and Their Minds Are in the Dungeon Lately, Blame Gamesman Gary Gygax." *People,* January 14, 1980, pp. 64–65.

Schuster, William G. "Critics Link a Fantasy Game to 29 Deaths." *Christianity Today,* May 17, 1985, pp. 64–65.

Subject Index

ABC (American Broadcasting Company), 127
Abstract thinking, 24; and individualism, 30; literacy as key to, 25; and writing, 22–23. *See also* Rational thinking
Addiction: electronic, 150; to mass media forms, 152, 179
Advertising: beginning of, 38; radio, 112, 115, 116, 139; TV, 139
Aggression. *See* Violence
Alienation, scientific advance and, 24
Alphabet: and abstraction, 22–23, 24; as evil, 31; history of, 21–25; significance of, 22–23, 24, 27
American: broadcasting, 110, 117; circulating libraries, 67–68; comic weeklies, 73; Congress, 71; heritage, literacy as, 30; mind and morals destroyed, 49; periodicals, use of photography in, 72; Puritan heritage, 6, 178–89; Revolution, newspapers' role in, 42. *See also* American colonies; American press
American Bar Association, 82
American colonies, the: circulating libraries in, 63; control of the press in, 39–43; the novel in, 58; popular literature in, 54–55
American Journalism (Mott), 73
American Marconi. *See* Marconi Company of America
American Nervousness, Its Causes and Consequences (Beard), 50
American press: beginning of, 39–43; censorship of, 40, 41–42; freedom of, 50; nineteenth-century, 67–68; and the Revolution, 42; 1765 Stamp Act and, 42. *See also* Newspapers; Press, the

American Research Bureau, 129
Amusing Ourselves to Death (Postman), 70
Antisocial behavior, theories of, 10–12, 99, 137
Anxiety, 180–81
Argument, persuasive, via books, 28–29
Art: Greek rationalism and, 23; and mass media, 147, 166; "real," vs. popular culture, 14, 163
Atari, Inc., 149
Atheists, 28
AT&T, 110
Audience: the comic strip, 74–75; the comics, 80; for doomsayers, 170; electronic media, 144; mass, 49, 159, 160–64, 171; mass culture and, 14; arrival of middle-class, 94, 161; movie, 91, 92, 93, 97; newspaper, 45–46, 47; passive, 12, 177; prose fiction, 56, 60; radio, 119, 120, 128; inventing, for radio, 110–14; role of, in mass media, 160; for sensationalism, 53; TV, 125, 128; VCR, 149; as victim, 150; video-games, 150. *See also* Reception
Audion, 109

Beadle and Company, 68
Book: -burning, public, 11, 29; production, history of, 25–29
Book-of-the-Month Club, 166
Books: banning of, 11, 29, 58; earliest known, 20; Greek trade of, 21; heretical, 29; Latin, 25; medieval, 26, 28; parchment, 25; and psychological changes, 30; religious argument via, 28; TV's impact on demand for, 128

197

Name Index

Media Index